Annabel Maule

THEATRE NEAR THE EQUATOR

Autobiographies

1. *Memoirs of a Biscuit Baron* - Madatally Manji
2. *A Love Affair with the Sun* - Michael Blundell
3. *Tales from Africa* - Douglas Collins
4. *The Illusion of Power* - G. G. Kariuki
5. *Nothing But the Truth* - Yusuf K. Dawood
6. *From Simple to Complex* - J. M. Mungai

THEATRE NEAR THE EQUATOR

The Donovan Maule Story

Annabel Maule

KENWAY PUBLICATIONS
Nairobi • Kampala • Dar es Salaam

Published by Kenway Publications
a subsidiary of
East African Educational Publishers Ltd.
Brick Court, Mpaka Road/Woodvale Groove
Westlands, P O Box 45314

East African Educational Publishers Ltd
P O Box 11542, Kampala

Ujuzi Educational Publishers Ltd
P O Box 31647, Kijito-Nyama
Dar es Salaam

© Annabel Maule 2004
First published 2004

ISBN 996625226-6

Typeset by Oakland Media Services Ltd
P O Box 56919, Nairobi

Printed and Bound by
AG Printing & Publishing Ltd., Kenya
Tel: +254 20 4446560 / 4449775, Fax: +254 20 4440167

Contents

Chapter 1	1
Chapter 2	13
Chapter 3	31
Chapter 4	67
Chapter 5	85
Chapter 6	105
Chapter 7	129
Chapter 8	151
Chapter 9	169
Chapter 10	183
Chapter 11	205
Chapter 12	229
Chapter 13	243
Chapter 14	265

Index

He was born in Brighton on June 24 1899 and died in Mombasa in 1982.

She was born in London on November 24 1897 and died in Mombasa in 1984.

They were married in 1920 and remained married for more than 60 years.

Together they built a theatre near the Equator.

Donovan Maule O.B.E.

CHAPTER ONE

SS ASCANIUS, a ship of the Blue Funnel Line, was labouring through the Red Sea. She had left Suez on August 18, 1947 and this was to be her penultimate voyage before the breaker's yard. Converted to wartime service, she had served as a troopship, with her peacetime passenger accommodation doubled and trebled for the purpose. She was old and overloaded and slow; her speed in these tropical waters was normally 10 or 11 knots, but due to a defective engine she couldn't make more than nine. She was bound for Mombasa and she carried personnel of British armed forces heading for a new life after the years of war.

There were wives, mothers and children going to join husbands, sons and fathers. There were also entire family units looking forward to a new start, in a new location, in "peace time".

Among them was an Army Major, Donovan Maule, and his wife Mollie.

Neither of them was young; both were approaching 50, and they were heading for Kenya with the idea of setting up a professional repertory theatre in Nairobi.

Donovan Maule's army career had ended in Egypt, as 'Director of Drama, Middle East Land Forces', but the work had dwindled as Forces personnel were demobilised and disappeared into 'Civvy Street'. Mollie had joined him in Egypt, thankful to escape the unwontedly severe winter of 1946 and an unheated house in London.

The suggestion of Kenya — and a repertory theatre — had been made by Don's superior officer, a Colonel who had served in Nairobi earlier in the war. Appointed to 'Army Welfare', his job was to provide entertainment for the troops. There were several venues: first and foremost among them being the Theatre Royal at the centre of the town on Delamere Avenue. Built in 1913, it had already been used for just such a purpose during the First World War. Mr. Medicks, the builder and owner, handed it over to the authorities in World War II to be used as a garrison theatre. There was also the Playhouse, the Empire and the Capitol Cinema, the NAAFI Canteen and the Military Hospital.

"I'll give you a list of contacts," the Colonel told Don. This conversation had taken place on April 1, 1947, which seemed an appropriate date when the Maules were later faced with ruin. But a fuse had been lighted and it now burned in Don's imagination as he set about making notes, outlines and sketches for his very own Theatre.

He had worked in a few in his time, and so had Mollie — in London and the English provinces, in Paris and New York. Born of theatrical parents, both had started their careers in melodrama, Mollie at the age of six weeks being "carried on" in her mother's arms in Hall Caine's *The Manxman* and Don, aged five, playing Little Willie in *East Lynne* with his mother, Lydia Donovan, in the leading role of Lady Isabel. As a small boy touring with his mother and step-father, he had criss-crossed England and was familiar with Sunday train-calls when different theatre companies might meet at large rail junctions such as Crewe and Darlington before continuing, on a branch line, to their next touring 'date'.

The *Ascanius* docked in Mombasa on September 4, 1947 and the Maules travelled up to Nairobi on the overnight train, reaching Kenya's capital in drenching rain. Accommodation was hard to come by. Nairobi's hotels were almost as overcrowded as the *Ascanius* had been, but Torr's Hotel managed to find two single, separate rooms on the third floor, which they would allow the Maules to occupy for that night only. The hotel's lifts being "Out of Order", they climbed the stairs, laden with overnight bags, and went their separate ways. It was still raining.

Don, impatient to begin work after months of enforced idleness, consulted his neatly inscribed list: Mrs. Edward Barret, stage name Gwen Alban, lived at the Queen's Hotel and an appointment was made. She told them bluntly that she couldn't understand why they had come to Kenya. If a professional theatre was possible in Nairobi, she herself — or others who had been in the town for years, would have started one.

During the war years, when the town swarmed with Service personnel, augmented by others coming there on leave, shows would be assured 'Full Houses'; but all that had changed and the theatres were now converted to cinemas under the control of New Theatres Limited based in Johannesburg. George Burrell was their representative in Nairobi and his office, at the Empire Cinema, was at the top of a flight of narrow stone stairs. A burly man with a marked South African accent, he sat behind his desk and listened to what the Maules had to say. Finally, his face broke into a grin: "You two must be crazy! You don't know what you're up against. You win a sweepstake, or something?" As they were leaving he called out "Good luck to you both, anyway!"

Things looked bleak: no theatres available and no home of their own. The 56 days' leave, before Don would leave the Army and his Army pay would cease, were melting away. How were they going to earn a living?

A small flat, attached to a larger house on Mua Park Road in Muthaiga, was available for rent and they moved in, thankful to be able to unpack at last. They also acquired, for £200 from the Car Controller, a 1936 Hillman 10 whose previous owner, the Acting Solicitor General, had rarely travelled beyond Nairobi's tarmac roads.

They met the Kenworthys: Eva was the Theatre Correspondent for the *East African Standard* and George was the Programme Manager for 7 L.O. Cable & Wireless Broadcasting Station. The Kenworthys gave them encouragement in their proposal for a professional repertory company in Nairobi and George suggested that they do a broadcast for the Children's Hour. The Maules adapted 'It's My Own Invention', the chapter in *Through The Looking Glass*, where Alice meets the White Knight in the forest with his 'gentle foolish face, mild blue eyes and kindly smile'. Cable & Wireless transmitted from a tiny studio at Kabete and was innocent of such luxuries as sound effects. Having adapted Lewis Carroll's fiction into a short play with dialogue, they had not only to hold their scripts and act their roles — Mollie as Alice, Don as the White Knight — but also produce all the necessary sounds.

The clip-clop of the Knight's horse (two halved coconut shells), the sound of the Knight's tin armour and numerous accoutrements as he fell off his horse (an array of hardware tossed over Don's shoulder). The few children who heard it judged the broadcast a success. There was no fee attached.

The Kenworthys introduced the Maules to Dr. Gregory, a delightful Irishman who had been in practice with Dr. 'Kill or Cure' Burkitt. Gregory was Chairman of the Conservatoire of Music. He was also a great theatre enthusiast and, together with the Kenworthys, was eager for Don and Mollie's plans to succeed. In his mémoir of Burkitt, *Under the Sun,* he wrote of their first meeting in London in 1928: 'During luncheon he asked me if I would like to go to a theatre... I accepted with alacrity... at St. Peter's Hospital for Diseases of the Rectum, we spent the afternoon watching Mr. Lockhart-Mummy operate.'

It was now 1948 and Don's diary noted: 'February 1 — Felt sick all day and very depressed. All our plans and designs for the future are hanging fire. Eaton Terrace [their London house] unsold. Heavy bank overdraft in England and Kenya. The Hillman tyres are wearing out fast.'

In March an article in *The Sunday Post* caught their attention. Headed 'A National Theatre for Kenya', it outlined the problems which would face any professional theatre in Nairobi. On the following Sunday *The Post* recorded: 'The remarks brought two interesting visitors to our office... Mr. and Mrs. Donovan Maule came to see what possibilities there were for doing just that — starting a permanent repertory theatre run on professional lines.' Quoting Don, the article went on: 'When a National Theatre exists, that'll be fine — somewhere for the Donovan Maule Players to move into, after they have thoroughly established themselves. But the initial step seems to be a *little* theatre, seating no more than 150 to 200 people.'

This bold statement must have surprised quite a few readers of *The Post*. Plans for a cultural centre, a home suitable for 'Music, Drama, Dancing and the Allied Arts', had first been launched back in March 1946: 'If all the ardent theatre-goers in the Colony... would give according to their means, the work of building the theatre would start at once.'

A theatre seating 'about 550' was mentioned, which would be only one of *two* theatres it was hoped would serve Kenya's theatre-goers. Now here was Donovan Maule proposing to move his players into the yet-unbuilt National Theatre! It had not been for his benefit that Shaw's *Arms And The Man* had been presented at the Theatre Royal to raise money for the Theatre Fund. The avowed aims of the Committee were for 'an inter-racial centre for the promotion of all the arts in the Colony' but the stark truth was that 'the ardent theatre-goers' were insufficiently ardent and now, two years later, the National Theatre was no more than some preliminary plans drawn by Mrs. E.D. Hughes. A great deal more money was required before even a foundation stone could be laid. Ultimately the Theatre Fund raised nearly £4,000. The contribution of £50,000 came from the Colonial Development & Welfare Department in Britain. The Kenya Government added a further £5,000 and building work began, but not before August 1951. The plot, opposite the Norfolk Hotel, was gratis.

The Sunday Post had quoted Don further: 'A step we want to take now, is to meet the right people — really keen enthusiasts who are ready and eager to work when the time comes; people who are prepared to form a nucleus of our technical staff and future cast... to build up a first class company of players on an ultimate professional basis which will be Nairobi's own Theatre.' These presumptuous declarations caused the ranks of the amateur theatre practitioners to draw even closer. They had been suspicious of the Maules from the moment of their arrival, and now it was clear that these newcomers would be poaching on their long-established territory.

Others thought differently, as letters to the Editor of *The Sunday Post* showed: 'I trust that Mr. and Mrs. Donovan Maule will receive full co-operation from all sides, i.e. Government Departments and the public, in their efforts to meet a need which must surely add to the importance and well-being of Kenya', was one such letter; and 'Mr. Donovan Maule, who is anxious to start a company of players, should be encouraged to the hilt, with the backing of the Press and the support of the public', read another.

Letters like these convinced Don and Mollie that they should pursue their goal. But lacking both capital and premises, just how were they to do it? The idea initially came from Dr. Gregory. It was vague and unformed, but gradually it took shape; they would create their own actors.

In April 1948 *The East African Standard* announced: 'As a start towards the formation of a company of repertory players, Mr. and Mrs. Donovan Maule are opening a School of Dramatic Art in Nairobi... Preliminary interviews with intending students at the Capitol Theatre.'

At 4.30pm on April 26, Mollie and Don waited for would-be thespians. "You going to allow *anyone* to join?" asked Tubby Block, who was there merely out of curiosity. The first term was launched on May 3 with classes from 5 to 7pm on Mondays and Thursdays, in front of the permanent screen at the Capitol Cinema, courtesy of George Burrell. Twenty students had enrolled, but at the end of the 12-week term, a few no-hopers were directed elsewhere.

On his 49th birthday, in June, Don wrote to me: 'We are plugging along with our students and giving a one-act play, *The Dear Departed* by Stanley Houghton this week before the film *Conflict* at the Theatre Royal, instead of the usual short features. This will be the first production of The Donovan Maule Players... It remains to be seen how much the cinema management gives us at the end of the week. So far, Box Office receipts have been, I think, slightly lower than if *Conflict* had been preceded by *Mickey Mouse*. On Monday 28th the Donovan Maule Studio Players are giving their first broadcast from Cable & Wireless which I hope will be the forerunner of broadcasting a regular play once a month... All these things constitute some sort of a start, I suppose.'

At the end of the week George Burrell handed over £25, but this first, rough little production was the birth of The Donovan Maule Players and the broadcasts *did* become a regular monthly feature. Don's letter to me continued: 'The big snag now is: how to cast full-length plays?'

Term two of the School of Dramatic Art was no longer at the Capitol Cinema. Students arrived instead at premises about fifty yards further along Government Road, 'directly opposite the NAAFI', and located above the Nairobi Provision Store. Mounting a steep flight of stairs between grey stone walls, they came into a room approximately 40 feet long by 20 feet wide. At one end the windows looked down on Government Road, at the rear a small-enclosed courtyard gave access to Victoria Street. This one-time Dance Studio was much better suited for the purpose of the school and work began there in mid-August.

"When are you going to do a full-length play?" people asked. George Burrell agreed to allow the Maules use of the Theatre Royal, for one week, in lieu of the usual film, on a 50-50 basis of net takings. They chose *The Guinea Pig* by Warren Chetham-Strode. The theme of the play dealt with social-class divisions within the British education system, while the plot centred on a young London Council schoolboy, son of a tobacconist, who gets a bursary to an old and tradition-bound Public School where he is regarded as an experiment (a guinea-pig).

On September 5, a short excerpt of the play was broadcast and it was Mollie who realised that it was the first anniversary of their arrival in Nairobi.

The Theatre Royal could seat a total of 511 people spread across Stalls, Circle and four Boxes, each one seating four. At the end of the week George Burrell posted a cheque for £355, adding: 'I would like to congratulate you on your first Nairobi production, and feel sure that the public of Nairobi will look forward to your future shows.' The Maules had taken their first tentative step towards the future Donovan Maule Theatre.

If visitors to the New Stanley or Torr's Hotel paused in either hotel lobby they might catch sight of display frames advertising The Donovan Maule Players' current or forthcoming production. Announced to open on November 15 was St. John Ervine's *Robert's Wife*. Among the cast were several students from the School of Dramatic Art with sufficient confidence now to appear before the public.

Gwen Alban and her husband attended the first night and so did Dr. Gregory, who wrote: 'Now that you have achieved such success with one Irish playwright, I hope you will be tempted to try another and put on *The Importance Of Being Earnest*.'

Despite its excellent position at the hub of Nairobi, the Theatre Royal (now the Cameo Cinema) was far from ideal from the actor's point of view. The dressing rooms had disappeared with the conversion to a cinema and the Maules had to contrive their own, under the stage, with bits of old discarded scenery. There were no chairs, other than those taken from boxes in the auditorium and as every seat, including boxes, sold on Saturday night, that left nothing in the dressing rooms. There were no washing arrangements, no lavatory, no stage staff and the house curtains didn't meet properly when drawn. Anything left on stage was liable to be stolen or nibbled by rats. But this was the only building they could get at the cost of about £350 per week.

Their Ideal Theatre, the one Don imagined and planned so carefully on the slow boat to Mombasa, was a 'Club' theatre equipped with club-room, bar and kitchen, able to serve light meals before and after performances. Writing to me, he estimated: 'I think we would get at least 500 members paying an annual subscription of, say, £1.1.0 a year and that the members would grow to over 1,000 within 12 months.' With this in mind, he was forever searching for premises. He met with the Commissioner of Lands and seven different sites were viewed, but none served his purpose. The search intensified when George Burrell was recalled to Johannesburg and New Theatres Limited told them the Theatre Royal would no longer be available in the evenings. One week a year, for matinées only, if booked well in advance, was all the Maules could hope for.

'If we chuck everything and come back to England now we shall have lost, through selling Eaton Terrace and having stuff shipped out here, fully £1,000 which we would have possessed had we gone straight home from Egypt... we would have no car, no home, no possessions beyond the clothes in our luggage. Our ages would be around 51... If we battle through and remain, we shall probably gain our permanent theatre in the end.'

To date five Donovan Maule Players productions had been seen at the Theatre Royal. Following *Robert's Wife* had come William Douglas Home's *The Chiltern Hundreds* in early January 1949, then *Saloon Bar* by Frank Harvey. Noel Coward's *This Happy Breed* — 'The Donovan Maule Players' fifth and best production', according to *The Kenya Weekly News* — was presented for matinées only, with all proceeds going to The British Legion 'Coming of Age' Appeal. This left the Maules out of pocket and without premises, but with a loyal following and letters appeared in the *East African Standard* lamenting their plight: 'Here we are with four partially filled picture houses as our evening's entertainment. Even when the show is 'in aid of,' the Maules have to be content with matinées... Cannot something, even if it is only an ex-Army hut on a suitable site, be put at the disposal of those who are prepared to entertain us in person?... I would hate our National Theatre to open without them,' said one. 'The Donovan Maules, during recent months, have produced a series of plays... All who have seen these productions must realise what an asset these artists are to the cultural life of Kenya. Yet owing to the fact that our theatres have been allowed to pass into the hands of one group... there is no independent theatre available to the Donovan Maules... It is a serious matter that the development of the theatre in Kenya should be handicapped or retarded because commercial interests are concentrated on the cinema... The Donovan Maules offer us cultural entertainment *now:* public opinion should insist that the opportunity be not lost through lack of a theatre...' said another.

Alas, Public Opinion (in the manner of Ardent Theatre-goers) remained supine.

Building number 12: until recently a Quartermaster's Store and the size of a hangar at Nairobi West aerodrome (now Wilson Airport), was being allocated to two young ladies operating The Prop Shop, a bar and restaurant in a nearby building scheduled for demolition. Building number 12 was however, too large for their purpose and the union of a theatre with The Prop Shop gave the illusion of a marriage made in heaven.

Suddenly it was full steam ahead: architect's blueprints were drawn, 250 special tip-up theatre seats were to be manufactured locally while an order, worth in excess of £1,000 for stage lighting equipment, was forwarded to London — the goods to be air-freighted to Nairobi soonest. So, too, were fire-proofed scene canvas and Dunlopillo seats for the tip-up chairs. Timber and Dexion steel girders were purchased and an order given for building the stage and the raked auditorium floor. Curtain track runner was purchased. Printing was put in hand and negotiations started with professional actors in England.

Approval was received from the D.C., the Firemaster and Public Works Department, the Director of Civil Aviation and the Mayor of Nairobi. The name would be New Venture Theatre. Solicitors drew up contracts. The Maules would soon have their Dream Theatre in which to present professional, continuous repertory. There now entered upon the hectic scene the mother of one of The Prop Shop ladies and the hitherto friendly atmosphere changed to one of distrust. Clauses in the contract were added, deleted, re-worded or questioned. Appointments were ignored, letters went unanswered and telephone calls were not returned. The Maules agreed to the ever-changing clauses until One-Restriction-Too-Many was imposed and their patience snapped. The deal was called off.

Sixty days had been spent in negotiations and £3,000 disbursed — money scraped together from all available sources: the sale of the lease of the Eaton Terrace house — a *very* desirable property — had resulted in just half the price originally hoped for, due to stretched lines of communication and dilatory agents. The small profit remaining from the productions at the Theatre Royal and the even smaller profit from the monthly broadcasts had been beefed up by Charles Markham, guaranteeing a hefty overdraft at the bank.

And now, with superb theatrical timing, the expensive stage lighting equipment arrived at Nairobi West — a few yards from Building number 12. To avoid further charges for demurrage, the load was hauled to the little studio on Government Road, where it filled most of the space. Rehearsals for the grand opening production of New Venture Theatre were abandoned. Now what?

Unable to sleep, Don and Mollie drove to Nairobi Game Park, arriving in the half light before dawn. Don halted the car at a spot facing east and switched off the engine.

A repertory theatre in Nairobi! Can't fail...

When and how had this brilliant suggestion been made? More than two years earlier, in Port Said on April Fool's Day 1947. Not such a brilliant suggestion after all: time wasted, money lost, hope gone.

Slowly the orange bowl of the rising sun silhouetted the black lace of an acacia thorn tree ahead and what had resembled a large rock, a few yards from the car, was shown now to be a full-grown lioness. She turned her head lazily in their direction and for a few long moments, lioness and forlorn, ruined impresarios stared at one another.

Finally the big cat squeezed up her amber eyes, opened her huge jaws and yawned cavernously in the Maules' faces. She then rose slowly to her feet and strolled away, tail swinging gently, without a backward glance.

In the deep silence Mollie's laughter sounded shocking. Then Don was laughing too. The indifferent lioness had put the Seal of Absurdity on their aborted endeavours in the world of mere humans.

Exhausted and breathless, with tears of laughter on their cheeks, they headed back to town.

CHAPTER TWO

"We heard you were trying to start a repertory theatre."

The man standing at the entrance to the Studio was tall, his gingery hair lay close to his scalp in tight waves and his nose was somewhat beaky. Basil Hurle-Hobbs had served during the war in the Fleet Air Arm and before that he had been a test pilot. He retained the jargon and was a great man for a party: a 'Jolly Up'. He was accompanied by Jean Parnell, also tall with auburn hair to her shoulders and an enchanting smile. She had served in the WRNS as a driver. Both had some stage experience, acquired at the Repertory Theatre in Worthing.

Deciding that post-war Britain was dull and bureaucracy-ridden, they had left it. Pooling all available resources, they had bought a single-engine ex-Naval plane and set off from Gatwick. On reaching Nice, they visited the Casino and won sufficient French francs to enjoy a two-week holiday before setting off again, flying to Sicily, Malta, Tripoli, El Adam, Cairo, Luxor and Wadi Haifa, where they came to a halt. Their little plane had no radio. A radio was imperative, so Basil arranged for one to be flown to Cairo, where the Egyptian authorities impounded it. He flew there to retrieve it and was imprisoned. After getting his transit visa renewed he was released, and with the radio under his arm, he hitched a lift in a Dakota. Running into bad weather, the Dakota deviated to Khartoum. Basil waited for a lift back to Wadi Haifa where he found his plane now covered with sand. He dug it out in sweltering temperatures of 125^0 and set about the complete dismantling and re-assembling job that the small and lightly built aircraft required following its smothering in baking sand.

This done, Basil prepared for a test flight accompanied by a young engineer. As they taxied down the runway, his passenger yelled: "Is that normal?" Flames were licking through the floor of the plane. Basil tipped a wing into the sand, bringing the plane to a halt. An Arab-manned firetender raced to the wreckage, but no water emerged through the hoses; the plane was a write-off.

Flying Sudan Airways, Jean and Basil reached Khartoum, then by flying boat, they arrived at Kisumu. From there they set off by bus for Nairobi and here they were, at the Maules' Studio, asking about the proposed repertory theatre.

Don recounted the story of New Theatres Limited followed by the débâcle of building number 12 at Nairobi West: "There are no premises for *live* theatre," he concluded.

"What's wrong with this place?" asked Basil, glancing round the Studio.

"This place?"

"You've got this marvellous new lighting equipment..." Basil was on his feet, pacing the length of the room used by the School of Dramatic Art "You've got the theatre seats, the timber, the Dexion Steel... it's a piece of cake!"

Work commenced on September 21, 1949. Basil was the designer and the 'Gaffer', Don his assistant; Mollie and Jean did anything they were told and the School's students also lent a hand. The stage, measuring 12 feet by 12 feet, was at the Victoria Street end of the room, with two tiny cubicles behind for dressing rooms. In the remaining space were ranged 55 Dunlopillo padded, tip-up seats. The remaining 195 seats remained with the manufacturer.

The last row backed right up against the windows overlooking Government Road. The Studio had to yield every possible inch, so Don arranged with the Army for prison cells to be used as a store. Dexion Steel, sawn to size then nutted-and-bolted together, like giant Meccano, was used for the main structure. The work continued all day, every day, Sundays included and was completed in nine and a half weeks with a cash outlay of approximately £1,800. News of the activity over the Nairobi Provision Store was speedily transmitted by bush telegraph: what were the Maules up to?

A few months earlier, when Mollie was spotted bidding for a large cabin trunk at an auction sale, the rumour flashed round Nairobi, "The Maules are off. They're quitting!"

Towards the end of the construction work rehearsals were held, in the evenings, for their opening production. Saturday, November 19, was set to herald the birth of The Studio Theatre.

Three days before opening night, from the top of a step-ladder, Don found himself looking down on the Fire Master, the Town Planning Engineer and His Worship the Mayor. They told him that much of the construction work at the School of Dramatic Art was irregular but, above all, unless a fire escape was installed before the audience arrived on Saturday night, the Maules faced closure and prosecution.

Their lovely new baby of a theatre was invaded by a horde of Sikhs who tore a gaping hole in the back wall behind the stage, installed a steel door and a fire escape to the yard below and departed leaving a pile of dust and masonry behind them. The dress rehearsal for *Outward Bound* was cancelled; instead, everyone set about clearing away the mess and repainting much of the scenery.

A three-part post card, the bottom portion a tear-off reply addressed to:

THE DONOVAN MAULE PLAYERS
STUDIO THEATRE
P.O. Box 2333
NAIROBI

had been mailed to a thousand addresses. It was an invitation to attend any one of 13 scheduled performances. Don wondered: 'Will anyone find our funny little place over a grocer's shop at the wrong end of Government Road?'

The following day, Sunday, he was able to record: 'Great artistic success. To theatre at 8am. Mollie and I cleaned the auditorium, stage and dressing rooms... 2nd performance tonight.'

The complimentary programme, handed to guests at the top of

the stairs, announced: 'It is hoped to obtain a licence to operate as a private Theatre Club... if we are granted a liquor licence as well for the convenience of members and their guests, so much the better. Meanwhile, we are presenting our opening production to invited audiences. If a licence is granted to us, the annual subscription will be Sh60 for a single and Sh100 for a double membership. The price of seats, which will be reserved for members, will be Sh5. If you would like to join the Club will you kindly fill up the application form below and leave it with our hostess'.

The following week brought letters of congratulations and cheques by every post: 'Your darling little theatre... a lovely idea so perfectly executed'; 'It is charming and comfortable, and the stage and lighting are models of perfection'; 'Most impressed by the theatre and particularly the amazing lighting'; 'I recognise the enormous amount of hard work — in the face of many obstacles — which you have had to put in to establish your Studio Theatre'; and 'Great asset to the cultural life of the town'.

They played to Full House at all 13 performances, but as Don said, "Not difficult with only 55 seats and everything free!"

When *Outward Bound* ended, 343 'Founder' Members of The Donovan Maule Players Club had paid their dues and the necessary licence — to operate a Theatre Club and sell liquor — was granted on January 1, 1950.

In the cast of *Outward Bound* was Gwen Alban, playing the role she had created 20 years earlier for The Railway Players. By agreeing to appear with the Maules she had set the Seal of Approval on these newcomers to the Nairobi theatre scene.

Now that they had the premises, and the nucleus of a permanent company — they had put 45 students through the school, several of whom were showing very real promise — Mollie and Don's original idea of a repertory theatre was possible and they began work on the production of *Jeannie*. At the end of the first read-through, Basil took a long, hard look at his surroundings. "You know, we've built this the wrong way round..." Reaching for a clipboard, he began to sketch. "If we switch the whole thing round we can get more seats into the auditorium and put in another lavatory, the sanitary boffins are insisting on that... a bar..."

"What about dressing rooms?" asked Don.

"Up in the roof, raise the existing roof: that will give us bags of space."

"Box office?"

"Here, at the head of the stairs, and then the bar here, then the back row of theatre seats. We can rake the whole thing... improve the sight lines."

It was a piece of cake! *Outward Bound* ended on December 3 and on December 7 demolition work began. Mollie couldn't bear to be a witness, so she was sent away to rest.

The radical reconstruction was completed in eight weeks. The stage, now at the Government Road end of the studio, was larger by four feet, measuring 16 by 16 feet with an area 5 feet wide on the prompt side, where a Dexion steel ladder led up to two tiny dressing rooms. On the Opposite Prompt (O.P.) side of the stage there was no space, merely the party wall to the neighbouring building.

The two windows overlooking Government Road had each been extended by a box-like structure at the rear of which a false window had been contrived. This gave the tiny stage an illusion of depth where none existed.

A further 21 tip-up seats were retrieved from Messrs Karam Singh, thereby increasing the seating capacity to 76. Over and above this was extra accommodation on bar stools and the bar counter itself: bringing the grand total to 83 play-goers. The 'bar' seats soon became favourites — they not only gave an uninterrupted view of the stage, but interval drinks could be obtained instantly.

Eva Kenworthy, writing for the *East African Standard* noted, 'The Little Studio has, once again, been completely reorganised, with better ventilation, more seats (all stepped up for improved visibility), a larger stage and other amenities, but it retains in full its delightful

'Little Theatre' atmosphere.'

Once again Charles Markham had come to the rescue with finance and Eva Kenworthy told her readers, 'Don and Mollie Maule are emphatic in stressing that this is only an interim theatre which has evolved out of their strenuous and almost despairing efforts to establish a permanent theatre here; rather than stand off the enthusiastic little company which they have gathered round them in anticipation of moving into much larger premises, they decided to 'make do' with what already existed.'

At the opening of *Jeannie* in early February 1950, a member exclaimed: "This is what Nairobi has been waiting for, for so long!"

Three months later 'Founder' membership was closed — it had reached 860. Henceforth an entrance fee would be charged: Sh40 for single and Sh60 for double. A matinée on Fridays was added for the benefit of the growing number of Country Members — those living '50 or more miles from Nairobi'.

No longer 'Those Maules', they were now becoming known as 'The DMs', and when a robbery occurred at the Studio Theatre, this merited mention in the press!

At about this time the *London Evening Standard* published an item under the heading: 'STAGE... by Bill Boorne'. It said: 'Another young actress whose work I have watched with increasing admiration is Annabel Maule. On Monday she opens in Leeds with Eric Portman in *His Excellency*. The show comes to London soon. In this play with Annabel is Arnold Bell. In his early days he was appearing with Annabel's parents in *The Right To Strike*. The Maules had been married only a few weeks and Mr. Maule suggested to Arnold Bell that he should refrain from kissing his bride too ardently in their love scene!'

At the first anniversary of the Theatre Club the Maules could look back on 11 productions, including Christopher Fry's verse play *The Lady's Not For Burning* — no easy undertaking on so small a stage. The setting is 'A room in the house of Hebble Tyson, Mayor of the small Market Town of Cool Clary. Time: 1400, either more or less or exactly'. The production was a success, being seen by 2,600 Club Members and their guests. They took the play to Nakuru and mounted it at the Athletic Club where 300 theatre-goers sat on seats hired from Nakuru Race Course. Shaw's *Pygmalion* and *Traveller's Joy* by Arthur McCrae were also taken to Nakuru.

The latter play travelled even further afield to Nyeri, where the single performance was put in jeopardy by a mini *crime passionel*. Vivian Pickles, later to make a name for herself in English films, was the 18-year old *ingénue* in the company and had caught the eye of two young actors. When none of this trio was present half an hour before Curtain Up, Don raced back to the White Rhino Hotel where he found members of the hotel staff pounding on a locked bedroom door as smoke curled from under it. One of the actors finally emerged, coughing and spluttering. The scenario was elementary: jealousy had impelled the thwarted lover to slice up his rival's new (as it happened) blue blazer, then squeeze toothpaste on the remnants before setting fire to the mattress in his hotel room.

The DMs paid the damages and the arsonist was himself fired.

Theatre Club membership had risen to 1,300 and Don declared: "Approximately 1,400 to 1,500 theatre-goers come to each production and to accommodate this number necessitates each play running three full weeks. We anticipate reaching our full quota of 1,500 members some time in the autumn of this year; that will be the maximum our present small theatre can seat, running each production for 28 performances."

Beyond this enclosed, self-regarding world of repertory productions and theatrical crises, Kenya was stirring.

In November 1950 the words "Mau Mau" were heard for the first time in the Legislative Council, uttered by the Attorney General. The fight for freedom from British rule was growing.

The Maules had moved into a larger home, still on Mua Park Road, and were joined by Mollie's mother, Sheila. I had accompanied my grandmother, then aged 78, to the air terminal in London. She had never flown before, but was happy to think she would be seeing her only child again after more than three years.

The reunion took place at Lake Naivasha, where she arrived by flying boat. Her life had been spent in theatre. Having married an actor, she toured with a company presenting Shakespeare plays but, widowed and left penniless in 1927, most of the remainder of her long life was spent with Mollie and Don.

With Theatre Club membership rising steadily, the number of performances for each play was increased to 34 and the Maules felt confident enough to offer contracts to professionals from Britain. The play *His Excellency* — mentioned by Bill Boorne in the *Evening Standard* — had settled into a London theatre in May 1950 where it became a big success, running until the end of June 1951. While we gave eight performances every week throughout this time, the Maules mounted 15 productions at the Studio.

His Excellency opened in Nairobi in October 1951 with Don in the leading role. Its appeal kept it running for six weeks to full houses, and the number of Theatre Club members reached a new high. Appearing in this production was Geoffrey Best, the first professional to come from England under contract.

'Scene designed and constructed in the Donovan Maule Workshops by Geoffrey Best' appeared beneath the cast-list in the programme for each new production at the Studio. Until 1950 the workshops consisted of a series of Army huts out at Nairobi West; they were one-time Quartermaster's stores, kindly loaned by the Army. This accommodation served well during the first dozen or so productions, but as the quantity of scenery, stage furniture, props, wardrobe and stage lighting equipment augmented, the congestion, as well as the distance from theatre to store, made it desirable to move into more central and larger premises. The new workshop, only a few hundred yards from the Studio Theatre, had a floor area of 3,000 square feet and was partitioned into scenic bay, furniture bay, carpenter's shop, paint shop, props department, electrical workshop, wardrobe department and Glory-hole for bits and pieces.

As with all repertory companies, a permanent staff was employed and kept busy all the year round designing, building and painting scenery. Props were either made, borrowed or bought. Local firms proved extremely co-operative; for a credit in the programme a range of items might be loaned, including beds and cookers, refrigerators and wheelbarrows, microscopes and lamps, radios and sports equipment, steel filing cabinets and negligées, medical charts and kitchen sinks. Don and Mollie's home was often plundered: sofas and armchairs one month, antique chests and bureaux the next. Seldom was their house furnished as Mollie had intended. The furniture bay in the new store was crammed with items bought at local auction sales. Plays might range from Biblical times, through Christopher Fry's '1400 either more or less or exactly', to *Tomorrow's Child;* set in the future so all manner of assorted chairs, tables, benches, foot stools, mirrors, console tables, candle stands, card tables, carpets and other unusual pieces — provided they were *small* had been acquired.

In the Studio Theatre, without 'flies' or off-stage space, solidly constructed 'rooms' had to be built, able to withstand the close scrutiny of an audience only a few feet away, over a period of up to 50 performances. Fire-proofed scene canvas being unobtainable, the heaviest weight of *americani* was used instead, and there being no seasoned non-warpable timber, hardboard or softboard was employed. Adaptation and improvisation was the key-note at the tiny Studio. An example: Noel Coward's *Present Laughter,* production number 20 at the Studio Theatre, May 1951. One set 'An actor-manager's London flat.' Simple! So it would be on any normal sized stage, but the Studio was not normal. Five doors are required, all essential to the plot. Or are they? Director and scenic designer study the printed script. Spare bedroom? Yes, imperative; there could be no play without it. The main door leading to the hall can't be scrapped either, people have to get into the flat somehow. The service door? A bit of compression there might be possible... suppose, instead of a hall door, there is an arch which affords a glimpse of the service door off-stage; that would save valuable acting area. There still remain Garry Essendine's bedroom and study. The study should be up a short flight of stairs, with its own little landing, clearly visible to the audience; but three steps up on the Studio Theatre's stage takes the actor's head out of sight and a staircase annexes one third of the acting area. There still remains the door to Garry's bedroom which can't be *down* right, again due to taking up acting area — and anyone making an exit couldn't get up to the dressing rooms for change of costume.

"Need we actually see the door to Garry's study? Can't we suppose that both his study and his bedroom are upstairs, leading off the landing?" After settling on this, the spare bedroom is placed *up* right, with a boxed-in space off-stage, measuring 2 feet by 2.5 feet, for the actress to change into pyjamas. The five 'essential' exits are now three, and in quite different places from those given in the script, which means positions of furniture must be altered, and all the given 'moves' for actors must be changed. But the actor-manager's London flat has been squeezed onto the Studio stage.

Many years later, Mollie recalled: 'To achieve an entrance from the left meant descending a cat-ladder from the pidgeon-loft dressing room and squeezing oneself: sardine-like, into the shallow triangle formed by diagonally-set scenery against the solid wall. If one was supposed to be coming from an adjacent room, the door had, of necessity, to open onto the stage, further restricting our extremely limited acting area. It is astonishing the number of plays in those days that required a French window leading out into a garden. To obtain this effect, trelliswork covered with greenery was attached to the solid wall. If two actors had to make a running entrance after a jolly game of tennis, for instance, it was a matter of "You breathe in, while I breathe out" while waiting for their entrance cue.'

By the end of 1951 Basil had left. He had envisaged the Studio Theatre then built it, followed by turning it back to front. He had designed and built scenery, made props, worked the electric switchboard, stage managed and acted. Now that repertory was established and running more or less routinely, he was bored. He looked for a new challenge and departed for Mombasa to work for a commercial firm. His last appearance was in *His Excellency*. Geoffrey Best now undertook the same variety of jobs. He had an assistant carpenter, Barnaba Onzere, known to everyone as 'Bonzo'.

The limitations and strictures imposed by trade unions were unknown in those early years. Bemused box office receptionists found themselves going on-stage, script in hand, to substitute for a cast member taken sick. The Bar manager might be whisked away to the lighting switchboard tucked away in a corner under the Dexion steel ladder leading up to the minuscule dressing rooms. Mollie, hitching up her elegant evening dress, would clean the lavatories while Don recorded the number of seats sold in his Author's Royalty book and answered the telephone in the matchbox-size box office. Jean Parnell acted, stage-managed, painted scenery and helped with costumes. When the frequent electricity failures plunged the stage into darkness, actors kept talking while lighted candles were brought on stage and set in pre-arranged areas. The show went on, no matter what.

At the start of 1952 an enigmatic but nevertheless significant entry appeared in Don's diary. 'February 1: Site between Connaught and Jackson Roads. 2 front corner plots nearest to Legco. 1/6th acre, 75 ft. x 120 ft. deep.' At this time it was just an area of soil and rocks, with a few trees and bushes greening the surface near Legco.

Meanwhile, the clamour for independence grew. In July that year a massive meeting was held at Nyeri, addressed by the leaders of the Kenya African Union (KAU), among them Jomo Kenyatta. The cauldron was coming to the boil.

Away from politics Don wrote: 'Ever since we started continuous presentation of plays with an all-professional company, we have had flattering and encouraging requests to take our productions further afield. We, ourselves very much wanted to do this, but the question arose — could it be economic? After five experimental visits to Nakuru, the answer was definitely 'No'. The audiences were enthusiastic, appreciative and supported us well, but since these visits necessitated the closure of our Nairobi theatre, with its subsequent loss of revenue and continual overheads, we found it simply didn't work out! Two subsequent visits to Turi for one night only, proved sounder economics but due to our increased Nairobi audience, it became inadvisable to close the Studio Theatre, even for one night. Only now, with our larger number of contracted artists from London, has it become possible to undertake an extensive tour throughout East Africa, leaving part of our company in Nairobi to present other productions to our Theatre Club audience of over 3,000 regular playgoers.

'In order to take *Bell, Book and Candle* on an extensive tour, it was necessary to engage further artists and staff. With unabashed nepotism we cabled our daughter Annabel, offering her the part of Gillian Holroyd because (a) it seemed possible she might be able to fit in a visit to Kenya between her London engagements, (b) she was just the actress we wanted for the part, and (c) well, she's our daughter anyway and we haven't seen her for six years!

'We have secured direct from New York the rights to John van Druten's play due to open in Nairobi on November 25 where it will run until the end of the year after which it will go on tour throughout Kenya, Uganda and Tanganyika. While the play is on tour the rest of the company will be presenting *The Little Hut* and *Dial 'M' For Murder* in Nairobi. This will be the first tour of any straight play attempted on such a scale in East Africa. With Annabel playing the leading role it will be the first occasion on which the entire Maule family have appeared together on stage. The company will take full equipment for the staging of the play: scenery, stage lighting with a portable dimmer switchboard, furniture, wardrobe, props and sound equipment.'

He estimated the cost of the enterprise at £3,000. The pre-planning had kept him busy, and happy, for weeks. With maps of East Africa spread across his bedroom floor, he selected 17 venues, leap-frogging towns on the Up-route which could be visited on the return Down-route. He wrote to the Secretaries of Amateur Theatre Groups spread across the three territories; an extraordinary number of groups existed at this time. His intention was to take the play to any town which could provide an audience. He enquired about electric power, seating for the audience, size of playhouse, hotel dining room, Club-room or even school hall. Was there a firmly-built stage or would rostra be available? What arrangements could be made for booking seats? Would hospitality be offered to all/any of the six people involved in *Bell, Book and Candle?* And more, much more.

Meanwhile, Mollie was auditioning cats. The play listed a cast of five persons: three of them present-day witches operating in New York City. Gillian Holroyd could cast spells but only her *familiar* could make them effective. Her *familiar* was a cat named Pyewacket. Applicants galore attended the Studio Theatre but all proved unsuitable until an elegant Siamese was set down on the stage. With feline fastidiousness she carried out a thorough tour of inspection which included the entire auditorium. She then returned to centre stage, sat down, curled her tail round her neatly placed front paws and fixed her blue eyes on the last row of seats. She was hired on the spot.

On the other side of Nairobi there was theatrical activity of another kind. The long-awaited National Theatre would be ceremoniously opened on November 6.

'In March 1946 a group of five people were determined to raise funds to build a theatre. The first production in aid of the scheme was a production of Shaw's *Arms And The Man*. Plans for the theatre were drawn by Mrs. Eugenie D. Hughes and gradually over the years these were modified until eventually the final plan was prepared and agreed upon... When the planning of this theatre was undertaken it was essential to consider two main features. First the auditorium had to be small enough to ensure full houses, for nothing is more discouraging than playing to a 'half empty house'.

It was decided that the auditorium should hold a total of 412 including a small circle holding approximately 70 seats. (A reduction from the originally proposed 550 seats.).

'The Centre of the Circle has been designed for the purposes of a Royal Box, and the Kenya emblem — a lion — is to be carved on the face of it by an African sculptor. To add to the feeling of intimacy a warm colour scheme has been designed bringing in the natural colour of the cedar panelling with terra-cotta in varying shades, rust seats and blue ceiling.

'Secondly, the theatre was designed as a multi-purpose hall where plays, concerts, pageants and films could be staged. For this reason it was necessary to effect a compromise in order to meet these varying conditions in the best possible manner.

'The key point which immediately presented itself was the necessity for the sake of music, to provide an apron stage where strings and soloists could be placed in front of the main proscenium curtain. An apron stage is also beneficial for the presentation of Shakespeare, Masques, Musical Comedy, Opera and Pageant Plays. It is not, however, always approved by producers of Straight plays.

'The Stage is 29 feet 6 inches deep from the Cyclorama to the Proscenium Arch with a 6 feet 0 inch apron stage. The Proscenium opening is 32 feet 0 inches wide by 21 feet 0 inches high. The stage itself is level... counterweighting has been installed and the safety curtain can be operated by hand as well as electrically. The air conditioning plant has been designed not only to cleanse the air, but also to control the temperature in the auditorium.'

The funding had been provided by:

Colonial Development & Welfare Fund	£50,000.00
Kenya Government	£5,000.00
Nairobi City Council	£2,000.00
The Theatre Fund	£3,975.3/4
	£ 60,975.3/4

The Land (Plot LR No. 209) had been gratis.
The cost of the building & equipment: £58,519.94

The National Theatre had been conceived in March 1946. Building had started in August 1951 and now it was being opened by Sir Ralph Richardson to a Full House of VIPs on November 6, 1952.

Nairobi now had two theatres; one somewhat too large and the other a great deal too small to accommodate its ever-growing number of Theatre Club Members, but neither the Governing Council of the National Theatre nor the Maules could have foreseen that on October 20 a State of Emergency would be declared in Kenya.

Don cabled me in London: did I wish to withdraw from my intended trip? On receiving my reply 'Certainly NOT!' he booked my air passage. On November 15, I set off from the London Terminal heading for Blackbushe airport in Hampshire in extreme cold with thick fog shrouding the forlorn English landscape. Finally a small Viking aircraft operated by a charter firm named Airwork took off and headed for Africa.

Upon reaching Malta, we spent the night at the Phoenicia Hotel. Open windows gave access to a balcony and deliciously warm air wafted into my bedroom. The night sky twinkled with stars. The Mediterranean glinted in the distance.

The next night was spent in an hotel in Khartoum in stifling heat while a sandstorm whirled. On Day Three we landed for lunch in Juba where the tarmac on the runway was frying in the heat, but on reaching Eastleigh Airport that same afternoon, I thought I was back in Hampshire. Grey clouds hung low and a chill wind was blowing. I had not been told about Kenya's rainy seasons. If Nairobi was only a short distance from the Equator, why — I wanted to know — wasn't the climate equatorial?

The Muthaiga house was full of flowers: arum and madonna lilies, roses and carnations, together with enormous globes of agapanthus and I knew then, this certainly wasn't Hampshire in November.

Next morning we plunged into rehearsals. We were scheduled to open just eight days later. Morning work took place on stage in the 'standing set' for the Maules' current production: Agatha Christie's *The Hollow* and the apprentice assistant stage manager stood in for the leading actor, a local 'Guest' who could join us only at the end of his day's work. From 5.30pm the entire cast came together but by 8.30pm the stage manager called: "Clear the stage, please..." This was the half hour call for the evening performance and Mollie, who was playing in *The Hollow*, scuttled up to her dressing room. Further rehearsals for *Bell, Book and Candle* continued elsewhere. At odd moments, fittings for costumes were squeezed in.

By opening night, November 25, I had developed laryngitis and was feverish. As I sat on stage, cradling Pyewacket in my arms, I could not be sure what sound, if any, would emerge from my throat. A few feet away, on the other side of the closed curtains, the first night audience (a Full House) chattered and laughed and this caused Pyewacket to prick up her chocolate-coloured ears in alarm. Would she take fright, leap from my arms and bolt when the curtains swung open? To date she had proved herself a splendid colleague and an affectionate companion. She had a whole repertoire of miaows and purrs and murmurings and sighs and she responded to my voice or any slight movement I might make when holding her. But with those unknown creatures assembled so very close she might decide, on the instant, that an acting career held no attraction for her.

The audience hushed, the curtains parted and, following the round of applause accorded to the splendid set (by Geoffrey Best) I spoke my opening line: "Oh, Pye-Pye-Pyewacket — what's the matter with me?" Dead on cue she answered with a small Siamese "Mmmmm... Purrrr" and was an instant hit with the audience.

We gave 41 performances over a six-week period, playing to just under 3,000 theatre-goers, paying Sh6 per seat and we ended in a blaze of glory on January 3, 1953. Pyewacket was now a 'Star'.

The leading actor — the 'Guest' — now dropped a bombshell: he declined to accompany us on the long-planned tour. This left us in a bit of a fix. Already the whole venture had been questioned.

The declaration of a State of Emergency and the arrest of Jomo Kenyatta had been the starting gun for the all-out struggle for Independence, and the Administration considered it unwise to allow a band of Strolling Players loose in areas which were deemed Mau Mau strongholds.

It was agreed, however, that we should continue with the tour, after certain proposed dates had been cancelled for reasons of security. Restraints were imposed: we must always travel in convoy; *never* after dark, and we had to be armed. A small revolver of Czechoslovak manufacture was duly licensed in our name and handed over together with 15 rounds of ammunition. This caused us more anxiety than any other hazard we were to face. There were draconian penalties for losing, mislaying or allowing any firearm to be stolen and here we were, forced to carry one while barnstorming outlying areas of Kenya where vicious, murderous attacks had taken place with equally vicious retaliation from Armed Forces.

Who would be responsible for our revolver? Where should it be kept? Who would fire it? Who *could* fire it? At each and every target practice the damned thing had jammed.

But this was insignificant set against the problem that now preoccupied us: we were scheduled to open on January 17 in Mombasa and we were without a leading actor.

CHAPTER THREE

"We'll motor to Mombasa through the night," Don declared, adding, "That way, we can do a full day's work either end."

A Morris saloon, fitted with a roof rack, was packed tight: four passengers and Pyewacket, luggage, cameras, picnic baskets, vacuum flasks, binoculars, cushions, rugs, maps and notebooks. In the trunk a first aid kit, a five-gallon jerrycan of petrol, containers of oil and water, tow ropes, a spade, a powerful flashlight and tools. It also carried Don's portable typewriter, a briefcase bursting at the seams with DM stationery — membership enrolment forms, receipt books, publicity matter ('The Little Theatre with the BIG reputation'), Royalty Return Ledgers, Desk Diary and a great deal more.

Following behind in a Land Rover were Donald Whittle, actor, and Jeremy Dempster, apprentice stage manager. In the rear was the steamer trunk — the source of the rumour "The Maules are quitting". In it, our stage costumes, make-up and an electric iron. An old bed-sheet was wrapped tight round the costumes, hanging from a notched rail. This was intended to keep the penetrating red dust of Kenya from reaching the expensive clothes.

Pyewacket had her own basket furnished with a cushion. She wore a collar, which she tolerated, but she loathed the restraint of a leash so I clipped it on to her collar only when absolutely necessary. She and I had been dozing in the rear of the Morris when we hit corrugations. Both of us woke with a jolt and Pye voiced a shrill cry of protest. The car juddered and shook while small items worked their way loose and scattered in the car's interior. Our teeth felt like they might do the same. There were two schools of thought on the best method of travelling over corrugations: either very slowly, which reduced the shuddering motion but prolonged the agony; or very fast in one uninterrupted session of chattering teeth and rattling windows, under a shower of dislodged objects.

We were enclosed by the velvety African night when Don announced, "This must be Sultan Hamud." Sultan Hamud. What a name! What visions of voluptuous luxury were evoked by the words... Sultan Hamud: gilded domes and arabesque arches, Houris in diaphanous trousers, delicately patterned tiles and tinkling fountains...

I peered from the back of the car, but all I could make out were a few pinpricks of light in the surrounding eiderdown of night. Soon we were beyond Sultan Hamud with nothing but darkness surrounding us. From time to time our headlights picked up eyes — some blood red, others incandescent gold. For an instant they hung in the darkness before being abruptly extinguished as the animal turned and was lost in the surrounding scrub.

At dead of night a large, tawny shape leapt from the dirt road ahead of us. The car slowed to a halt and a pair of eyes flashed in our direction. A full-grown lioness stood no more than five yards away, another lioness at her side. From the tall grass at the road's edge two great heads were raised to focus on us while a fifth lioness came strolling from behind the vehicle to join the pride. For a few moments all was still, then the big cats lost interest and turned away, disappearing from view in an instant.

As the sky lightened and acacia thorns took on familiar outlines, we drew to the side of the road, somewhere in the Taru Desert. Begrimed and stiff: we emerged from the cramped car. Across the limpid air came the sound of cattle lowing while smoke from village cooking fires rose in lazy coils.

I attached Pye by her leash to a small thorn bush and set water — which she preferred to milk — and food before her. She surveyed her surroundings, sitting neat and elegant, faintly surprised at this turn of events.

The sun now came into view over the rim of the horizon, molten gold as it gilded the dawn sky.

When we reached Mombasa, we headed directly for the Little Theatre Club.

The Mombasa Times had told its readers: 'The Donovan Maules... East Africa's pioneers, are bringing us something we need... and for which we have waited many years.'

Michael Watson, a keen amateur actor and, at that time, a Big Wheel at Allsopps Brewery, had agreed to take on the lead role in *Bell, Book and Candle* for the performances in Mombasa. He would take part of his annual leave to do so.

But before he could even join us at the Coast, he had company meetings to attend in Uganda and Tanganyika. Clutching the script of the play, he assured us he would learn his lines and join us for rehearsals a few days later. Meanwhile, we cabled London urgently requesting a substitute actor to arrive in time to play Shepherd Henderson for the remainder of the tour.

We opened on schedule. Michael had done a magnificent job, with only minimal rehearsals. Applying make-up to a face slicked with sweat, I could hear cicadas shrilling nearby. Then came another sound, a high wailing cry: "Allah is Mighty!" Jeremy rapped on the dressing room door. "Half an hour, please."

Three calls — the insect to mate; the faithful to prayer; the actor to work.

The heat was stupefying. Side doors the entire length of the auditorium remained wide, to catch any little breeze blowing. This attracted a variety of insects, lured by bright stage lights. We blinked away salty sweat from our eyes and tried to remain focussed on our lines as moths fluttered and flies buzzed near our ears. An amiable mongrel dog ambled into one performance and sat quietly watching until boredom sent it ambling out again. Bats swooped, executed a few circuits of the stage then swooped out.

No replacement for Shepherd Henderson had arrived from London; nevertheless, during the length of the run in Mombasa, I acted with Michael Watson at night, while rehearsing each morning with Basil Hurle-Hobbs.

Basil had heard of our dilemma. He already knew about the upcoming, first ever 'Fit-up' tour of East Africa. It presented the opportunity for some action, possibly even some excitement, with Kenya under a State of Emergency. The prospect appealed to him. In fact, the outlook was bang on.

We would be leaving Mombasa the following morning, heading for Arusha. Our final performance at the coast was to a Full House with bouquets for Mollie and me and tributes to Pyewacket: a tin of sardines and a large plate of cold, cooked sausages — two of her favourite foods. Her star status was now assured and her fame spread with frequent mentions in the press.

That night, on their farm on the Kinangop, Mr. and Mrs. Ruck and their young son Michael were murdered by Mau Mau.

Don kept a log book. *Bell, Book and Candle* was the first full-scale tour of East Africa and our experiences might be of use in the future.

'Arusha. Tanganyika. School dining room. Seats approx. 150 on flat floor. Rental Sh75 a night. Awkward stage. No proper dressing rooms. Off stage wing space: None!'

Leaving the ever-changing colours of the Indian Ocean and the coconut palms of the Coast behind us, we headed for Voi where we would turn left. The landscape was dry, the sun hot overhead and Pyewacket was complaining about the bone-shattering corrugations. Now the windshield in front of my face began to darken ominously as an avalanche of luggage, shaken loose from its moorings on the roof, slid slowly towards the bonnet of the Morris.

Mount Kilimanjaro was camouflaged in cloud as we continued towards Moshi. Reaching Arusha at dusk, the Land Rover was unloaded at the Primary School before we scattered to our various hosts for the night. When we unpacked the following morning, we found our costumes, curtains and drapes deeply creased and wrinkled after the steam-heat of Mombasa. Mollie and I set about a marathon ironing session: she on the ironing board, me on the floor using a second iron borrowed from the school matron. Basil was rigging the lighting. Don was seeing to bookings, and arranging for programme sellers and ticket-tearers. Jeremy and Donald hammered nails and hung curtains as they came away from our irons.

"They're going to dress up!" exclaimed a small girl when she glimpsed my costumes hanging from the edge of a shelf. Props were unpacked. I re-wrapped the Christmas gifts used in the opening scene; they were much the worse for wear after nine performances in Mombasa. "D'you get prizes for doing it?" enquired a small boy.

At noon the dining room filled with children eager for lunch. As noisy as a flock of starlings they swarmed in, setting up a great surge of chatter and giggles as they speculated on the activity taking place at the end of the hall. They would not be attending either of the two performances, timed for 9pm, but the level of excitement as they watched our labours grew to fever pitch.

'Cloakroom — Girls' was equipped with rows of gleaming basins and lavatories, all at knee height. Using them induced a Groucho Marx lope.

At 6pm, with much yet to do on the set, we tried to give Basil a run-through. This was his opening night. Now it was supper time and the starlings were out in full force. Filthy, dishevelled, exhausted, we raced back to our hosts for a quick bath and a sandwich, the first food since breakfast, before returning for the evening performance.

Poor Basil — never a quick or diligent study — had only a sketchy idea of Shepherd Henderson. We battled valiantly through the performance with much improvisation and many departures from the script, causing Jeremy to flutter desperately through the prompt book in an effort to keep track while I steered Basil back to the plot line.

Only rarely was he 'on the beam'. At the end of the fraught evening — Don's description of the stage: 'awkward' was an understatement — the German matron offered us piping hot coffee and delicious home-made cakes.

Famished and grateful, we wolfed them down. In a conciliatory gesture Basil laced my coffee with a stiff slug of brandy from the flask which had sustained him through his ordeal.

The next day we were allowed a respite. A short drive from Arusha was a lake, said to be immensely deep: it filled the crater of an ancient, extinct volcano. High above it was a lovely villa with a terraced garden and flowering shrubs spilling down the sheer rock face to the water below. In the distance, shimmering above the water, was Kilimanjaro. A glorious spot for our picnic before returning for the second performance at Arusha. At its conclusion we stripped the set as far as we could in the dark. The rest would have to wait for daylight. 236 seats had been sold over the two performances. Next day we packed up, loaded up and set off with the assembled starlings, noisier than ever, waving us off.

In Nairobi we packed and reorganised. The following day we would be heading for Nanyuki with a further nine locations to follow, hauling everything needed for the production. To date we had received much help from the Little Theatre Club in Mombasa and the Arusha Amateur Arts Society, but from now on we would be on our own. Coupled to the rear of the Land Rover was a trailer capable of carrying up to three tons. Constructed of Dexion steel and timber, it had been designed by Basil and was dubbed the Dexion Special.

Scenery consisted of folding screens — 14 in all — made of plywood, 8 feet high with a scroll design at their top. Some, or all, would be set up, dictated by the size of the stage in school, hotel, club or hall. Furniture had been carefully selected for its compactness. The sofa seated two (and *only* two) intimately. Carpets, curtains, loose covers and cushions went into a skip. The portable switchboard: 5ft by 3ft, was complete with cue lights, bells and dimmers. We had a set of footlights, two lighting battens, three baby spots, a chandelier and wall brackets together with yards and yards of cable, dozens of spare light bulbs and sheets of coloured gelatines; a back-cloth and six battens furnished with curtain hooks from which to fly it; and also, House Curtains for anywhere without their own; twelve frames of production photographs and a huge crate of programmes with other necessary stationary.

A further quantity of glazed frames had been dispatched ahead of us by rail. Paint, distemper and brushes for touching up the set, a box of tools and mirrors to furnish the often improvised dressing rooms were packed into the Morris, sandwiched between cushions and rugs. There were two enormous canvas banners displaying, in giant letters, THE DONOVAN MAULE PLAYERS. These were to be strung, after obtaining the necessary permission, across the main street of each of our tour dates. The Dexion Special was emblazoned in the same manner along each flank. Four huge crates of props went into the Land Rover together with the cabin trunk. Donald, Jeremy and Basil sat in front.

On January 29 the Morris, with luggage firmly roped to the roof and three Maules and Pyewacket in the interior, headed out of Nairobi. The Land Rover, hauling the Dexion Special, followed behind.

We attracted a few curious glances and well-wishers waved us on our way, shouting "Good Luck!"

'Nanyuki — 124 miles from Nairobi. Sports Club seats 150 on flat floor, stepped at back. Stage: not bad. Flimsy transparent tabs. One rather cramped 'dressing room' back P. side of stage.'

We were scheduled to give two performances on the last two days of January 1953, intended to 'take settlers' thoughts off their worries for an hour or two.' These worries had increased sharply since the murder of the Ruck family the previous Saturday.

At the insistence of the authorities in Nairobi, our own armoury had expanded to three revolvers.

Our route lay through a green landscape of maize and bananas. Streams of brown water tumbled, fed by the multitude of small rivers springing from the slopes of the Aberdares, crouched like a great beast to our left.

Thatched rondavels and grain stores dotted the surrounding hills. Kikuyu women, bent double, worked the red fertile soil — digging, hoeing, and weeding — cultivating sustenance for their ever-growing, ever-hungry families. Others, their backs loaded, trudged the miles, their hands busy weaving a sisal *ciondo*.

Glossy-flanked goats nibbled and tore at bushes and rust-coloured sheep, bemused and disoriented, prepared to cross the road: some moving forward, others turning back, until a little herdsboy, stick in hand, appeared over the brow of a hill. Swiftly he set about concentrating their woolly minds. The road again clear, the car moved on. From time to time we caught a glimpse of Mount Kenya, emerging from cloud cover.

Nanyuki swarmed with uniforms — Army and Kenya Police Reservists. A busy little spotter aircraft buzzed overhead.

Arriving later than expected, we received a warm welcome from the Sports Club housekeeper. "We've all been looking forward to your visit so much. I hope you don't mind, but we thought it better for the shows to be at five o'clock — not nine. Security, you know. People like to get back home before dusk, if possible. Is that all right? And we thought the dining room would be the best place for the play. We'll clear it for you after breakfast tomorrow."

The Land Rover now lumbered into the car park. The Dexion Special was uncoupled and we dispersed to our various overnight hosts. When I reported for duty the following morning, I found Don surveying the wreckage of the production pix sent by rail: frames smashed, glass shattered, photographs slashed. I repaired as many as possible and then hawked them round Nanyuki, requesting any likely hotel or shop to please be kind enough to display this publicity. If accepted, a note of the location, together with trading hours, was made — all frames had to be collected again before we moved on.

Meanwhile, Don was making arrangements for flying our two overhead banners. With only two performances, the first a mere eight hours later, speedy and visible promotion was essential.

The Dexion Special, a hybrid vehicle of Basil's own invention, had sustained a bent axle on the way to Nanyuki, causing a tyre to chafe against the side of the trailer. The wheels were not of standard size and we carried no spares, none being available in Nairobi at the time of our departure. The contraption was taken to a garage for attention.

Our new, adaptable set was not yet familiar to us. Errors were made and time wasted. A set of curtains required shortening. The ever-helpful housekeeper introduced me to a treadle sewing machine, possibly one of the very first to reach Kenya. It was all heavy wrought-iron, and with a stubborn mind of its own. I set to work but it was no contest. To save time I admitted defeat quickly. Instead I raced into town in the Land Rover (Don was using the Morris) and found the Star Tailoring Company who guaranteed a set of new curtains — ready for collection by four o'clock that afternoon.

While in town, I shopped around for a desk blotter, required on the set. At last an accommodating chemist loaned me an impressive presentation ICI number. "Very jolly, isn't it?" He smoothed the impeccable leather margins. "You will return?" I swore I would. "It is for the drama," I told him. "Today and tomorrow."

"OK. You will return?"

Basil worked all day on the lights: hanging battens, fixing lanterns, wiring up and testing.

An elderly Club member clad in khaki shorts as commodious as a tent, golfing stockings and a sleeveless khaki jacket, wanted to know why lunch was being served in the Bar, not the dining room. "What's goin' on in there?"

He was told: "There's the play tonight."

"Play, eh? That accounts for it! Thought I saw someone in fancy dress in town this mornin'." Chortling at his joke, he sipped his first pink gin of the day. His chortle back-fired and he was overcome in a paroxysm of coughing, his face turning purple.

Lunch over, the Club staff ranged all available seats for an audience. Just after four o'clock, I sped back to the Star Tailoring

Company. A well-made set of lined curtains were still being pressed under a heavy charcoal iron.

Ripping them away from the astonished African, I raced back to the Club, flinging the bundle to Jeremy before I went on to my dressing room.

Nanyuki Sports Club featured a race course. The ground was rough and the tiny grandstand somewhat shaky, but it could boast the most magnificent backdrop possible: Mount Kenya rising in all its majesty behind the starting post. Some distance from the Club, the housekeeper had her own quarters and had planned that I should use this accommodation. As I sprinted the furlong, I was thankful that it was without hurdles!

The *Kenya Weekly News* reported: 'Nanyuki had been fortunate in being included...' (Nyeri had been scratched). 'This splendid little company is greatly to be congratulated in deciding to tour the 'affected areas'. Very sensibly they decided to put on two performances at 5pm so that farmers in outlying districts were able to avail themselves of the opportunity to see the first professional show ever to be put on in Nanyuki... It was extremely well dressed, and it was interesting to note the clever use of scenery and miniature furniture which gave the impression of space and size on the very small stage... It was unfortunate that, on the second night, the electricity failed, but undeterred and without a minute's pause the company carried on by the light of torches, without any loss of continuity at all. Annabel Maule and her Siamese cat rather 'stole' the show; Pyewacket answered all her questions with 'miaows' at all the correct places and is a superb little actress...'

The *Kenya Weekly News* correspondent could not know that Pyewacket had had a nasty experience the previous night, soon after our arrival in Nanyuki.

As my hostess drove me to her home she told me that she had a Siamese of her own. This news alarmed me. Pyewacket did not like other animals. I had witnessed her spitting viciously at her very own son. She only tolerated humans — and even then, not all of them. I was apprehensive.

I smuggled her, in her basket, into the bedroom and closed the door. She explored the room thoroughly then attempted to exit through a window, only to find herself imprisoned by sturdy security grills. While I went to run a bath, she managed to escape and came face to face with the other Siamese. For a silent, tense moment the two cats glared at one another then there was a screech from Pye as she took off: racing down the highly polished corridor with the resident cat in hot pursuit. As I chased both creatures, wisps of *café-au-lait* down flew in my face or settled gently on the shining floor boards. Retracing her tracks, she fled into our bedroom and I followed while restraining the resident cat from entering. The door shut, I called softly. Once assured that we were alone, she emerged from under the bed, thoroughly shaken. I placed her on the bed where she examined her wounds: a few scratches on her hindquarters, which she began to lick. Much the greater wound was to her self-esteem. How could that creature not know about her star status, her renown, her press notices? How could he have been so crude as to fail to pay homage and — worse — actually attack her? She had done nothing, nothing at all to provoke him. The whole thing was most uncalled for. After much soothing and some warm milk she settled down.

The *Kenya Weekly News* had continued: 'Basil Hurle Hobbs is to be congratulated on undertaking the part of Shepherd Henderson at such short notice.'

There had been an interval of two whole days since we had played Arusha, and if Basil had been 'shaky on lines' then, his mind now, following hours of strenuous work, had truly slipped into neutral. At every moment when Mollie was off stage she positioned herself behind a screen and hissed his lines at him.

None of this troubled the wonderfully enthusiastic audiences, totalling 230 over the two performances. Clapping wildly, shouting "Bravo!" and "Come again!" they made the whole thing worthwhile. These were the 'prizes for doing it.' As I sprinted up the race course one last time, a full moon silvered Mount Kenya, highlighting the snow on the peaks. Mau Mau gangs used caves up on the mountain; how many pairs of eyes had observed our comings and goings in and around the Club? What reports of our activities had flashed along the swift, mysterious bush-telegraph?

Following our second performance on Saturday, Club members were spurred to 'Make a Night of It', and soon a dance was in full swing and we were not allowed to leave.

There still remained the stripping and packing. We got very little sleep that night.

Next morning, feeling distinctly frail, I was ready to depart from my hospitable hosts when I realised that Pyewacket had gone AWOL. She wasn't in the bedroom so I searched the garden, calling her name and whistling. Previously she had always responded, galloping towards me on velvet paws but on this occasion it was the resident Siamese who made his appearance, not Pye. He was confined to barracks and the search party now included both my host and hostess, the cook and two house servants. My arrival on Thursday night, with a cat attached to a leash, like a dog, had caused some amusement among the Africans. My behaviour now, as the minutes passed and I grew more agitated, calling and whistling and searching, was even more ludicrous. The gardener, together with a few women and children, materialised and joined in the fun. At the foot of every tree, peering into every flowering shrub, was an African crying: "Poozz... Poozz..." before succumbing to uncontrollable laughter.

Finally Pyewacket made her delayed entrance, strolling up the drive to come and roll in the dust at my feet. Swiftly I clipped the leash to her collar and snatched her up before she could launch on further escapades. We were late already with a long day ahead. We were expected in Molo before nightfall. Africans, doubled up in mirth, witnessed my departure.

Arriving at the Club I asked Jeremy for the borrowed ICI blotter. "Haven't you got it?" he asked. "I left it out, as you asked."

The dining room was searched. The impromptu dressing room was searched. I had promised, so sincerely, to return it. But where was it? Don now appeared. "Blotter? I've packed a blotter — with the programmes. I thought it might come in handy..." The skip was located, unloaded, re-opened. The blotter was reclaimed and returned. It was 11.30 by the time we left Nanyuki.

We would be travelling due west, almost on the Equator, heading for Thomson's Falls. Travel arrangements were altered. Don, Basil and Jeremy rode in the Land Rover, taking with them two of our three firearms. I would drive the Morris with Mollie, Donald and Pyewacket. The unreliable Czech revolver lay to hand near the steering column. The Dexion Special, back from the garage, still wasn't right. I followed behind, watching the trailer waddle like an uncertain duck until, travelling at 25 miles an hour in their dust cloud, we could bear it no longer and passed them.

With Mount Kenya etched sharp against a brilliant blue sky at our backs, we travelled over an empty, sunlit plateau. Tommy gazelle raised their small, neat heads at our approach. Giraffe stared over flat-topped acacia thorns. The shadows of clouds raced along the ground, keeping pace with the moving vehicle.

We reached Thomson's Falls after one o'clock and drew into the car park of Barry's Hotel, anticipating the first gulp at a pint of chilled shandy. "Shall we wait for the others?" I asked. "No," Mollie said. "We'll eat now. We're running very late." The dining room was crowded with khaki-clad figures and bristling with firearms: revolvers, rifles, even a sub-machine gun or two.

We were at the coffee stage when I caught sight of Basil's dust-covered face peering into the room.

"What happened? Where are the others?"

"Tyre burst on the Dexion Special. I'm looking for a replacement."

"But where are the others?"

"They're with the trailer. About 15 miles from here. God! I'm thirsty..."

The proprietor of Barry's Hotel 'swung into action' — he pointed out a diner who owned a garage nearby. He swiftly assembled two lunch boxes, remembering beers and a bottle opener. He undertook Pyewacket's welfare in my absence. "Does she like cold sausages?" Mollie insisted on coming with me. I checked with Basil, now demolishing cold beef and salad and swallowing his second beer, "Just the job..."

"15 miles you said?"

"As near as dammit."

Mount Kenya was now ahead of us. Behind us was a swirl of grey dust as I trod on the accelerator. We scanned the empty landscape. "I see something..." — "Can't be them, we haven't done 10 miles yet." The sepia coloured scrubland flew by.

"There they are!" The tiny object ahead grew larger and took on the recognisable shape of Basil's brainchild — lopsided, one flank resting on rocks. There was no sign of either Don or Jeremy. I slowed to reduce the dust and drew up behind the crippled Dexion Special.

Slowly, painfully, two figures emerged, on their hands and knees, from beneath the trailer, their eyes bloodshot, their faces a mask of dust. They had been lying, each with a revolver at his side, in the only shade available to them — facing in either direction of the lonely road. We handed over the beer.

All doors to the Morris were open to catch any breath of breeze. The packed interior was like an oven. We were waiting for Basil's return. An occasional passing motorist offered help. The sun was well over the roof of the sky and making its afternoon descent when Basil slewed to a halt, covering all of us with dust. He set to work immediately. The Dexion Special carried three tons; it wasn't an easy job. The trailer, upright and roadworthy once more, was coupled to the Land Rover. Jeremy was collecting the scattered tools when Don observed, "The Land Rover's got a flat..." Someone breathed "Holy cow!"

Back at Barry's Hotel we tried to telephone Molo but were unable to make a connection. "We must stay in convoy until we reach Nakuru," Don ordered. Pyewacket, bulging with cold bangers, was sleeping it off in her basket and remained unaware of an apricot-coloured Labrador puppy that came gambolling up to us, eager to join this fun party. It made a determined effort to get into the Morris with Mollie... Its look of abandoned misery as we drew away was heartbreaking, but almost instantly a passing butterfly caught its attention and it gambolled off in pursuit.

The sun was setting as we left Thomson's Falls, outlining the crest of a hill ahead of us in a fierce shade of pink. Dense, dark forest enclosed the road on either side. A line of figures, silhouetted against the evening sky, came into view over the brow of the hill, occupying the width of the road. They appeared hooded and as they moved forward we caught the flash of metal.

I urged the Morris to greater effort, to gain ground... to reach the brow of the hill. As we cleaved through the centre of the cordon it scattered to either side of the road. The way ahead was clear. We had escaped the ambush.

Donald, from the back of the car, gave his verdict: "Poor things. You've frightened them to death."

The African women, heavily-laden with firewood, their metal ear ornaments swinging, scrambled back to the road to continue the miles to their destination.

In the Bar of the Stag's Head Hotel in Nakuru, we held a conference. It was long after dark and Molo was 40 miles away. Molly Ryan had given clear instructions. "We've cut a new approach road to the farm. Don't take the old one. It's impassable now, just a *ng'ombe* track. My son will be there to guide you."

The three Maules and Pyewacket were to stay with her while neighbours would be hosting the boys. Instructions on how to reach them would be given after our arrival at Garryowen — due many hours ago.

This was the plan: The Maules and Pyewacket would head for Garryowen with all speed. Don, given the details of where the boys would be staying, would then head back toward Nakuru, meet the slow lumbering half of our convoy and lead it to its destination. The Land Rover, hauling the lengthy, inflexible Dexion Special, was incapable of reversing. Even a simple turn required the space needed by a span of oxen.

We set off. Some distance from Nakuru, on the open road, we spotted a light being moved horizontally ahead of us. Trouble? We slowed, a woman in a light flowered cotton dress stood hugging a cardigan to her chest. It was a cold night. "Can you take us to Turi? There are two of us..." They squeezed into the Morris, rousing Pyewacket from her sausage hangover. "Are you the Donovan Maules? This must be Pyewacket. We are so much looking forward to your show."

The détour to Turi delayed us. Back on the road to Molo, Don said, "Look for the sign 'Ryan'. On the left."

We saw a left turn. We took it and laboured up a rough track until the Morris took a sickening lurch, causing Pye to protest and Mollie to declare, "This can't be right. We'd better go back." Turning was out of the question; the car's wheels were embedded in ruts and the sump scraped the overgrown ridge in the middle of the track. Mollie and I got out to guide Don. The chill night air made us catch our breath.

Over the rim of the hill ahead a lantern gleamed and a voice called, "Are you the Maules?" Mrs. Ryan's son confirmed what we had already guessed: we had taken the wrong track. It was at this moment that I caught sight of headlamps approaching on the main road. The boys were about to make the same mistake. I set off at a run. At an altitude of 9,000 feet the air was thin and cold, causing my lungs to pump painfully, while stinging sinuses brought tears to my eyes. Fine powdery dust rose from under my pounding feet. There had been no rain for a long time.

Basil was on the point of making the turn when I stumbled, arms threshing, into the beam of his headlamps. I couldn't speak. I could do no more than signal violently: 'NO...NO!...NOT THIS WAY...STOP!'

When we got to Garryowen, Molly Ryan, catching sight of my scarlet face, asked, "What's wrong with you?" She was convinced I was drunk. It was bliss to lay my throbbing head on soft pillows, cosy under two blankets and an eiderdown, cuddling a hot water bottle. Pye curled up close, sharing the warmth as well as adding her own.

Molo had been deemed an 'Unaffected Area' until the morning of our arrival, when it was discovered that Mau Mau oath administrators were operating on several of the big farms in the neighbourhood. All Kikuyu men had been hauled in for screening, carried out in a large goods shed alongside the railway line. Their womenfolk squatted in the dust outside. This development led to a shortage of farm labour, and arrangements were made for non-Kikuyu workers to undertake the more urgent tasks, such as milking; moving from farm to farm.

'MOLO Club. 'Little Theatre' seats 150 on club chairs on flat auditorium. Stage has to be erected on trestles specially for performance.'

Three performances had been scheduled — now we offered to move straight on to Kitale. "No! No. Certainly not... we've been looking forward to your visit, but... perhaps just two performances? Possibly both on the same day? People don't want to drive long distances now — not after dark."

We had anticipated theatre-goers coming from Kericho, Elburgon, Njoro, Rongai and Londiani. Now, a great many would cancel. It was agreed that we would play at 2.45 and 9pm on Wednesday, February 4.

We drove the few miles to the Club, walking further to the Little Theatre, a somewhat bleak building with a great many uncurtained windows. On the steeply raked stage was a standing-set of 'too, too solid' timber.

"Oh yes... perhaps nobody told you? We've all been so busy. The Amateur Dramatic Society did *Little Lambs Eat Ivy*. It was so good! We thought you could use the same scenery for your play."

This presented problems. So did the number of windows, allowing sunshine to stream in. How were we to play a matinée? Sheets of brown paper and rolls of sticky tape were bought and Mollie and I started work. Basil, trying to hoist a lighting batten, called for a ladder (an item we didn't travel with). Following a lengthy delay, three saplings, loosely lashed together to form a tripod, were manhandled up onto the stage. When the apex made contact with the roof one of the treads fell away. A second gave way soon after. Basil decided to forgo the ladder, which left a trail of twigs and leaves in its wake.

Throughout the matinée, before 103 patrons, the wind gnawed and fidgeted at the papered-over windows. At the second performance, played to a mere 84, it grew fiercer, moaning round the building and tearing away what remained of the paper blinds. The cold was intense. It was difficult to control our chattering teeth.

Sanitary arrangements were set apart. A log-cabin privy at some distance across rough terrain housed an Elsan Chemical Toilet. There being no back stage exit, once an audience was in place the only way we could reach the loo was to climb out of the dressing room window, sprint across the field, sprint back and call to a colleague for help to climb back in.

Shivering, we removed our costumes but exhaustion and numb fingers forced us to delay packing the cabin trunk until next day.

Now came the good news — hot soup and Irish stew awaited us in the Club's kitchen. Molo was sheep country; Molly Ryan the premier pedigree breeder at the time.

We huddled over a charcoal brazier, plates of mutton and potatoes on our knees, gulping down brandy. As I mashed down potato with the back of my fork to soak up the last of the gravy, I could feel some life returning to my frozen toes.

East African Standard

THEATRE
ROYAL

All This Week at 9 p.m.

**MATINEE SATURDAY
5-15 P.M.
BE A FIRST NIGHTER!**

THE DONOVAN MAULE PLAYERS
by arrangement with
NEW THEATRES LTD.
present
The Well Known
London Stage Success

THE
GUINEA-PIG

In Three Acts

By Warren Chetham-Strode
PRODUCER DONOVAN MAULE

**ONE OF THE MOST DELIGHTFUL
PLAYS SEEN IN LONDON
FOR YEARS.
LOOKS INTO THE SOUL OF
ENGLISH
PUBLIC SCHOOL LIFE.**

CAST:
Donovan Maule
Mollie Donovan Maule
E. A. Vasey.-Bob Woodford
Tessa Woodford.-W. David
R. Scott.-Winlow
Fred Hutton
Mrs. K. Fraser Allen.

MATINEE: 7/50. 4/50, 3/50.
PRICES 10/50, 7/50, 4/50.

PLANS FILLING BOOK NOW.

THEATRE ROYAL
NAIROBI

Week Commencing MONDAY 13th September, 1948

THE DONOVAN MAULE PLAYERS

PRESENT

By arrangement with NEW THEATRES LTD.

THE GUINEA-PIG
by
WARREN CHETHAM-STRODE

Programme   One Shilling

The DONOVAN MAULE SCHOOL of DRAMATIC ART

STAGE TECHNIQUE IN ALL ITS BRANCHES
VOICE PRODUCTION
ELOCUTION
DICTION
MIME
FENCING
BROADCASTING

(Adult Students accepted for class-work only after preliminary private audition)

CHILDREN'S CLASS
SATURDAY MORNINGS 11—12.

INDIVIDUAL TUITION

Private lessons by arrangement in accordance with needs of individual student (child, or adult): dispelling of shyness, awkwardness, speech defects, improvement of diction, ease of movement, bringing out of personality.

Apply for brochure:
THE DONOVAN MAULE SCHOOL OF DRAMATIC ART
P.O. Box 67, NAIROBI.

or

Call at STUDIO in Government Road (50 yards past Capitol Cinema). Office Hours: 9—12-30. Telephone 3853.

Rear wall of studio - where first stage was built for *Outward Bound*.

Other end of Studio, windows facing Government Road. This became rear of auditorium for *Outward Bound*.

In desperation - as a theatre of some kind - we decided to turn our studios into a Studio Theatre of 55 seats.

Work began 21 September, 1949 and continued from 8am until 9pm and later every day for nine and a half weeks, Sundays included. Cash outlay approximately £1,800. Stage erected at Victorial St. end measured 12ft X 12ft with two tiny dressing-rooms behind. Flat auditorium floor contained 55 tip-up seats.

Jean Parnell,
Donovan Maule,
Mollie Donovan
Maule.

Basil Hurle-Hobbs,
Donovan Maule,
Mollie Donovan
Maule

The Donovan Maule Players

request the pleasure of your company at a performance of

"Outward Bound" by Sutton Vane

at their Studio Theatre, Government Road
(Just beyond the Capitol Cinema)
at 9 o'clock in the evening of

....

It is hoped to form a **THEATRE CLUB** to provide Nairobi play-lovers with well-staged, professionally produced plays.

The **STUDIO THEATRE** is an interim measure to foster dramatic art in Kenya and provide entertainment of high standard until a permanent repertory company can be launched in a larger Theatre.

R. S. V. P.
On Attached Postal Reply-Card
By **RETURN** Please.

....

I am able (not able) to be present at the STUDIO THEATRE on the evening of .... and shall be glad to have two seats reserved for me.

Signature..

Address..

Telephone No..

STUDIO THEATRE

NAIROBI

The
DONOVAN MAULE PLAYERS

Present

OUTWARD BOUND

by
SUTTON VANE

Programme

THE DONOVAN MAULE PLAYERS
present

OUTWARD BOUND

by Sutton Vane

Characters in order of their appearance

Scrubby	Donovan Maule
Ann	Ruth Hogan
Henry	Michael Partridge
Mr. Prior	Basil Hurle-Hobbs
Mrs. Cliveden-Banks	Gwen Alban
Rev. William Duke	R. Scott-Winlow
Mrs. Midget	Mollie Donovan Maule
Mr. Lingley	Roy Cable
Rev. Frank Thomson	R.C. Laming

Directed by
Mollie and Donovan Maule

Stage Manager . . Jean Parnell
Assistant Stage Manager . Jill Browse

Scenery designed and executed by
Basil Hurle-Hobbs and Ruth Hogan.

SYNOPSIS

The action of the play takes place in the smoke room of a ship.

Act 1. In Harbour . Morning
Act 2. At Sea . . The same evening
Act 3. About Six Days later

    Scene 1. Afternoon
    Scene 2. The night of the same day

Miss Ruth Hogan's hair styled by LENEE
Wrought-iron furniture   Hutchings, Biemer & Co., Ltd.
Cigarettes   Arcade Tobacconists.
Electric Fan   E. A. P. & L. Ltd.
All Dying & Cleaning for the Donovan Maule Players by The Pearl Dry Cleaners Limited.
Programme   Taylor's Advertising Service.

Front of House Hostess   PAM FENTON
Lighting Effects by   ALLEN BRAMLEY

"JEANNIE"

by
Aimee Stuart

The STUDIO THEATRE in its first version, before it got turned back to front. See daylight through window at top of the picture on the left. Don in the foreground, with script, Basil Hurle-Hobbs behind him and Mollie in the third row.

The STUDIO THEATRE after conversion with the Bar at the rear - everyone's favourite seat.

Don and Mollie at work in the little STUDIO THEATRE

Don in the Box Office of the Donovan Maule Theatre.

Production number 24 at the Studio Theatre, Government Road. HIS EXCELLENCY by Dorothy & Campbell Christie. October 1951. Don 2nd from left as H.E. Mollie seated.

DONOVAN MAULE & MOLLIE DONOVAN MAULE in BREATH OF SPRING By Peter Coke THE DONOVAN MAULE THEATRE 16 JUNE 1959 (Prod . 101).

Production no. 123, March 1961 - *The Rainmaker* by N. Richard Nash. Donovan Maule as H.C. Curry and Dorothy Primrose as his daughter Lizzie. Setting by Bill Piggott.

Production no. 132 - *Oliver!* December 1961. Setting by Bill Piggott.

The Hostage by Brendan Behan. Production no. 145, February 1963. Joseph Gichure as "Princess Grace" 3rd from right.

The Merchant of Venice - production no. 162, April 1964. From left: John Gardiner, Kerry Jordan and Kenneth Mason.

Billy Liar, production no. 149, May/June 1963 celebrated five years in the new Donovan Maule Theatre. Mollie Donovan Maule (above) and Annabel Maule (below) as mother and daughter in the play.

A Man for All Seasons by Robert Bolt - production no. 173, March 1965. Donald Kiboro, centre, as The Common Man. Others, from the left: Robert Beaumont, John Gardiner (seated), Kenneth Mason, Kerry Jordan and Bernard Hickley.

10th anniversary of the Donovan Maule Theatre, June 1968. Left to right: Bill Ryan, famous professional hunter, Don and Mollie.

Next day, in brilliant sunshine tempered by a chill breeze in these highlands, we packed, loaded and moved on.

We were getting the hang of this fit-up 'lark'. The best method of packing our vehicles was always in the same manner: First in, Last out. Mirrors cushioned between rugs and cushions; lampshades placed on top of crates full of props. But no matter how much care we took, lampshades sustained new dents and scratches on every journey. Mollie and I tied cotton squares over our heads to keep at bay the ever-present dust. Damp face flannels, kept in sponge bags, wiped away grime from face and hands. The boys rolled their cotton squares into bandannas and tied them round their heads, pirate-fashion. They smeared their lips and nose with cold cream to guard against wind and sunburn.

In the worst dust they tied scarves over their nose and mouth. When I groomed Pye, clouds of dust flew out of her coat.

Jeremy, an almond-white blond, wore an old Panama hat when painting scenery at the Studio. It was said that several productions could be identified through the layers of colour. The hat accompanied Jeremy on tour, and if the hat was missing at the moment of departure, the convoy must wait. The Dexion Special, fully loaded and tarpaulin-covered, stood ready. The Land Rover, Basil at the wheel and Donald beside him, needed only Jeremy. The Morris, with Maules aboard and Pye's basket carefully placed so that she might take note of everything that occurred, made up the band of travelling Players.

"Are we fit?" Basil shouted.

"Right. Who's got the guns?" came from Don.

"All right, then. Let's go!"

A cry came from Jeremy, "My hat!" He dashed away to recover his unique and disreputable headgear. Grinning, he would reappear with the disgraceful object on his corn-coloured hair.

"OK, let's go!" he ordered as he climbed into the Land Rover. It was his sole opportunity to wield a little bit of authority over the rest of us.

We headed north west, under brilliant blue sky, through forests of cedar and podo. Ghost-grey 'Old man's beard', a delicate lichen, hung, swaying in the breeze. We laboured up and over Timboroa, making the blood pound in my ears, relieved only when we dropped down into Trans-Nzoia. Ahead was a vista of ripening wheat dotted here and there by a Nandi flame tree flaunting great glowing scarlet blooms.

Kitale, well away from the 'Affected Areas', was relaxed and tranquil. Jacaranda trees shed their mauve tubular blossoms on the lawns of the Club. Crowned Cranes leaped in the ritual of their courtship dance: prancing on broken-match-stick legs, their wings outstretched. The plumage of their tiny heads resembled a fashionable Victorian lady's 'best-go-to-church' bonnet. Bush fires burned on the horizon, the acrid smell of smoke came to us on the breeze.

'KITALE. 251 miles from Nairobi. 119 from Molo. Kitale Hotel can seat approximately 250 in dining room on flat floor. Stage has to be erected specially behind permanently installed adequate tabs. No proper dressing rooms but enough room either side of the stage to rig small accommodation. All this placed in front of doors to kitchen.'

There could be no question of Kitale Hotel guests being diverted to the Bar for their meals, which meant we couldn't start work until the following morning, when breakfast was finished. With a matinée set for 5.30 the same day, this was cutting it fine. Nor could we haul our stuff through the entrance to the hotel — it had to come through the service entrance and the kitchen, under the curious gaze of potato-peelers and pastry-makers.

The three-foot high rostra only just held our set — we were at the limit either side, and without any steps available, this made every entrance difficult and every exit hazardous. There being no room for Pye's basket, she was handed up to me for each of her appearances. She made an occasional murmur of protest but was remarkably forbearing.

We gave three performances, seen by a total of 432 people, which helped to balance the poor figures at Molo. It was also a great deal warmer.

Back in the 1920s, gold had been found in the blue hills around Kakamega and a miniature gold-rush had followed. Prospectors settled and homesteads were erected. Rosterman's Mine boasted a Social Club, complete with a dance floor. Later, the gold proved insufficient, the rush slowed and the prospectors left.

When we visited, Kakamega was an unlovely town of earth roads lined with Asian *dukas*. At its centre stood a clock tower 'Built in 1935 with subscriptions from all races to commemorate the Silver Jubilee of King George V.' There was also 'King Georgi's Hoteli', a large Government Prison where the meals came *gratis* and the work was not too arduous, thereby offering a stress-free sojourn to the convicts housed there.

We would be giving only one performance in Kakamega, scheduled to be at a school. This proved unsuitable as it was without electricity, so we cast about for an alternative venue. The residual population of Europeans, just 87 of them, appeared sunk in terminal despair. "There's the Club... but hardly anyone goes there these days."

We had arrived 30 years too late! Back in the Roaring Twenties, Kakamega could boast several hotels. At one, the Corkscrew Inn, champagne flowed and on truly wild nights miners shot the necks from the bottles ranged behind the Bar. Now, there was only the deserted Club. On inspection we decided we could adapt the tiny circular dance floor to our purpose.

We needed runner rails from which to hang our curtains and Don, poring over a road map, said "Kisumu is only 35 miles away. You can shop and I can check on publicity and bookings." Three Maules set off in the Morris unaware of the Nyando Escarpment ahead. Huge boulders, 50 feet and more in diameter, littered the landscape: 'A feature of the terrain round Lake Victoria.' We were thrown off our seats as the car bucked and plunged. The very special, adjustable shock absorbers died of shock and, on a steep hill, we ground to a halt. Wedging rocks behind the rear wheels, we waited for the engine to cool.

A country bus came labouring up the hill, the familiar load of beds, bicycles and bananas on the roof. At every window grinning black faces witnessed the scene of three *wazungu* standing beside their visibly steaming *gari*. Their laughter set off a cackle of alarm from the chickens travelling with them. As the vehicle crept past us, it lurched dangerously as passengers came from the off-side to get a closer look. When at last it drew ahead, the rear window filled with grinning faces intent on one last, hilarious glimpse.

The Kisumu chemist, acting as our Booking Agent, showed Don the seating plan. "Booking not good... you coming at wrong time. Pakistani Rovers! Very good booking!"

"Rovers?"

"Hockey Team. Very popular! All... Everybody going to Rovers!" Runner rail, looped into a circle, would not fit into the car's trunk, so I sat in the back with it round my neck as we set off on the appalling 35-mile return journey. The identical thought was in all our minds: Pyewacket's reaction to this road when we returned to Kisumu in two days time. One of us spoke: "Do you think we could drug her?"

Donald and Jeremy fixed the runner rail and attached our own curtains. They were found to be too long, so I sat on the dance floor shortening them. All this unaccustomed activity dislodged a number of live creatures from the thatch roof. These scuttled away, fast. Dead carcasses were swept up before the performance. Basil had placed both our lighting switchboard and the prop table behind the Bar. In his final scene, Don threw back a neat whisky instead of the usual coloured water. He gasped, his eyes bulging, trying to find some breath for his next line.

The Club's 'Ladies' acted as our communal dressing room. Searching for chairs, we found a few frames with seats of interlaced strips of hide stretched slack by age. Our weight caused them to sag near ground level. We resembled nets of pink onions ranged round the room — they left their impression on us.

Le tout Kakamega came to our performance: 87 seats sold while two bats took it upon themselves to enter free. On joining our hosts, after striking and packing, a re-awakening of the uproarious 1920s was evident. "Don't expect this Club will see anything much after you're gone. Let's set fire to the place!"

Dropping down the final two or three miles to Kisumu, we could see a heat haze shimmering over Lake Victoria and the town.

'KISUMU — 221 miles from Nairobi. Garrison Theatre (very austere and arid) can seat 250 on flat concrete floor. Chairs have to be hired and transported. Hire fees: 25 cents per chair per day. Dressing rooms in Army hut about 20 yards away. Good lighting and switchboard.'

Constructed entirely of timber, the Garrison Theatre stood on a patch of scuffed earth. Clearly it had not been used for a very long time. The lavatory, for the use of players and audience alike, was a sociable wooden two-seater. Our opening performance (it was Friday 13th) played to row upon row of hired chairs costing us 25 cents each. Only 78 were occupied. Good God! We had played to a larger audience in near-defunct Kakamega! Saturday's performance fielded 124 customers. We sweltered and sweated and blamed the Pakistani Rovers as we swiped at swarms of lake flies busy settling everywhere: on the soap at the filthy wash-basin, round every light bulb, on the mirrors... those floundering in the tin of make-up remover had to be picked out individually. Before the Dexion Special could be loaded on Sunday morning, it had to return the hired seats.

"Have your passports handy — you'll need them at the border." It was very hot as our convoy left Kisumu. Initially our route lay along the shore of Lake Victoria under a canopy of flamboyants in full bloom — beautiful and soothing. All too soon the road turned away from the Lake and we began to climb, causing Pyewacket, who was feeling the heat and in a bad mood, to voice her displeasure. Prior to leaving Nairobi I had obtained, from the Department of

Immigration, a Re-entry Permit for myself. I enquired about "touring a Siamese cat". This query was not made too frequently, I fancy. Department after department failed to come up with an answer, so Pye had no travel documents.

'KAMPALA. Uganda. 444 miles from Nairobi. 223 from Kisumu. Makerere College Theatre. Auditorium: 500/600 and includes a Circle. Press: *Uganda Herald* (Tue. Thurs. and Sats). Plenty of advance publicity needed including press announcements in *Uganda Herald* and *E.A. Standard*. Stage: very good. Two very good dressing rooms. Good lighting.'

Approaching the border at Busia, a billboard proclaimed: WARNING! Halt at Police Post.

Pye stood on her hind legs, placed her forepaws at the open window of the Morris and shouted "Miaooowww!!"

"Attach her leash," Mollie advised Don, who was sitting in the back.

ALL DOCUMENTS TO BE SHOWN. RABIES!! The movement of DOGS is strictly controlled.

It seemed prudent to remove Pye from view. Don tried to put her in her basket and a violent battle of wills ensued. Don only just won. He closed the lid of her basket as we slowed at the barrier. From the Police Post came an *Askari* smart in puttees and tarboosh. Through the car window he handed Don a large ledger. "What date is it?"

"15th of February." The sound of creaking wickerwork grew louder as Pye tried to heave her way out of her prison. "My God! She's strong." Don muttered. "Passengers: three. Name: Maule. Let me have your passports..." Pye let out a howl of frustration and pushed harder.

The *Askari,* joined now by a colleague, was taking an interest in the crowded interior of the car. Oh, Lord! They wouldn't want to carry out a search, would they? Pye could no longer be controlled; in spite of Don's restraining foot she pushed and clawed her way out of her basket yelling, "Sssssshhhhhit!!!" She then jumped onto the back of the driver's seat, eyes flashing and every hackle raised. A low rumble came from the back of her throat: she was one very angry Siamese. We waited meekly for the summons to the Police Post. Instead, one after the other, the ebony faces broke into grins, displaying perfect teeth. "Pousssee! Pousssee!" they exclaimed in delight, stretching long, elegant fingers towards her. Mollified by their admiration, she refrained from spitting or scratching and allowed herself to be stroked by loving fingers.

Don returned the ledger, the *Askaris* gave smart salutes, the barrier was raised and we crossed into Uganda. We drew up at the Border Inn still weak with laughter. Pye, however, was unrelenting for a great many more miles.

Hot, dusty and dishevelled, we reached Kampala at 7.30 that Sunday evening. The Imperial Hotel was full of men in dark suits and highly polished shoes, but where was our 'Liaison Officer', the man who had all the information regarding our visit to Kampala? We enquired at the desk. "Donovan Maule Players. You're not expected until Thursday." Don put a call through to Entebbe. The Liaison Officer arrived just 30 minutes later. "Why are you here? Why aren't you in Mbale?"

"Didn't you get my letter?"

"What letter?" Our proposed date at Mbale had been cancelled long since and here we were — three days ahead of schedule in Kampala, which was hosting a Conference of African Courts (which accounted for the suits and shoes) and there was not a bed to be had in any of the hotels. Don delved into his bursting briefcase. Somewhere among the diaries, notebooks and receipt books he had made a note of a 'contact in Kampala'. He called the number. "This is Donovan Maule. Three of us and a cat are homeless until Thursday..."

"You must come to us, of course. Have dinner at the Imperial and we'll come and collect you. You would never find us in the dark. You did say three of you?"

"Yes. I have my wife and daughter with me." The boys were not expected until the following day.

Three hungry Maules found a table in the crowded dining room. Pyewacket allowed herself to be offered a portion of fish (without Sauce Tartare). She then drank water from a wine glass, neatly and elegantly, before attending to her toilette. Our Liaison Officer was impressed. "Now I've seen everything!"

Our hosts arrived. There was no difficulty in spotting the travel-stained Barnstormers among the Sober Judges.

"Oh, thank heaven you're an adult," said Mrs. Fraser when Don introduced me. "We wondered whether we should borrow a cot!"

They bore us away, leading the Morris out of town and finally up a steep hill. Mollie and Don were conducted to the guest house, taking Pye with them. This allowed her direct access to the garden. No security grilles here. I was shown to a suite of rooms in the main house, normally occupied by the Frasers' son, now at University in England. It was sheer luxury! Daylight revealed all Kampala spread out below. Murchison Bay, a tongue of Lake Victoria, curled away into the shimmering Lake, where currents feathered the surface in delicate shifting patterns. In contrast to Kenya, a subtle sepia photograph of sun-baked colours, dust and corrugations, Uganda was startling: a bright travel poster with green the dominant colour.

Bananaland!

The Baganda belles, standing tall in flowing robes of scarlet, purple and cyclamen-pink with turbans twisted high, strolled past. Their head-loads made them taller yet. Travelling light, one lady bore nothing more than an empty Coca-Cola bottle on her head. Every blade of grass, every palm leaf gleamed. There was no dust. All roads were tarmacked.

The prospect of Makerere College Theatre, accommodating '500/600 and includes a Circle', was daunting. Was there no alternative? Don's journal disclosed 'Kampala Club has useful stage with good proscenium and tabs and can seat 150 to 200.' So why weren't we playing there? 'Committee reluctant to let in 'Play Actors'.'

We made use of the time in hand to touch up our travel-worn scenery, to beat the dust from all our soft furnishings, to smooth and repair injured lampshades and look over our costumes — washing and repairing where necessary.

'A cold war seems to be raging in Kampala amongst the play producers and supporters.' Don noted. 'Much grumbling over Makerere College Theatre, which has no Bar... Three amateur societies here, with the usual strife and jealousy arising. The KATS; John Henderson's Amber Club Theatre (96 seats) but refused a Licence by the Fire Master and Makerere College Players.'

Warring amateurs notwithstanding, we played to 614 playgoers over our two performances and received wonderful hospitality, including a reception by the Mayor of Kampala.

Makerere College, later a University, was beautifully situated in spacious grounds. New residential quarters were under construction. Every student would have his own room, at a cost of £25 per year.

The *Uganda Herald's* theatre correspondent dwelt exclusively on the manner the KATS might have interpreted *Bell, Book and Candle* had *they* been presenting it. Mollie got a brief word of praise, but that was all.

It was an easy ride to Entebbe. 'A beautifully-laid-out garden city on the shores of Lake Victoria. There are extensive Botanical Gardens which, besides a fine collection of tropical flowering plants, contain gigantic rain forest trees with buttresses, stilt roots and Liana.' This information came from a guide book — Don's journal noted 'Entebbe Club. Charming little theatre with stepped-up auditorium with 144 comfortable chairs. Well equipped and practical stage. Good lighting. Two good dressing rooms.'

Mollie and I occupied one of these. It was crammed with superb Victorian mahogany bedroom furniture. Pye purred her approval as she stretched luxuriantly on a well-upholstered sofa.

Hippos, coming ashore at night to graze, might be seen in gardens bordering the lake and had even been sighted at the Main Post Office. The Comet, on its inaugural flight to South Africa, touched down at Entebbe and I was shown over the interior: roomy and air conditioned, with a delicious all-pink 'Ladies'.

We played to two Full Houses at Entebbe Club. Our visit was all too brief. We were relaxed and happy as we set off for Jinja, just 76 miles away, where no welcome of any sort was accorded us.

We were refused permission to hang our banner across Main Street, or any other street. We had not been offered private accommodation so instead we put up at the Ripon Falls Hotel, shabby and run down, where the manager declared, "I hate this damned country. Can't wait to get back to a pint in the local and a soccer match."

Clearly, touring actors found little favour with him.

'JINJA. Garrison Theatre. Seats approximately 250. Seats have to be hired from Kampala, costing, with transport, about 400/-! Bookings by Mr. Hira: Chemist.'

We went to inspect the Garrison Theatre, several miles out of town. Finding it locked, we pounded on doors and shouted at windows until a somnolent watchman allowed us in. His huge feet were encased in army boots without laces. An old British Army greatcoat, lacking buttons, hung from his gaunt frame. Following our arrival he returned to an alcove marked CLOAKS, lay down and slept for the remainder of our visit: two days and nights.

God only knew when Jinja's Garrison Theatre had last housed a show. There were no lights in either auditorium or dressing rooms. The latter held no furniture of any kind. Dust lay thick everywhere. I set off, heading for the Army huts on the far side of the compound. I climbed wooden steps to OFFICER'S MESS and knocked; receiving no answer, I tried the door, which was unlocked. The Mess was deserted. H.Q. OFFICE was the same and so, too, was C Coy OFFICE. Had there been a mutiny? Or an order to evacuate? In B Coy OFFICE I surprised a solitary subaltern at a desk. He sent for the Sergeant Major, who promised me a Fatigue Party and furniture from the Sergeant's Mess. Back at the theatre I found Basil surveying the scant lighting equipment. "Pretty duff stuff."

Don had gone to town where he found Mr. Hira's Chemist shop locked and shuttered. He turned into the neighbouring shop, 'Jinja Suitable Stores', and enquired of the whereabouts of Mr. Hira. "Not knowing. Gone on Safari — maybe."

"Squad... HALT!" Twelve *Askaris* of the King's African Rifles, a Corporal in charge, stood to attention at the entrance to the theatre. It was explained to the Corporal that the interior needed cleaning — a play was to be presented — an audience of many people would be seated here. He shouted an order, the *Askaris* scattered in all directions, returning with branches torn from the few remaining trees languishing at the perimeter of the compound. With these makeshift brooms they raised clouds of choking dust, most of which settled back, now mixed with twigs and leaves. A small proportion was swept outside the entrance and left there. An Army lorry rumbled up and ground to a halt. More shouting, whereupon the *Askaris* cast aside their denuded brooms and unloaded great chunks of furniture. This was all carried through to the dressing rooms at the rear. None of it served our purpose, so all of it was carried back to the transport. Had the hired seats arrived from Kampala, the *Askaris* could have been of use unloading them, but as matters stood, we decided we would soldier on without them.

Under the stage, buried beneath piles of rotting rubbish, I uncovered a broom with a few remaining bristles. There were also some cartons and boxes which would serve as dressing room furniture.

Don returned to Mr. Hira and found him behind his counter. "Your drama... not many seats sold. Look at Friday — rotten, isn't it?" Don studied the plan. "This block booking for Saturday looks quite good."

"That is for my family. 10 seats I am taking. That is my commission, isn't it?"

An unresponsive audience of 83 sat on the expensively hired seats on Friday. On Saturday it was increased to 135, fronted in Row A by the chemist's unsmiling progeny, while torrential rain thundered on the tin roof through most of the performance. Don's journal gave the final verdict: *'A date to be avoided!!!'*

We spotted a brass plate in Jinja's Main Street: 'Mandatali Devraj. BA (Failed).' We felt a certain kinship.

We turned our backs on Jinja and headed back to Kenya. We had reached the limit of our safari, now we were on the home stretch with just two more tour dates. By 12 noon on March 1, the Maules were once again crossing the border at Busia. Pye made no fuss on this occasion, remaining fast asleep in her basket.

Kenya was bleached a pale shade of straw. There had been no rain.

'ELDORET. 210 miles from Nairobi. HILL SCHOOL: seats 150 on hired chairs which have to be transported. Three Hotels: New Lincoln, Grand and Pioneer. Private hospitality available. Two amateur societies: Bristow-Hopper Players and the Eldoret Players. Two cinemas: Roxy and Lyric. Very friendly atmosphere throughout the town.'

What a relief. Dusk was falling when we reached the New Lincoln where our 'friendly' hosts were waiting. An hour later there was no sign of the boys.

My hostess for the following four nights explained, on the drive to her home, "Our friends in Kitale told me that Pyewacket is not too good with other animals." Pye was travelling on my knee, quiet and happy. "We've got an old bull terrier and a Labrador puppy, so I've put an earth box in your room." Our arrival at the house was greeted by furiously barking dogs. Pye straightaway pricked up her ears and started a low rumble of apprehension. I smuggled her into the room allotted to us and shut the door. The moment she was freed from her basket, she sprang to the windows, only to find them all secured by metal grilles. No way out; dammit!

I introduced her to the earth box, placed on clean sheets of newspaper. Whiskers twitching, she made a careful inspection, then turned away with a flick of her tail. There was a knock at the door. "Dinner is ready. I've brought Pyewacket's." I left her settling down to a large plate of sardines. That, I thought, should keep her happy.

The home comforts offered by my Eldoret hostess were in sharp contrast to the sagging, lumpy bed, the threadbare, inadequate sheets and unwelcoming atmosphere at the Ripon Falls Hotel. After dinner I sank into a comfortable bed and immediately to sleep. Pye curled up nearby, reeking of sardines.

At some point I woke to find Pye trapped in the small space cut in the security grilles which allowed access to the window catch. Her front paws and head were through, but a sardine-filled tummy had stuck fast. I released her and took her back to bed. Soon I was asleep once more, and dreaming of barking dogs... As I swam up to consciousness I found it to be true; dogs were howling outside and Pyewacket was not in the room. Peering out into the black night I could see nothing. What to do? Useless to wake the sleeping household. She might be up a tree, she might have absconded altogether, she might now be dead... Whatever the outcome, it had to wait until daylight. I was worrying about the last awful thought and the need to find an understudy to appear in the play when I drifted off to sleep again.

"Memsa'b. Jambo!" The house servant placed a tray of early morning tea on the bedside table then padded away on silent feet. At that instant I got a whiff of sardine. Pye was just where she had curled up the previous night. She stretched chocolate-coloured paws and yawned hugely, exhaling further clouds of Sardine Fragrance. Every night we spent in Eldoret she performed her Houdini trick just as she wished. Not once did she use the earth box. Not once did she fail to appear on stage.

The boys finally reached the New Lincoln Hotel. Basil, flak-happy as ever, had elected to take a different route out of Uganda, and this had been the undoing of the Dexion Special. The rear axle broke, and both Land Rover and trailer went off the road. The Dexion Special was a dead loss, its load scattered.

An Asian trader with a lorry was located and hired. Our equipment and what remained of the smashed trailer were loaded aboard and we, at Hill School, were impatient for its arrival.

Scattered across a large compound were a number of timber huts. We were assigned the Concert Hall: a concrete-floored area with a space at the back of the stage, down three steps which served as our communal dressing room and prop room. Thoughtfully, a highly polished antique commode had been placed there for our use, but we viewed it in much the same way as Pye viewed an earth box.

Our equipment arrived. The damage was extensive. The screen-flats, now very insecure, were rain-spattered, scratched and smudged. Two small tables were reduced to firewood. The armchair had lost a leg. Glass and china, already depleted over the previous weeks, was now at a bare minimum. Saucers smashed, cups minus handles and the electroplated teapot a mangled wreck of no further pouring capacity.

With an opening matinée at 5.30, we 'got cracking' instantly: repainting, repairing, replacing, improvising and opening on time.

'Dramatic Society very warm and friendly. Generous hospitality and a real welcome for the DM Players.'

Four hundred and thirty one theatre patrons came to see *Bell, Book and Candle*.

Mollie and Don stayed with Mrs. Pretty. In her beautiful garden, Crowned Cranes watched us with suspicious beady eyes as they sat on a clutch of eggs in their ramshackle, jerrybuilt nest at the water's edge. They still wore the elegant little Victorian bonnets tied under their bills.

Next stop — Nakuru: 'date' number 12 and the final one of our Tour. 'Athletic Club. Small theatre. Can seat approximately 200 on flat auditorium floor. Chairs or benches have to be hired from the Race course. Quite good stage, but with low beams. Fair lighting equipment. Good sound equipment. Very good dressing rooms (2).'

The Maules had already taken several productions to Nakuru and knew just what to expect. I laid out make-up and hung costumes in one of the dressing rooms as if settling in for a lengthy run. This made a nice change from some of the conditions we had faced — no furniture, no mirrors, no hanging space, no lights and NO privacy!

Setting up for the last time, I compensated for the pitifully reduced props by re-wrapping the Christmas gifts. These, at least, would make a good impression. At the opening matinée a gigantic grasshopper made its entry, whirring like a mini-helicopter from mantelpiece to sofa, to table and back to mantelpiece.

Our final performance, at 9pm on Saturday March 7, attracted a Full House. At its conclusion, we flung costumes into the cabin trunk; there was no longer any need to pack carefully, as everything would be going to the dry-cleaners (or to the garbage can) when we got back to Nairobi. We enjoyed a final 'Jolly up' at the Bar: bacon and eggs washed down with champagne.

Mollie and I had ironed and ironed; on boards set across the backs of two chairs, on counters, on tables, on the floor. Curtains had been shortened, then lengthened then shortened again. Nails had been hammered in then plucked out. Carpets had been beaten, running repairs had been made on all the costumes, cushions and lamp shades. Stages had been swept over and over again. Just as the curtain was due to rise, fingernails were given a quick lick of varnish to hide the broken, dirty evidence of all this labour.

The Pioneer Tour was nearing the finishing post. 12 'dates' spread over three East African territories had taken us 2,300 miles. We had sold 4,185 seats at an average price of Sh8.50; we had been on the road for seven weeks and now we were on our way back to Nairobi. Mollie and Don had enjoyed it, I think. They were certainly a lot easier to live and work with than had been the case at the Studio. The setbacks, triumphs, frustrations, hazards and laughter had been shared by us all.

Basil never got on top of his lines — to the very end he was paraphrasing and surprising me at every turn. But he kept the show on the road. His ability to 'cope' got us over several sticky situations. We had been a good team.

Had it been a financial success? Certainly not! A loss was shown: Transport costs had absorbed any possible gains — Hire of lorry from Jinja to Eldoret, hire of chairs (with so many remaining vacant!) and transport, repairs to the eccentric Dexion Special, accommodation for six people where no hospitality was offered... But Don was well pleased. The fame of the Donovan Maule Players had spread far and wide. It had been a good job of PR. Some new members had signed up and we had taken professional theatre to areas which had never before witnessed it.

The work had been tough but the socialising had been tougher, coming as it did after hours of strenuous work with an early start the next day. We received wonderful, generous hospitality and were indebted to many.

As we bowled along the tarmac road the Aberdares lay outlined against the clear March sky. Ahead, three figures at the roadside came into focus: *Morani* gazing across to the Mau Escarpment. Barefoot, dark skin glistening, plumes stuck in their hair, coloured beads in their ears, they carried bows as tall as themselves with a quiver of arrows hanging from a shoulder. What could they know of touring actors? Or care?

Pye woke and settled herself to watch the passing landscape. She couldn't know that she was now in retirement. Her acting career was over. She had been an unequivocal success at every appearance and this without even trying! The rest of us 'worked for laughs', 'lifted a scene where it had gone flat', 'picked up the pace' or 'slowed down the tempo' as required. And for me personally, steering Basil to keep somewhere near the script. All Pyewacket had done was to come on stage in my arms and instantly all attention was on her. And she loved it! She had never swept and carried, scrubbed and ironed, hammered and lifted, packed up and unpacked, stowed and repainted. She had never been called upon to help change a car wheel nor did she have to memorise where the guns were concealed.

She had been taken to 14 temporary homes, many of them with resident, alien animals. True, she had held up the departure of our convoy more than once with a last-minute escapade. She had never gone sick, or bitten anyone. She had never fouled anywhere indoors. She had travelled all the miles we travelled, complaining when road conditions were not to her liking but taking an interest in the scene or sleeping as the mood took her.

Truly Pyewacket was a *non-pareil* among cats. As for me, the tour of *Bell, Book and Candle* had been an unforgettable experience. It had first brought me to Kenya and it was to change my life.

CHAPTER FOUR

While the struggle for Independence continued, 1953 was Coronation Year in Britain. In Nairobi, theatre-going expatriates were offered two productions to celebrate the occasion. *King Henry VIII* presented by the Railway Players, the oldest theatre group in Nairobi, founded by James Master in 1929, and *The Young Elizabeth*, produced by the Donovan Maule Players. The play sprawled across 13 scenes with a cast of 22 characters... clearly impossible to present on the tiny (16 x 16 foot and no wing space) Studio stage, so Don hired the National Theatre where 11 performances brought in 3,520 patrons. The play spanned the period 1547 — the death of King Henry VIII — to 1558, when Elizabeth came to the throne on the death of her half sister, 'Bloody' Mary Tudor. Eleven turbulent years in the life of the 'young' Elizabeth. April 24 was Opening Night.

Earlier that day Nairobi was proclaimed a 'Special Area'; anybody failing to halt when challenged by a member of the Security Forces was liable to be shot without further ado. Some responsible leaders advised "extreme caution", even suggesting people should not go out after dark.

Under the circumstances, would *The Young Elizabeth* attract an audience?

Three hundred and forty six first-nighters ignored the gloomy warnings. The production received an excellent press — and made a substantial financial loss, due to heavy production costs: theatre hire, extra guest artists and costumes galore, designed by Mrs. Ambren Garland, previously of the Old Vic Theatre Company in London who had already dressed several shows for the DMs. With the help of extra seamstresses the satins and brocades, silks and velvets bought by Mollie in Bazaar Street, were transformed into glittering Elizabethan raiment.

In June, Don wrote: 'The theatre, like every business in Kenya, is passing through a difficult time and the Emergency is hitting us hard. The oldest member of our staff, Basil Hurle-Hobbs, joins the Kenya Police Reserve in July... called up for full-time duty. Others of us are doing Home Guard patrols at night. *Who Goes There?* is on tour, playing to troops and civilians in a number of towns, including such trouble spots as Nanyuki and Nyeri.'

Basil failed to join the Kenya Police Reserve, deciding it was time to bale out. He flew out of Kenya just ahead of his call-up, abandoning a queue of creditors.

Jean Parnell had left the DMs to marry Charles Hayes. They had met on stage at the Studio the previous year, when both appeared in *Born Yesterday*.

In August 1953 the first of a series of setbacks hit the DM. Players. The actress playing the eponymous *Claudia* came down with chickenpox. Roles were re-assigned to allow the play to continue.

This production was followed by *The Day's Mischief*, where the same actress collapsed with appendicitis. Next came *Private Lives*, where the leading lady who was deputising for the appendicitis patient, died in a shooting accident. In January 1954 came production number 46, *The Deep Blue Sea*. A new actor, fresh out from London, received advice from his doctor that he was gravely ill and must return to England without delay. The *Sunday Post* told its readers: 'Certainly it required a lot of stamina and an almost fanatical love of your job to work uncomplainingly through the hours which the Donovan Maule Players have had to put in lately, due to illness and other mishaps...'

It was said that Don proposed forming his own airline, 'Actors Special', to fly the artists who came (and went) so speedily.

Theatre Arts an American publication, headlined a feature '*Footlights In Darkest Africa*: It is probably true that, barring the theatre capitals of New York, London, Paris and Tokyo, Kenya has proportionately more professional and amateur activity than any other part of the world... there is a steady theatre-going audience of about 2,500 people... There is a remarkably large number of amateur dramatic societies — more than two dozen in all. Each of the main towns has at least one amateur group, and several, such as Mombasa and Nyeri, have two each. The core of professional theatrical activity in East Africa is the Donovan Maule family. The profound debt which Kenya, in particular, owes to the Maules is obvious, even to the visitor. They were the first professional actors to come to Kenya and settle there.'

Nairobi was the centre and base from which freedom fighters' operations were mounted in the forests. It was also the main source of supplies and recruits. Break-ins and robberies increased. The Studio Theatre wasn't spared and the nearby workshop and store in Victoria Street (now Tom Mboya Street) was routinely plundered, causing Mollie particular anguish when irreplaceable period costumes disappeared.

'The accountant squirmed his way in among the CID (yet another robbery) and the Insurance people during yesterday's rehearsal,' Don wrote to me in London. 'Apparently the theatre did £20,000 this year but only £2,000 for us with all the work and incessant worry... Better than a kick up the arse, I suppose.'

On April 24 (just a year after *The Young Elizabeth* had opened), Operation Anvil was launched. More than 30,000 Kikuyu were taken from Nairobi to reception areas for screening. Mau Mau were removed to detention centres. The immediate result was a reduction in the crime rate in Nairobi and a dwindling of funds to the fighters in the forest.

In August 1954 a new artist joined the DMs, under contract for one year. Almost immediately he had to take over a small role in the current production, *I Am A Camera,* due to illness among the cast. A few months later Kenneth Mason was playing Doctor Sloper in *The Heiress* and showing the full extent of his talent.

The Studio Theatre was bursting at the seams. Both 1954 and

1955 were buoyant years: Club membership increased steadily and productions were kept running for five or more weeks. The offices, workshop and wardrobe departments were transferred to premises in nearby Duke Street (now Ronald Ngala). If the Donovan Maule Players were to expand, larger premises were a MUST.

Suddenly, a golden opportunity presented itself. The 'Site between Connaught & Jackson Roads. Two front corner plots, nearest Legco' noted in Don's diary back in early 1952, was offered to the Maules. A preliminary approach had been made to Club members in January 1953 to enlist their support for the erection of a new theatre on this land but, doubtless as a result of the Emergency conditions then prevailing, the response was inadequate and the matter had been dropped. Now, in January 1956, another developer, for a different purpose, was anxious to be granted the plots and was in possession of the funds necessary for their development.

The Maules, unfortunately, were not in possession of the funds necessary to build a theatre.

The plots remained on offer to the Maules until February 28 but, 'If the required proof of financial ability is not furnished by then the offer by the Government would be withdrawn.'

It was decided to appeal to the public. A prospectus offering for subscription 60,000 shares at Sh20 each at par, opened on Friday, February 10. There were just 18 days in which to raise 'proof of financial ability.'

Don was the first subscriber, buying 5,000 shares funded by the sale of blue chip equities. His mother-in-law, Sheila, put her widow's mite: £10. So, too, did ex-students of the School of Dramatic Art, together with artists and staff both past and present.

From the very first moment Don's diary recorded nothing beyond the number of shares bought each day. At the close of the first week 12,285 had been sold.

'If this venture fails it will represent the Maules' last attempt in a long, hard struggle to bring first-class theatre to Kenya. Nairobi must not let it fail!' implored the *Sunday Nation* on 19 February.

If a minimum of £43,000 was promised, the Bank of India would lend a further £20,000 at 6% per annum.

The following week Don's diary noted a further 11,755 shares sold. The total now stood at 24,040, and only four more days to go. On February 24 the *East African Standard* told its readers: 'Seven years' hard work, enterprise and expenditure have gone into the creation of the now-famous company which plays throughout the year in Nairobi. When they embarked upon their theatrical adventure in 1948 the pundits prophesied disaster — "You'll never do it!" they said. "Never!" The Maules now wish to strike out afresh and once more risk their lot on a new theatre which, if it comes to fruition, will make theatrical history. Although they are the prime movers in this great endeavour, it is too big financially for even their broad shoulders to bear alone, and they look to the public which they have served so well to back them with the confidence they have shown in the past.'

At the deadline, 12 noon on February 28, the Share Register showed 27,655 applications. The very next day — 1956 being Leap Year — Don wrote to Club members: 'The Government considers the initial response to our Prospectus has been sufficiently satisfactory to ensure the probable success of the new Theatre in City Square. The Commissioner of Lands is therefore arranging to issue immediately a Letter of Allotment of the site... This must be accepted or rejected within one month... We have one month in which to get the minimum balance of £13,000 to enable us to take up the site.' He himself reduced the figure to £12,500 by purchasing a further 500 shares.

'MUST WE LOSE THE MAULES FOR £6,000?' asked *The Sunday Post* on March 25. 'The first crisis was averted when the sum of £30,000 was raised in three weeks and, on the strength of this, an extension on the time limit for taking up the plot was granted. The situation now? Shares to the extent of £37,000 have been applied for (including £5,500 of the Maules' own money) leaving a balance of £6,000 short of that minimum target of £43,000. The city of

Nairobi must face the danger of losing not only the prospect of a fine new theatre but, if the scheme has to be abandoned altogether, the very real danger of losing the Maules as well, for they have no security of tenure in their present theatre premises... Nairobi is not so rich in cultural amenities that we can allow one of its few assets, many say one of its greatest, to go by default... The challenge for that extra £6,000 still remains to be taken up.'

At a meeting of the Directors in April 'The Chairman reported that applications had been received for 44,350 shares. As this figure now exceeded minimum subscription, arrangements were going ahead to incorporate the company... Steps should be taken for the erection of the theatre so as to lose as little time as possible.'

During the stagnant, idle, frustrating days in Port Said back in 1947, waiting for a Movement Order to bring them to Kenya, Don had given a lot of thought to his 'ideal' theatre. Here was the opportunity to realise his dream.

He knew what he wanted and almost more important, he knew what he did not want. Now that the moment had arrived, Frederick Wilkinson of Inglis, McGuiness & Wilkinson (who had never before designed a theatre) listened to what Don had to tell him. Together they planned the Donovan Maule Theatre.

The Company was incorporated on April 26, 1956. 'Horrid to think we are limited after September this year.' Mollie wrote to me. 'I spent yesterday signing my soul and freedom away...'

Having reached this point, they flew to London. Immediately after take-off, Don settled to study the imposing-looking document, bound in blue, headed: Memorandum and Articles of Association of DONOVAN MAULE THEATRE Limited.

He was astonished to learn that now he might carry on business as 'General publishers and printers, booksellers, stationers, designers, advertising agents... painters and decorators ... contractors, engineers, electricians... The Company could prepare building sites... construct offices, flats, houses, factories, mills, warehouses, shops, restaurants, hotels, breweries, distilleries, gas and electrical works...

and conveniences of all kinds. Further, the Company could plant, pave, drain, farm and cultivate... Carry on business of tavern, beer house, refreshment room and lodging house keepers, licensed victuallers, wine, beer and spirit merchants, brewers, maltsters, distillers... Garage proprietors... Dairymen, grocers, poulterers, butchers, bakers, confectioners and ice merchants... importers of Live and Dead Stock... Hairdressers, perfumiers, chemists... Agents for railway, shipping and air-plane companies and carriers...' and so on and on, covering six pages of close print.

On the last day of April, Mollie and Don reached my London flat. They were fêted in theatrical circles where they had become well known for creating the 'Little Theatre with the BIG Reputation' in Nairobi.

When a theatrical 'Great', Dame Sybil Thorndike had visited it, she told the Maules "You've got to be a little mad to get anywhere in the theatre, and you are two of the most delightfully mad people I've ever met!"

The news of the proposed new Donovan Maule Theatre, funded entirely by subscription, caused amazement tinged with envy. In England, in the past year alone, 80 provincial repertory theatres had closed due to lack of support attributed to the arrival of commercial television.

The Maules' days and nights were crowded. Plays to see, artists to interview, authors' agents to meet, Strand Electric & Engineering Company to visit, specialists in theatre seats, house curtains... the list went on. Away from London, they toured the remaining repertory companies and all the time there were so many friends to see, after an absence of nearly 10 years. On June 5 we left for Europe and motored up the Mosel, down the Rhine and along the Danube before doubling back to Venice where Mollie and Don boarded the *Europa* bound for Mombasa.

Once home again, they were required immediately for rehearsal of *The Burning Glass,* due to open two weeks later.

What of the 'new' theatre? Preparation of the site would start soon, but a further £10,000 was needed if the entire project — without any modification — was to be achieved. Don, in optimistic mood, felt sure this would be forthcoming and gave the go ahead. Already nearly £4,000 had been swallowed in fees: to architects, quantity surveyors, Company Secretaries, auditors and advocates.

'Erection of Hoarding' was item number one, and by September a billboard fronted Connaught Road proclaiming: SITE OF THE NEW DONOVAN MAULE THEATRE. Behind it could be glimpsed grass, shrubs and trees.

'Bulk Excavations' was item number two. Beneath the grass, shrubs and trees lay the topsoil that nourished them. When this was removed, 'excavations' hit hard rock strata.

In November Don wrote from the Maia Carberry Nursing Home where he was being treated for lumbago: 'The new theatre consists of an enormous hoarding... inside which is a vast hole carved out of solid rock... I have also had to pay the City Council rent to be allowed to dump the said rock and earth, for a maximum of nine months, on the adjacent piece of waste ground.' Meanwhile, their Muthaiga landlady wished to repossess her property and Mollie told me: 'In our spare time we go and view houses, all equally expensive and equally ugly.'

She was anxious about her mother, now 84, who suffered recurrent minor heart attacks and who, left alone at home, pined for company and conversation. Invariably, the only topic at lunch dealt exclusively with problems concerning their work and an air of preoccupied gloom prevailed, as I had experienced at the time of *Bell, Book and Candle.*

In December, Don reported: 'The Quantity Surveyor's Bill of Quantities has reached me, the *abridged* version runs to 150 close-typed pages... The enormous hole which forms the understage of our theatre is practically finished... What we all want to see now is things going UP instead of DOWN.'

At the Studio a Noel Coward comedy, *South Sea Bubble,* ran for seven weeks, which took them into the new year, 1957, and the expectation of the much-needed larger premises by October. The year just ended had been the 'Best Ever' at the Studio... the new theatre would be a Godsend.

It was now that the 'long' rains began, and soon Nairobi wags were asking: "Is Donovan Maule building a theatre or a swimming pool?" The architect presented his first Progress Report: 'Some delay is being caused by the present inclement weather, and the contractors will have a legitimate claim for extra time... It is anticipated that, subject to favourable weather, the first concrete will be poured in about a week's time, and from then onward there will be more obvious signs of progress.'

Mollie reported: 'We have at last seen a house we feel we could bear to live in and we are buying it. Just 3¾ miles from the theatre. Nice locality, Riverside Drive.'

Early in March, Wilkinson's Progress Report number two noted: 'Work on the building has been considerably delayed by the heavy rain which fell from January 25 to February 14. The delay was extended beyond the rainy period because of a steady flow of water into the basement excavation under the hard rock strata which has only recently been brought under control... Orders have been placed for all items of building equipment which are not normally stocked in this country and the delivery dates are quite satisfactory.' President Nasser of Egypt having nationalised the Suez Canal in July the previous year, all such equipment would now have to travel the 'long way round' — and cost more. Mollie wrote to me from her bed in a nursing home: 'Of course, I knew I was overdoing it outrageously, but what can one do? Dress rehearsal was a 23-hour day...' The following night she collapsed at the end of Agatha Christie's *Spider's Web*.

'The opening of *Toreadors* and the move to Riverside Drive within two days of each other was a bit of a nightmare.'

Jean Anouilh's play *The Waltz Of The Toreadors* opened at the Studio in early April. It brought forth a howl of disdain from the local press and the bar manager chose that moment to abscond with a good deal of the management's cash. Her letter went on: 'I was very ill with Nairobi tummy... sick and faint. Low blood pressure.'

In June the Nairobi City Council forwarded a Valuation for the Purpose of Rating the non-existent new theatre.

In July the Directors met to discuss Ways and Means. Exploration of the former due to the inadequacy of the latter. Further injections of cash were needed and it was clear that no new theatre would open in October. Another appeal went out, restricted to Theatre Club Members, for a further £13,000.

The Balance Sheet for the first year of operating the Donovan Maule Theatre Limited showed a loss: abnormally high administrative costs, two lots of rental to pay, extra costs for printing and stationery and a drop in box office sales at the Studio compared with the year before.

This had been caused partly by sickness and accidents among company members but mainly by alterations to Government Road. These had made it near impossible for patrons to reach the Studio and despite the assurance 'There is plenty of parking space in Victoria Street and one can easily reach the box office by coming in the back way up the Fire Escape staircase...' theatre-goers had delayed until they could, once again, reach their theatre club by more conventional means.

There was another reason for the drop in sales: the composition of the resident company of actors. The delicate balance of an ensemble of players can be overturned by only minor changes taking place. Teamwork is required in the theatre, as much as on the playing field. If a management is blessed with a 'Dream Team', the choice of plays is made that much easier and everyone is that much happier including audiences. But contracts come to an end, one or more linchpins leave and somehow nothing is the same again. The team that had been at the Studio through 1954 and 1955 was dispersed.

Another factor was the National Theatre. Since the opening at the end of 1952, it offered a venue for other entrepreneurs, including at least one ex-DM artist immediately he had concluded his contract at the Studio.

In November 1956, a new group presented *The Love of Four Colonels* (sometimes misprinted as *The Love Of Four Colonials*) at the National. The Nairobi City Players had come to town. At this time there were only a few weeks throughout the year when the National Theatre was without a show.

Eva Kenworthy, reviewing the theatrical year 1952 for the *East African Standard;* focused mainly on the new theatre, but she made the point: 'If one thing emerges from this year's work more than another, it is that the choice of play is all important, and upon that more than anything else, depends success or failure... it is wiser to choose a good play than a popular play.'

Good advice, but not always easy to follow. Without any subsidy of any kind from any quarter, the DMs were totally reliant on box office income. And B.O. income told Don that 'popular plays' were almost always light comedies and thrillers. Choosing the right play, at the right moment, for the actors under contract, became ever more difficult. Experimental or post-modern plays were not popular with their patrons. And Repertory-throughout-the-year used up a lot of plays.

Reviewing the year 1957, a local critic wrote: 'About productions at Nairobi's Studio Theatre, I am afraid the least said, the better.' Commenting on the year's Drama Festival: 'I found the most interesting features the imagination displayed by the Asian and African societies, particularly the Orient Art Circle and the African Drama Society.'

At the Studio the year ended with the ludicrous romp *Doctor In The House,* doing better business than any previous show that year. It continued drawing audiences until well into 1958, when they could expect the new theatre to be ready in April.

On the opening night of *Doctor In The House,* Don received a cable with the news that his mother had had a stroke. She died a few days later. Lydia Donovan, born in 1879, first appeared on stage in London at the age of 18. Receiving a legacy of £500 and already the mother of an only son, born in 1899, she went into Theatrical Management.

As a small boy, Don toured with his mother until the outbreak of the First World War in 1914. Thereafter their paths diverged and only a tenuous, uneasy relationship existed between the two of them.

Following her death there remained in her tiny two-roomed London flat — 'The Haven' — the accumulated evidence of her life: press clippings of plays, poems both published and unpublished, souvenirs and knick knacks, resplendent stage costumes and make-up boxes, love letters and prompt scripts and photographs... a great multitude of photographs. One of her notable successes had been the old melodrama, *East Lynne*. 'Miss Lydia Donovan stands alone in her magnificent delineation of Lady Isabel.' The detritus of a life spent in the theatre and three marriages.

The tarnished reputation of the Studio was redeemed in a spectacular manner by the arrival of Sonia Dresdel, at that time a very considerable Star. Warned that the Studio — 'The Sweat Box' lacked star dressing rooms and that the audience in row A rested its feet on the stage, she replied, 'I am not interested in salary or conditions in your small theatre... I would love to see East Africa.' Don promptly obtained a work permit.

More good news arrived early in the new year: 'The Company could proceed with the Full Project for the new theatre.'

As the skeleton of the building grew; Don conducted small groups round the concrete shell of his new kingdom. These tours took place on Sunday mornings when the site was free of workmen. As his visitors gazed at blue sky overhead, he explained: "That's the proscenium arch opening. You're standing about centre stage! Now, through here... careful! It's still a bit damp, will be our dressing room, Mollie's and mine. Direct access to the stage, you see, and it'll double as an office, so I can do the Royalty Returns during my stage waits. Now, along here..."

Sonia Dresdel opened in *The Queen And The Rebels* on January 28. 'My God! How she knows her job. It's wonderful to work with her,' Mollie told me. Miss Dresdel was wonderful for the box office too — the play continued for seven weeks, doing great business. Famous as a 'Tragedy Queen', she wanted to do a comedy and chose *Come Live With Me,* intended to be the final production at the little theatre, taking them to April and the long awaited new Donovan Maule Theatre.

'The course of True Love never did run smooth, neither it seems, does the course of building a theatre,' Don declared. The date for completion was now May... but the good news was that Sonia Dresdel would stay on and play *Hedda Gabler* at the Studio. She had enjoyed enormous success in this role in London and at the Edinburgh Festival. Nairobi would be privileged to see her.

Bill Piggott designed the superbly evocative scenery. His list of credits was amazing: desert islands and Baronial Halls, penthouse apartments in New York and country cottages in Yorkshire, luxury flats in Mayfair and dingy digs in Dungeness. More often than not he was on stage as well, and stage managed.

Terence Rattigan's *Separate Tables* was scheduled for the opening of the new theatre. The date: June 3. Miss Dresdel would be superb casting for the contrasting women's roles in the two-part play.

THE HEAVIEST STORM IN THIRTY YEARS was the banner headline in the *East African Standard* dated May 17. 'Nearly 5½ inches of rain fell in Nairobi... Power lines destroyed... The basement of the new Donovan Maule Theatre was flooded and pumping went on all night.'

A second electric pump had been installed following heavy rains when milder flooding had occurred, but with total power failure all over the city, both were put out of order. Floodwater burst through the walls in great spouts. The Maules' worst fear was for the choke dimmers housed in the basement. If water got into them, it would cause thousands of pounds worth of damage to the expensive, brand new electrical equipment. The Fire Brigade was called in and pumped all night at the rate of 500 gallons an hour, but as fast as they pumped out from one side, it flowed in at the other.

The damage caused by the flooding led, of course, to another delay, so *Hedda Gabler* continued beyond May 31.

The especially manufactured tip-up seats, 220 of them, were due to reach Mombasa on June 6, but Mombasa knew nothing about theatre seats. A cable went to Johannesburg: DEFINITE SHIPPING DATE FOR THEATRE SEATS URGENTLY REQUIRED AND WHICH BOAT. The answer came: 'The consignment is being shipped from Lourenço Marques to Mombasa. The goods were railed on Friday May 16 in order to connect with the *Oldekerk* which sails on May 20 or with the next available vessel.'

Had the seats connected with the *Oldekerk?* Were they in the hold of another ship? Nobody knew.

Back in March, when the Grand Opening was expected in April, a list had been opened of Club members wishing to be present. Two months later, the list far exceeded the theatre's seating capacity. A further 40 or 50 might be squeezed in, sitting on the side aisles and the cross-over which separated the front half of the auditorium from the second tier, but this still left a great many theatre-goers disappointed. It was decided to hold a ballot. This was done, as near the deadline as possible, the winners were informed, but still there were no seats.

Frederick Wilkinson, the architect, gave details of his creation: 'It will retain the present air of intimacy. The auditorium will be in the form of a gradually sloping amphitheatre... There will be offices, workshops beneath the stage, a play library, wardrobe department and flats for 12 artists and members of the staff. The stage will be 30 feet deep with a 25-foot proscenium arch and 15 feet of off-stage space which will enable the company to put on plays which are impossible at the Studio Theatre. Dressing rooms and the Stage Manager's room are next to the stage... One feature will be a Club lounge and dance floor, where members can dance while a show is going on in the sound-proof theatre.' But still there were no seats...

On June 15 *The Sunday Post* published a full-page feature headed BEFORE THE CURTAIN RINGS UP. It reported: 'Donovan Maule these days is obsessed with this theatre, a dream for many years, which the other day gave an impression of semi-controlled frenzy as the *fundis*, the carpet layers, the painters, carpenters, stage managers and dozens who defy lay description, laboured to have everything ready for next Tuesday's first night... talking rapidly as we evaded painter's ladders and paint pots, he said: "You know, this place was supposed to cost £60,000 but the final figure is likely to be in the neighbourhood of £100,000. Of course, the flood damage is included in that and we can't be sure what that has really cost. Come downstairs and I'll show you." I followed him below stage. One side of the very large workshop was packed with stage property such as sofas, chairs, cushions etc, which had been salvaged after floating on three feet of water during the night of the great flood. Expensive, seasoned timber had suffered the same fate. Donovan Maule led me to the root of the trouble: his own private river running below, and into, the basement of the theatre. He explained, "Because the road outside will eventually be lowered two feet, we had to build the theatre two feet lower than the present road and now we've become Nairobi's main drain." The river flowed into a small concrete hole and when it reached a certain height two automatic pumps came into action. Provided there was power.

'Donovan Maule was still extolling. "Look at Oswald Fischer's décor. All done with a few pieces of rope and paint — isn't it wonderful?" He leapt into the auditorium and I clambered after him. "Had a terrible feeling," he said, "that the seats wouldn't turn up in time. We were going to ask the audience to bring their own cushions." *Fundis* were putting the seats in position and a tall gentleman was supervising the carpet laying. He emitted an anguished shriek: "You're treading on a wet bit — get off it." On to the tastefully furnished flats for 12 members of the staff. There are six single flats and three doubles. Each contains its own kitchenette and toilet facilities. The doubles cost each person Sh50 a week and the singles Sh60. As we rushed upstairs and along corridors Donovan Maule threw a never-ceasing string of facts at me. "We played 2,986 performances at the little theatre. Starting with *The Guinea Pig,* in 1948, which played to 78% of capacity and on to 106% of capacity in recent years... My wife and I sank all our money, £11,000 into the little theatre and didn't start to get it back for four or five years: Now, we've sunk everything into this place... Here we have a theatre, a club, night club and business luncheons available." I walked miles pursuing the dynamic little man... enthusiasm is a rare quality in this blasé 20th century; it was refreshing to meet it... This new theatre, when the curtain rises on Tuesday night, must represent a tribute to two very dedicated people, who will have realised a dream.'

'God, why do we do these things?' Mollie asked me. 'Why not be content with a nice, quiet life somewhere? This terrible compulsion which drives one on to fresh achievements... Instead of looking my best I'm looking a ravaged old hag... We have worked in a haze of utter exhaustion for the last few weeks, never getting more than four or five hours' sleep at night.'

She was playing in *Hedda Gabler,* rehearsing for *Separate Tables,* equipping the twelve flats in the new theatre, attending (she was a Director) the frequent Board Meetings and running the Riverside Drive house where Musa, the cook, handed her a scrap of paper, his shopping list, as she dashed out each morning: *'Siagi.* Floors. Gravy B. *SUKARI.* Polis. Deapperin. Vim. Coco. Chivers.'

Kenneth Mason was putting the finishing touches to the Souvenir Programme of *Separate Tables.* Beginning with production number 78 in April 1957, he had been the Editor and Sole Contributor to *On Stage*, the newly-designed magazine programme of the Donovan Maule Players. It extended far beyond a mere cast list. He included theatre news from around the world, potted biographies of playwrights, 'Gossip from the Theatre Bar', articles and anecdotes and frequent, erudite information on Things Theatrical. A theatre critic declared: 'The magazine programme adds considerably to the pleasure of visiting the Maule Theatre. It is the only theatre programme I know that is worth the money charged for it.' The bumper issue for the opening of the new theatre was truly a 'souvenir'. He traced every production, from the very first at the Theatre Royal, to the final one at the Studio, listing the casts, accompanied by photographs. Most of these had been taken by John Karmali. Comedies and thrillers, dramas and farces, faces, sets and costumes; John had photographed them all. 'Stage photography is a specialised business and on the Donovan Maule stage, it is even more so. There is hardly room to set up a tripod. The photographer has to clamber over the seats and various props lying about in the auditorium. I shall be happy when the new theatre is ready...'

Club members, seized with nostalgia, were anxious to attend the final performance at the Studio, thus ensuring the last overfull house on Saturday June 14, when 84 of them packed tight the tiny playhouse. As the curtains closed for the last time, when Hedda has shot herself, it could be said — paraphrasing T.S. Eliot — 'This is the way the Studio ends: not with a whimper, but a bang.'

'*Outward Bound;* that was the name of the very first play we performed in our tiny Studio Theatre, way back in November 1949.' Don wrote, 'And now after eight and a half crowded years we are outward bound again. The Studio has housed 83 productions... Lack of space was never an excuse for lack of enterprise. Thus a 76-seater theatre with a stage 16 by 16 has paved the way to a 220-seater theatre of sufficient dimensions to enable us to present anything we have a mind to, without having first to consider 'geography' too much... Our sincere congratulations must be extended to our architect Frederick Wilkinson who has designed the building so superbly... Because of the increased seating, the run of the plays will be much shorter, three or at most four weeks, depending on the popularity of each particular production.'

The original 343 'Founder Members' had convinced the Maules that a professional repertory would be supported. Club membership currently exceeded 4,000.

'How we managed to get open at all is a miracle and part of that strange alchemy of theatre that produces some sort of order out of utter chaos at the very last minute,' Mollie reported. 'The painters and builders were round our feet until the hour of opening. The front of the theatre isn't nearly finished yet, the scaffolding is still up and the bastards have now all gone off to another job!'

"The essence of theatre is make-believe. Even the opening ceremony is good theatre, because you are being asked to make believe that the substitution of the Mayor of Nairobi for his Excellency the Governor is a perfectly acceptable change of character... Few people are privileged to open new theatres in these days of the 'telly'... I want to congratulate all those who by their membership and investment have made the building of this theatre possible. It is going to be a wonderful attraction and amenity to this city and one more reason why tourists will find Nairobi a happy choice as a stopping-off place," Alderman Harold Travis then declared the Donovan Maule Theatre open.

Don recorded: 'After the many delays lots of people no doubt had serious misgivings (we had quite a few ourselves) whether we would really open on the 17th June. As anybody who happened to pass the theatre at any time up to an hour before the official opening ceremony would have seen, work was going on till the last moment. Thanks to superb help and co-operation from everybody concerned, when His Worship the Mayor, Alderman Harold Travis, Sir Charles Markham, Mollie and myself walked on to the stage at 6.30 prompt on the Seventeenth day of June One thousand nine hundred and fifty-eight, everything was ready, the auditorium was crammed to capacity, and there was a large overflow in the lounge and foyer. It was a thrilling moment for us and we are deeply grateful for the wonderful generosity of your support... this was the proudest moment of our lives.'

CHAPTER FIVE

'It is not given to everyone in this contrary world to realise a life's ambition — the fulfilment of a dream. We count ourselves among those fortunately blessed to have done so,' Don wrote.

The dream was now reality — THE DONOVAN MAULE THEATRE — standing proud 'Between Connaught & Jackson Roads, 2 front corner plots, nearest Legco...' There it was, well equipped, awaiting the staging of plays: '... anything we have a mind to...'

The Opening had been a triumph, but *Separate Tables* fell short of true success. Sonia Dresdel had been unable to prolong her visit to Kenya and her lustre was sadly missing.

Within a month, Don was in hospital. 'I do feel that it was an absolute brainwave that I should come here,' he wrote from his bed in Mombasa Hospital, 'perfectly delightfully situated just round the corner from Fort Jesus, overlooking the creek.'

His doctor had sent him there, deliberately distancing him from his office at the theatre.

'I have spent a lot of time at my favourite occupation — fiddling with and chewing over masses of figures. I even read the old D.M. Prospectus ...to see how guesswork of three years ago is likely to compare with actuality. I'm willing to bet a tranquilliser against a jab in the backside that the overall Gross Income for the new theatre will reach £60,000 during the first year...but we need 6,000 members to near-fill our theatre over a four-week run and thus provide us with sufficient assured income to afford an extra producer and more artists.'

Calling himself 'criminally' optimistic from time to time, Don admitted, 'Once set on a goal I go for it with almost fanatical concentration that makes me difficult to live with.'

It fell to Mollie, the practical half of the team, to bring to his attention the hurdles and pitfalls ahead. This, of course, didn't go down well: 'Every time I try to be practical and point out facts, I'm a dampener — a wet blanket.' Don had, indeed, been over-optimistic in estimating £60,000 income for the first year. In spite of the wonderful working conditions available to artists and staff, 'management' now faced new problems. Shorter runs of plays used up more scripts and the problem remained: choosing plays that would appeal to theatre club members. John Osborne's *Look Back In Anger* had exploded on the London stage just two years earlier in May 1956 and from that moment this type of play, dubbed 'Kitchen sink', influenced much new writing; plays by and about 'Angry Young Men'.

Prevailed upon by a Method actor under contract at the time, Osborne's play followed *Separate Tables*.

'The angry young men on the stage of the Donovan Maule Theatre on Tuesday night were as nothing compared with the number of Furious Old People in the audience loudly declaring that they couldn't understand it,' wrote a Nairobi critic. A letter to the editor offered a little praise: 'The Donovan Maule Theatre must be wholeheartedly congratulated and encouraged for attempting a play which is not obviously acceptable to people who believe that the theatre's role is solely to 'amuse and uplift'.'

The play did very poor business, and confirmed Don in his opinion that 'Lavatory pan' plays, as he dubbed them, were not for Nairobi.

The capacity houses they had known at the Studio — not difficult with only 76 seats — were infrequent at the larger theatre. At the end of the first year an average of 60% of capacity was recorded. The larger building required a larger staff and whereas the Bar became popular with executives from neighbouring commercial firms — they named it 'The Auxiliary Boardroom' — few, if any, passed through the double soundproof doors into the auditorium.

Operating the popular Bar proved a near perpetual headache. Don reported to his fellow Directors, just two years after the Company was formed: 'There is little that I can say at this moment about the disastrous business of our ex-Bar Manager who, having been deported by Immigration Authorities, left this theatre with the keys of the new Cash Register and owing several self-written IOUs for cash taken from Bar receipts. It also came to light during the course of the stock check, when he handed over to our new Bar Manager, that he had 'borrowed' a case of brandy and a case of whisky from our store (and, no doubt, several cases of minerals) which he used to stock some 'party' he gave at the Nairobi County Hall before the night of his departure. Latest information, gained last night, is that Mr. X was forbidden to land at Dar es Salaam by the Tanganyika Immigration Authorities, and that he is therefore perforce sailing onwards to South Africa, after relieving a fellow Rhodesian friend of £25 cash. I am afraid this was just a thoroughly bad business, making the third Bar Manager who had worked for the DM Players who has ultimately been deported by the authorities.'

1959 heralded a visit to the DM Theatre of the great Shakespearean actor Sir Donald Wolfit. He came at Don's invitation, bringing with him his wife and leading lady, Rosalind Iden. Together they presented *Scenes from Shakespeare* for a three-week season.

Wolfit, mainly under his own management, had played more of the big leading roles in Shakespeare than any other single actor and his *King Lear* was considered outstanding. During the dark days of the Second World War, he and his troupe of players toured blacked-out Britain, taking Shakespeare to unlikely venues, often under difficult circumstances. He did much to popularise the Bard of Avon but was also known as a flawed Colossus, a blustering tyrant, a spoilt child and a Grand Old Man — at once cussed and courageous. He gave many of the greatest and a few of the worst performances of his time. It was said he had accused a colleague of "deliberately *under-acting* to make *me* look ham!"

His performance in the title role of *Tamburlaine The Great,* at

London's Old Vic theatre in 1951, was one of his greatest and that of Lord Ogleby in *The Clandestine Marriage* one of the funniest. The Nairobi press, while acknowledging Sir Donald's great talent and stage presence, nevertheless had reservations about the 'Scenes', 'The staging of excerpts of Shakespeare makes unusual demands on both audience and actor. The audience has repeatedly to adjust itself to a fresh portion of the Shakespeare universe, while the actor has the additional task of projecting in a single monologue or short scene the quintessence of a character which can normally be developed gradually over five acts.' The opening week of the season, comprising eight different scenes, played to somewhat poor business. The visiting Star was displeased. Don, over-optimistic again, had forecast Full Houses and on this assumption had guaranteed the Wolfits 50% of the Box Office Gross, or a minimum of £1,000 plus airfares. He reported to his Board: 'The visit of Sir Donald Wolfit had been an economic failure and this had changed his plans for other guest artists.' Box office income had fallen far short of £2,000, but a Guarantee is a Guarantee. Writing to me, he said: 'It's better for us to remain a team with no star billing and all engaged to play as a cast.'

In spite of the financial disappointment, *Scenes from Shakespeare* appealed to many patrons and must have come as a revelation to students from the Kenya High School, the Duke of York School and others who attended matinées at specially reduced prices.

For those averse to the Bard, *The Boy Friend* played at the National Theatre.

The DM Theatre's first birthday was celebrated with *Breath Of Spring* by Peter Coke. Twelve productions had been staged by the resident company with the Wolfits' season making it a baker's dozen. Both Maules played in *Breath Of Spring* and Sheila, Mollie's mother, attended on opening night as she always did. It would be her last visit to the theatre. In July she had another, final heart attack. It was the end of a long life beginning in China in 1872 and ending in Kenya 87 years later. She had never known financial security, nor had she ever had a home of her own. In earlier years she had toured with a minor Shakespearean actor-manager named Henry Baynton, playing small roles and generally making herself useful, persuading her not-always-sober employer to get on stage in time for his entrance in *The Melting Pot* or *Hamlet*. As soon as he was safely "on", she would search for the bottles cunningly strung outside the dressing room window, or concealed in the lavatory cistern. Widowed in 1927, she had made her home with Mollie and Don — lacking financial means, she had few options. She was not perhaps the stereotype of a Grandmama... there was no ample lap or fairy stories, no scent from the kitchen of fresh-baked pie. I never saw a piece of tapestry or crochet work in her hands; instead there would be a book and a cigarette. Proudly she told me once, "I've given up cigarettes!" adding, "Except other peoples."

Ever tolerant of sexual deviants, she was a loyal and steadfast friend. 'If the slightest opportunity occurs, forgive,' she wrote to me.

When a new young beauty joined Baynton's company and homosexual jealousies flared, she might attempt to mediate. 'I'm sick of living in a small community, where gossip is so rife,' she wrote of life in Nairobi. 'As a family, we have been pretty free, living in London most of the time.' Unlike Don's mother Lydia, she left very little behind. There were no day-bills of her Star Appearances, no photographs, no love letters.

'It comes as something of a pleasant surprise to find such a modern well-run theatre where not many years ago there was only a frontier town on the edge of a wilderness. The theatre is named for Donovan Maule, a short peppery British actor who came to Kenya in 1947 with his wife, Mollie,' *The New York Times* published a feature in September '...their partnership started a long time ago. They met in 1906... both were children of theatrical parents and the families were appearing together in a production of *The Soldiers Of The Queen* that was touring the British provinces. "My mother was an old leading lady of the melodrama school. She toured with all sorts of dreadful things like *Her One Great Sin."* ' The feature continued: 'His own career took him to New York in 1923 with the British war play *Havoc* that was presented at the Maxine Elliot Theatre by Lee Shubert. Later he was stage director at such London theatres as the Garrick, Wyndham's and Strand... speaking about his Nairobi theatre, Mr. Maule declared: "I got an architect who'd never done a theatre before, so I got what I wanted. The trouble with most theatres is they are not designed by actors who have to work in the bloody things." '

'I haven't seen the Balance Sheet yet, but I'm told we made a profit of £8,000 last year.' *Inside East Africa* was quoting Don, and continued: 'Despite a skilful and economic organisation (the players are their own stagehands) it still costs £5,000 a month to run the theatre.'

Mollie wrote to me, 'The picture is really very rosy and gratifying... I do hope *Lock Up Your Daughters* catches the public fancy. I'm frankly terrified of it... a most complicated set, very expensive costumes and not suitable for children, which everyone demands over the holidays.' A gamble indeed, for a small repertory company (without a trained singing voice among them) to embark on a musical. Based on Henry Fielding's novel *Rape Upon Rape* — a "Savage satire on the practices of the law" embodied in Justice Squeezum, 'It is as brave and ambitious an experiment as any the Maules have attempted since they opened their splendid new theatre 18 months ago.' — *The Sunday Post.* Unable to run to a live orchestra, the music was recorded by Bela's Band, normally playing live at the New Stanley Hotel.

Lock Up Your Daughters opened in January 1960, scheduled for a four-week run. '...a tremendous success... presented with a polish that made Wednesday's first night one of the most triumphant I can remember in Kenya... A production which as a whole excels.' — *East African Standard;* while the *Nation* proclaimed: 'I think it would be impossible not to enjoy *Lock Up Your Daughters.'* And Nairobi theatre-goers did so, in large numbers. The four weeks extended to five and then six. Houses were Full. Production costs had been high, but income had been higher. 7,258 seats were sold. While going into their second week, on January 12, the State of Emergency was rescinded. Most people were unaware that it was still in existence, with the possible exception of Mr. Jomo Kenyatta, who remained in detention at a distance from Nairobi.

On February 3 Harold Macmillan, the British Prime Minister, made a speech in Cape Town. "The wind of change is blowing through the continent..." The implications of this declaration were not immediately apparent to those getting the next production on stage at the DM. The non-stop conveyor-belt mode absorbed everyone in the theatre. Production number 110 opened in March: *The Summer Of The Seventeenth Doll* written by Australian Ray Lawler, told of two sugarcane cutters who spend their five-month lay-off season in Melbourne, shacked up with a couple of barmaids. The men have money and are eager to spend it and enjoy a good time before they leave once more for the cane fields. Each year Roo brings Olive a kewpie doll — there are 16 of them strewn about the set. This summer is that of the 17th doll, but the good times are ending; nobody is getting any younger and dreams give way to raw reality. Mollie, playing Olive's mother, made her first entrance slung across Kenneth Mason's shoulders.

The planned reconstruction and lowering of Connaught Road began in April. Don recorded, 'Ghastly racket of mechanical drills and one-way traffic only from Whitehouse Road towards the Post Office ...lunchtime trade particularly affected... Nearly impossible to work in our offices due to noise... Artists and staff uncomfortable in staff flats... Noise so bad Easter Sunday and Monday that we were compelled to close club altogether... seriously affecting our business.'

In June they flew to Rome where I met them. On reaching London they went to work, visiting 39 theatres, shopping for plays and players. Back in Nairobi in September, Don growled: "The theatre is saturated with 'Kitchen sink' productions which jaded critics write up."

Politically Kenya was moving fast. The ban on political meetings having been lifted, KANU — the Kenya African National Union — came into being, headed by James Gichuru, until such time as Jomo Kenyatta was released from detention. KADU — the Kenya African Democratic Union — was led by Ronald Ngala.

Back in his office again, Don was dismayed to see the graph on the main wall indicating a marked downward slide. This chart showed the attendance at each production and the total cash taken at the Box Office. It meandered up and down; a success gave it a healthy boost UP before the next dip. Observing it now, Don saw the steep ski-slope descent ending in a tumble with G.B. Shaw's *Candida*. The current acting team was not a team, there were some noticeable weaknesses and, as always, there remained the choice of play. As John Counsell, the Managing Director of the Theatre Royal in Windsor wrote, 'Good, light escapist entertainment is fast disappearing for all of us. The London critics are quite determined to kill it and consequently both authors and managements are tending to give up the unequal struggle. It is a very serious development because there is no doubt that it is what 90 per cent of playgoers want.'

Nairobi critics, it seemed, were following suit. A series of unnecessarily harsh opinions were penned by a sour, albeit anonymous, critic writing for the *East African Standard*

A theatre manager discovers very quickly that he can Displease Some of the People All of the Time. Month followed month when the DM show displeased both the *Standard* and *The Nation* critic, until recently himself an actor on contract at the theatre. It reached the point where a letter to the Editor of the *Standard* asked: 'Who on earth is this long-haired intellectual type fellow... shortly after each opening night at the Donovan Maule we turn to our *East African Standard* — not to ascertain whether the play is a good one and how it has been produced, but to discover just what new jets of venom will have been squirted forth by your critic... so far as choice of plays is concerned, I think Donovan Maule knows his public. *The Amorous Prawn, Dry Rot* and now, perhaps *Rookery Nook* are the kind of plays which, despite your critic's best endeavours, seem to command full houses...'

The Amorous Prawn had indeed extended to a fifth week. *Dry Rot* had not much appealed and as regards *Rookery Nook*, — Don wrote: 'Lucky if we do 30% ...and serve us damn well right. — It really is *pitiful!*'. He was writing to Mollie who was enjoying a few days at Nyali Beach Hotel 'just eating, sleeping... and lazing in the sun.' Don continued: 'But never mind, let's learn by this lesson... and carry out your policy of doing reasonably good plays.'

Alongside the series of lacklustre productions, the uncertainty of the political situation affected business. At the company's AGM early in February 1961, the Chairman stated: "We were very worried about so many members leaving the country ...This loss must be expected over the next year or so." At the end of that year the official figure for departed expatriates stood at 6,052.

The theatre was not the only one to suffer. Kenya was experiencing the worst drought for many years. Famine loomed, cattle died, crops failed. 'This is about the only thing we can't blame on Macmillan and his bloody 'Wind of Change'!' Don proclaimed.

Following the dismal *Rookery Nook* came a reasonably good play, *The Rainmaker* by N. Richard Nash 'set on the Curry's ranch in a Western State of the USA on a summer day in time of drought.' Don played H.C. Curry, a widower, father of two sons and a daughter.

He loved the play and his role in it and the *East African Standard* critic — a new man, not old sourpuss, wrote: 'The man to be thanked for much of the pleasure in this production is Donovan Maule himself. His is a thoroughly likeable performance as the old rancher, father of a family and peacemaker in a hundred and one domestic squabbles. With one eye on the heavens for a sight of rain and the other on his family for a sign of squalls, he has to be ready always with a sample of homespun philosophy or humour to smooth over difficulties. Cooking breakfast, hunting down a beau for his daughter or trying to look as if he had not just spilled whitewash over his clean shirt, Donovan Maule's is a crisp and witty portrayal of this crusty individual.' A regular theatre-goer wrote: 'I think this is DM's play. I'll never see a nicer performance where so much was expressed with the use of so few words. It is nice to see some father-love (which is often inarticulate) for a change. We get a lot of the theme of mother-love.' Praise, too, came from the ex-actor critic writing for *The Nation:* 'Mollie Donovan Maule's production is unquestionably one of her best ...So, too, the setting by Bill Piggott — excellently conceived and executed.'

A new publication, *Reporter* appeared at this time. 'One of the big problems of theatre managers, in East Africa and elsewhere, is to gauge accurately the taste of the public, if not all the time, then most of the time. 'If anyone can do this all the time,' says Donovan Maule, 'he would become a millionaire. I can think of no impresario or actor-manager, who hasn't at some time backed a loser.' In Nairobi neither Don nor Mollie expected *The Rainmaker* or *She Stoops To Conquer* to be good box office. Yet both proved box office winners. They say the next production, *The Aspern Papers,* is a play they like. It is a lovely, delicate play, but they will not prophesy whether or not it will be good box office. The task of gauging public opinion has haunted Don and Mollie for years. In the early 1930s, when Don was Leon M. Lion's stage director, he and Mollie were connected with eleven 'losers' in a row. Don recalls that most of the West End theatres were having a sticky time around 1930 and 1931. Leon M. Lion leased the Royalty Theatre in Dean Street. It was the era of 'Two seats for the price of one' in London, the theatres were doing so badly... Then Mr. Lion handed Don the script of a new play written by a young Naval officer, which bore the unpromising title *That Excellent Woman.*

'After reading it Don felt sure that Lion was in for yet another failure... Following a great deal of re-writing, the play, now titled

While Parents Sleep, ran for three years in London.' The playwright, Anthony Kimmins, wrote more plays, one of them being *The Amorous Prawn.*

The Aspern Papers caused the *East African Standard* critic to declare, 'There are no two ways about it; this has to be a 'rave' review.' Once again Bill Piggott produced a masterly setting: that of an old, decaying palazzo in Venice. Next came a knock-about farce, *Simple Spymen,* which had audiences 'rolling in the aisles' due mainly to the two leading players, both experts at the genre. Trousers fell, false moustaches sprouted and mistaken identities multiplied — never allowing a moment for the audience to consider how ridiculous it all was. Making his début at the DM was Mike McCabe, a clever young actor who went on to give many wonderful performances in Nairobi before moving on to South Africa.

Harold Pinter's *The Caretaker,* guaranteed to displease some of the people, hit the target! A club member wrote: 'My wife and I saw *The Caretaker* yesterday, and we consider it the nastiest play we have ever seen. It is a pointless play about three mentally defectives, written apparently by a lunatic for imbeciles to enjoy ...Our sympathies are with the actors, and we wonder what they really think of the play.' The *Nation* critic gave the answer: 'From the actors' point of view it is a heavenly exercise, and, make no mistake about it, at the Donovan Maule Theatre the three actors have risen magnificently to the occasion.' More than 3,000 'imbeciles' came to see what all the fuss was about.

Beyond the roller-coaster of continuous repertory, a moment was being enacted in the history of Kenya. Jomo Kenyatta was released from detention. Within two months he had taken over the leadership of KANU. The road was now clear to Kenya's independence.

At the DM, preparations for the most elaborate and quite the most expensive production they had ever undertaken were underway. *Oliver!* would be the Christmas attraction in December 1961. The Maules had seen the London production — twice, in fact, with Mollie, who would be directing it, scribbling notes all through the performance on the second occasion. They were granted the rights — the show was still packing them in at the New Theatre in London with bookings well into the following year — with a higher than normal royalty to pay.

'I reckon we'll need to take at least £13,000 over the six-week run, just to cover costs. My agreement with Donald Albery stipulates that we must run a minimum of six weeks — I hope to run seven.' Don declared. This time they would have a 'live' orchestra — playing in the Orchestra Pit — created by the removal of all 13 seats in Row 'A', thereby reducing the seating capacity. Extra lighting was ordered, a Musical Director was appointed, over a hundred costumes were required. Mollie researched early copies of *Punch*, founded in 1841 shortly after Charles Dickens' novel *Oliver Twist* had been published in monthly instalments. The line-drawings of kitchen skivvies, street urchins and Undertaker's Mutes gave her all the details she needed.

As well as the lead role of Oliver, 12 other boys — workhouse orphans and members of Fagin's gang of pickpockets — were needed. Nairobi school boys, mainly from the Prince of Wales School, entered wholeheartedly and convincingly into the on-stage pickpocketing business. Dozens of boys attended the many auditions, some returning over and over again until Mollie made her choice. The hugely taxing role of Oliver went to 11-year-old Desmond Kenny, a St. Mary's schoolboy.

The ambitious venture might have foundered had it not been for Oliver Wigmore, the headmaster of the Prince of Wales School. His help and enthusiasm smoothed the way to production. He rehearsed the boys in all their songs, thereby saving hours of valuable theatre time. He liaised with parents and made adjustments to the school timetable to avoid overworking young Thespians kept late at the theatre.

Performances were 9pm on week nights, 9.30pm on Saturdays with matinées on Friday and Saturday. There were no performances on Sunday or Monday. The boys were divided into two teams, the A team and the B team, either team able (and always eager) to go on stage. The resident company was augmented by 20 guest artists.

On the evening of Monday December 18 the whole cast, together with musicians, came together for the first time and a dress rehearsal started. Chaos set in. Singers couldn't hear the music; the orchestra pit had been built too deep and the musical director couldn't see the singers who were up on stage. Bill Piggott's ingenious revolving stage, set between two permanent flights of steps, made so much noise when revolved, that it quite drowned the bridging music. The long-drawn-out evening was exhausting, disheartening, shambolic... How could they possibly open on Thursday?

'Well done DM. *Oliver!* should be a smash hit... The Maules have shown very great and laudable courage and ambition in tackling a musical which, technically as well as musically, is extremely difficult and, one might have thought, beyond the scope of their resources. Their battle with the seemingly impossible has been handsomely won... Fully 50% of the success of *Oliver!* is dependent on its mobility and the ability to flow from scene to scene, and the ingenuity of Mr. Piggott has enabled the producers to achieve this. Supreme on the acting side is Desmond Kenny's Oliver Twist... a half-pint sized Rock of Gibraltar, he dominates and carries the show along on his shoulders with the aplomb and unconcern of Atlas. His counterpart among the grown-ups is, not unexpectedly, Kenneth Mason's Fagin... a delightful creation... And don't let us forget the confidently exuberant teamwork of the boys of the Workhouse and Fagin's gang... Ambition has paid off and the Maules have a smash hit which should fill the theatre for many, many weeks.' — *Daily Nation*.

'You will love *Oliver!;* superbly dressed and staged and well acted and sung... All the numbers are punched over with tremendous bounce and verve particularly when the Workhouse Boys and the Fagin's gang are involved. Oliver is a winner,' commented the *Sunday Post*.

'*Oliver!* should break records in Kenya... Dominating the proceedings is Ken Mason's wily Fagin, an expert mixture of cunning and pathos.... This exhilarating show deserves to be more successful than the record-breaking *Lock Up Your Daughters*,' — the *Sunday*

Nation.

Oliver! filled — over-filled: cushions up and down the aisles — the theatre for eight weeks, sweeping them into February 1962. Fifty seven performances. Nearly 13,000 seats sold. Royalties paid to the London management approached £800. The National Theatre of Uganda requested the Maules to take the show to Kampala. Don delighted in marking up his wall chart.

Following the opening of *Oliver!*, Mollie was treating herself to a morning in bed, where she was handed a Cable: MEET FLIGHT EC 713 DECEMBER 23 1130 TO RECEIVE CHRISTMAS PRESENT. SANTA CLAUS. "What on earth is this?" she asked Don. "Can't you go without me?" He persuaded her to accompany him to the airport and as I stepped off the plane from London she squeezed her eyes against the December sun to confirm that the figure in fire-engine red trousers with boots to match was really her daughter. When she knew there was no mistake, she burst into tears.

Don had engineered the whole thing (Kenneth Mason compared the planning to that of Operation Overlord!) and sprung the surprise on her. He also had a 'hidden agenda.' I would be seeing his beautiful theatre for the first time. He would soon be in need of an actress.

Following a month of Kenya sun and sea: I took Mollie down to the coast for a rest; I was back in my flat in London and rehearsing for a popular BBC television soap named COMPACT. After the first episode was aired, I received some fan mail. Expecting the subtlety of my performance to have been recognised by a connoisseur, I read 'That cardigan you're wearing is lovely. Can you send me the pattern?'

In the run-up to *Oliver!* the *Sunday Nation* reported: 'Let it be remembered that the Maules, without subsidies of any kind, sank everything they possessed into the theatre, and when the new DM Theatre and Club opened its doors in June 1958, there was an overdraft in the bank of £20,000. The original cost of the building was in the region of £62,000, but with constant additions of fittings, alterations and all the permanent 'props' that go into the making of a first-class theatre (by any standards), the cost mounted to more than £100,000. Yet the position today after just over three years, is that the bank overdraft has been transformed into a credit and there are strong hopes that a dividend will be paid to shareholders.'

The company's AGM took place in February and Kenneth Mason wrote, in the next issue of *On Stage:* 'Take a look at the scene back in the United Kingdom, which is still the principal home of the repertory movement: there, in spite of subsidies from the Arts Council or local town or city councils, repertory theatres are finding it hard work to make ends meet even, let alone make a profit... Here in Nairobi we take pride in the fact that the theatre has been built entirely on private enterprise.'

In mid-April cheques were dispatched to 1,100 shareholders. Following the long haul of *Oliver!* Kenneth left Nairobi for some leave. He was away for 13 weeks, first in England and later New York. Amazingly, during his absence, *On Stage* continued to appear, on time for the opening night of the four productions mounted at the theatre during his absence. Just how he managed this long-distance conjuring trick remains a mystery. Each number contained the normal quota of five substantial items over and above the centre page cast list. No matter where he happened to be, he got his copy back to the Nairobi printers and met every deadline. The only occasion when *On Stage* failed to appear on a first night was for production number 137 in June, *The Irregular Verb To Love*. This was due to a printer's strike in Nairobi and this was the play in which we appeared together for the first, but not the last time.

Don's 'hidden agenda' had worked — I was now under contract to the DM for... at least six months.

Six months were absorbed, incredibly fast, doing monthly rep. Rehearsing for the next play, *The Deep Blue Sea*, while playing at night in *The Irregular Verb To Love*. Then came *Boeing-Boeing*, followed by *The Gazebo* at night, while rehearsing *The School for Scandal* in which all three Maules would appear together on stage.

In early October we were in our dressing rooms donning extravagant 18th century costumes topped off with powdered wigs before driving to the Sorsbie Gallery for a photo call scheduled for 8.45am. The classical architecture made a suitable background for the shoot. As we drove to Muthaiga, we attracted remarkably few glances, despite our extraordinary appearance! Sheridan's classic was followed by a thriller, *Signpost To Murder,* and my six months were up. Had I been wise, I would have returned to London and picked up the threads of my career there.

Despite losing 2,276 club members during the year, the DM paid another dividend and its future appeared reasonably assured.

It was another story on the opposite side of town. At the end of January 1963 an *East African Standard* headline trumpeted: THEATRE MAY HAVE TO CLOSE and in the same newspaper the following day the leader was headed: NATIONAL THEATRE TRAGEDY. It was the same old story: Lack of cash. The theatre had been living on its reserves for the past two years and 'Unless something is done this year it looks as if I shall have to go to the Government and hand them the keys of the building and say we cannot go on because we shall be bankrupt.' Thus announced Sir Richard Woodley, the Chairman of the Governing Council of the Kenya Cultural Centre. 'The fundamental financial trouble is the National Theatre's obligation to pay for the Cultural Centre' — where the new Memorial Hall had opened in 1961 — 'As this commitment is written into the original terms, the Ordinance will have to be altered to remove the burden.'

In February 'Representatives of dramatic societies in Nairobi met ...to draw up a plan of campaign...' while we at the Donovan Maule opened with Brendan Behan's wild Irish comedy 'with music and songs' — *The Hostage* — which was not much enjoyed by our patrons! Without pausing, we went into rehearsals for a thriller, *Kill Two Birds,* and Mollie and Don set off for Johannesburg, leaving me to 'Mind the Shop'. The leading man under contract had already thrown several tantrums; now with 'Management' absent, he really let rip. True, a very thin little comedy *Don't Tell Father;* that was being rehearsed at the time, wasn't too brilliant, but his contemptuous manner toward everybody working on it reached crisis point. Kenneth and I conferred: would the Diva feel happier if the roles they had been assigned were switched? He sighed deeply, inferring that the situation was so hopeless that it was beyond salvation, and we resumed rehearsals while he shook his head and muttered imprecations under his breath. On opening night he gave a splendidly funny performance, thereby ensuring he received a 'rave' press. Thereafter he 'walked through' the following 26 performances, a trick he employed from time to time. When the casting for the following production was announced, he demanded: "Why can't you choose plays that fit the company?" and we were once again treated to mutterings and head shakings.

Mollie wrote to me from Durban: 'We spent all day yesterday going into the possibilities of a theatre club here ...a lot of people are very enthusiastic about the idea.' Don enlarged: 'Durban has truly BIG possibilities for a DM Theatre Club.' An architect had ready-drawn blueprints; and money, they were assured, was no problem! They sailed from Durban in a freighter of the American Farrell Line, and enjoyed a quiet, relaxing interlude until they reached Mombasa. 'The Head Steward is a Mr. Wang, who looks like Matheson Lang as 'Mr. Woo' and speaks impeccable American... The Cabin Steward had once been dresser to Otis Skinner.'

At the start of May they were back in Nairobi and no further talk of a theatre club in Durban was heard. Instead it was rehearsing for *Billy Liar;* a splendid 'vehicle' for Mike McCabe with Kenneth as his father, me as his long-suffering mother and Mollie as his near-senile old Gran; a team working together and enjoying it, now that the 'Abominable Showman', as Don dubbed the Diva, had departed.

The play opened at the end of May and on Saturday we had two performances as usual. We had spent the morning up on the theatre's roof, which offered a splendid vantage point to observe the nearby Parliament Building. Jubilant crowds spilled across Connaught Road (soon to be renamed Parliament Road). The air vibrated with shouts and cries of joy and women ululating. The newly elected African Government, with Mr. Jomo Kenyatta as Prime Minister, had been sworn-in on June 1, 1963: Madaraka Day brought Kenya a step closer to independence. Our own, minor celebration occurred later the same month.

On the 17th, the theatre was five years old and we gave a 'Gala' performance that night to a full house followed by a champagne party in the Bar. Kenneth wrote: 'Although nobody knows what the next five years will bring, certain things can be guessed at. History will grind relentlessly on, Kenya will become Independent… and approximately 60 productions will run their monthly course at the Donovan Maule Theatre.'

September brought the end of the Company's financial year, and although theatre club membership was down to fewer than 4,000, finances allowed the payment of another dividend, the third in as many years.

In December a local publication opined, 'At first sight, a French farce of the 'naughty nineties' seems the oddest possible choice as a theatrical offering during the independence celebrations of an African state in the wind of change sixties. But after a week of pomp and ceremony, it was relaxing to enjoy a quiet chuckle at some inconsequential nonsense, and the Maules' intention in choosing the entertainment *Look After Lulu* became clearer.'

Following a strenuous day of rehearsals for the Feydeau farce 'Set in Paris in the year 1898', three Maules armed with rugs, cushions, sandwiches and a flask, headed for the stadium on the Lang'ata Road. Until midnight, the familiar Union Jack flew from the flagstaff. At the appointed hour the stadium was plunged into darkness. When the lights once again flooded the arena, the Kenyan flag was now aloft, fluttering in the breeze. The night exploded with cries of joy.

All ceremonies concluded, Mr. Kenyatta circled the arena in a Land Rover, flourishing his trademark fly whisk. The boisterous crowd went wild, roaring its approval, its euphoria, its victory, its Independence.

CHAPTER SIX

In the newly-independent Kenya, in a rapidly changing environment, what of the expatriate repertory-system Donovan Maule Theatre? Business as Usual for the time being. But for how long? 'The big problem for the Maules at present is how to please capricious theatre tastes in 1964.' *Reporter,* February.

Running costs now averaged £5,700 a month. *The Merchant Of Venice* opened in April and Don's wall chart improved a little, driven by extra Schools Matinées. Caltex Oil (Kenya) sponsored children at Sh5 per seat and a total of 520 young people, chosen from 16 secondary schools in districts outside Nairobi whose pupils seldom had an opportunity to see a professional stage production, came to Nairobi.

They travelled in battered school buses and traders' lorries, some journeying more than 100 miles over some of the worst roads in Kenya at the height of the rainy season. Mr. J.D. Otiende, Minister of Education, addressed the first matinée audience, employing many an apt quotation from the Bard. These schools matinées were the most responsive audiences we ever had. Their excitement communicated itself to us up on stage and created a vibrant rapport. In spite of the archaic language, the young Kenyans followed the action closely and reacted with all the vigour of the groundlings at Shakespeare's Globe Theatre. Elizabethan jokes, the bawdier the better, sparked howls of laughter. The performance over, we would go down into the auditorium, still in make-up and costume, to chat to the children, answer their questions and ask a few of our own. Their eager faces, displaying wide smiles, rows of perfect teeth and bright shining eyes, were beautiful to behold. Harassed teachers tried to shepherd their charges, unwilling to leave, back to their ramshackle transport for the long ride home. The evening performance couldn't come near the response we had enjoyed earlier.

To the question "Why don't you do Shakespeare more often?" The answer was simple: "We can't afford it." Extra guest artists, extra costumes ...for *The Merchant,* 18 pairs of tights for the men were ordered from London, cost: £18.15 — when they finally reached the theatre's wardrobe, having passed through several Government Departments, the cost had risen to £34.61! 'Cheerful Comedies & Bloody Murders' kept Don's chart above the poverty line — all dubbed 'Trivial' by the critics.

"The theatre is now hardly holding its own, in fact losing money," Don told a friend. "It may not be possible for it to continue very much longer." Two months later he was hospitalised with bronchitis and asthma, the first of a number of bouts of ill health which would dog him to the end of the year and be the start of health problems which, increasingly, affected the years to come.

I ended at the DM in September, following two and a half years and 25 plays, usually in a large role. I was past my 'sell by' date. Audiences needed a new face, a new personality and I needed a rest.

When the Directors met in February 1965, concern was voiced about 'the indifferent health which Mr. Maule had been subject to recently.' He was urged to see a specialist who diagnosed emphysema, and the Directors insisted that a proper holiday away from the theatre altogether was indicated. Before sailing for Durban on the *Rhodesia Castle,* Don was able to announce, at the AGM, "that they had now got approximately 40 African members and hoped that this would increase."

At the same time, the next production, Robert Bolt's *A Man For All Seasons* would feature a Kenyan actor, Donald Kiboro, in the role of the Common Man, a gift for any actor, encompassing as it does that of the narrator of events, studded with 'cameos': a steward, a boatman, a jury foreman, a jailer and — finally — an executioner, while he himself remains a survivor.

'It is sheer delight through and through. It is theatre at its best... To give the Common Man to Donald Kiboro was an inspiration which he more than justifies.' *Reporter,* March 1965. Interviewed by the *E.A. Standard;* Mr Kiboro admitted: 'I cannot bear to go to any theatre. Sheer jealousy is to blame. I simply cannot sit in front of the footlights without wanting to go on to the stage and take over one of the roles.' The play was on that year's school syllabus and once again Caltex sponsored extra matinées for schools and 2,300 students came. The good news, however, was that so many others did too — total attendance reached 6,400 and the run extended to a fifth week.

Kiboro wasn't the first African to appear on stage at the DM; Joseph Gichure had already 'trodden the boards', first in *The Miracle Worker* in 1961, followed by *The Hostage* in 1963. Joseph was an astonishing, versatile character. He came to the DM first in 1959, having previously been a house-painter. He was put to work assisting Don in altering the theatre's 47 advertising frames situated round and about Nairobi. A photograph of the new production would replace the existing one (to be returned to the office for the records), followed by re-setting, with white plastic letters, the title and author of the upcoming production. "A simple job with such a title as 'Gigi' but 'The Happiest Days Of Your Life' takes time! I know because I simultaneously do the same job in the outlying districts with the car!" Don said. In order to get round central Nairobi with the pile of photographs and a big box of plastic letters, Joseph had been taught to drive and travelled in a three-wheeled vehicle emblazoned with the theatre's logo, but he proved so useful that the scenic workshop and the stage staff quickly pinched him, turning him into a Jack-of-all-Trades. He helped build scenery, he washed in background colour for the scenic artist, he assisted the theatre's electrician and sometimes operated the switchboard. He worked the Act-drop curtain and was chief property master, helping the stage crew with scene changes.

He renewed burnt-out light bulbs throughout the theatre and

club, he wired up table lamps and other stage 'practicals' at set-ups. He renewed burnt-out elements in electric irons for the wardrobe, the laundry and the dressing rooms. He redecorated the offices and artists' flats at the theatre. He took props and pieces of furniture from the theatre to the Riverside Drive house for storage, bringing back replacements for the next play. He was sent to fetch anything urgently wanted, from a load of timber to a packet of screws for the stage or further supplies of butter, cheese and biscuits for the pantry, doing a big lunchtime trade. He took prescriptions to the chemist and returned with the *dawa*. The theatre's programme named him General Assistant.

"But," Don lamented, " we have come to the conclusion that Joseph is accident-prone. He has had yet another accident: overturning the *piki-piki*. He has already written off two vehicles. The third — comparatively new — spends much time in General Motor's workshops and when it is unavailable, extra transport has to be hired to get Joseph home at night and for carting stage furniture and props."

Joseph's skill on the switchboard — these were pre-computerised days — got him promoted to Chief Electrician and he could operate a slow-fade with utmost sensitivity, enhancing the mood of a scene on stage.

Mollie and Don sailed round much of Africa before landing at Malaga at Easter, where I was waiting to see them off the Spanish ship which had brought them from Las Palmas. "What's the flat like?" were Don's first words. "Not bad, bit small. There's a marvellous view." We had leased an upstairs apartment in a small modern block. I had already installed myself in the second bedroom which was the size of a broom closet, and soon we were made aware of the imperfections of the plumbing (and other utilities) in hastily-erected Spanish apartment buildings. But the view *was* marvellous.

Six weeks later, Mollie and Don sailed from Gibraltar, reaching Nairobi on June 17, the eighth anniversary of the DM Theatre, where they received 'a wonderful welcome from everybody and saw an excellent matinée of *Waters Of The Moon.*' Two days later Don was confined to bed with bronchial asthma. 'Very difficult to breathe. Unable to lie down all night...'

Mollie too, went sick, 'It's really too humiliating if not comic for both of us to be ill after a three-month holiday,' she wrote, 'I feel so ashamed!'

This did not portend well; neither did the news in Don's next letter to me: 'The theatre lost money again last month. The profits from the Bar just subsidised it but the precarious financial state is a constant worry. We have a host of air fares coming up... which will plunge us into the red... The problem of the right kind of play is ever with us.' A rollicking farce, *Diplomatic Baggage,* achieved some £700 at a special Gala performance, but not for the benefit of the theatre. It went to boost the campaign funds of the National Freedom from Hunger Committee. The Speaker of the House of Representatives, the Rt. Hon. Humphrey Slade, received the donation with "very many thanks." His two sons, Nigel and Laurie, were both to become associated with the theatre in their separate ways.

'The DM has just become the first theatre outside Britain to be accepted into the Council of Repertory Theatre,' — *East African Standard,* September 1965. 'Quite a privilege for a theatre so far from the theatrical beaten track and rather an unusual tribute to its reputation. CORT (as it has been known for 21 years) is valuable to theatre managements in their continual struggle to find out what the general public wants. It provides them with a pool of information and opinions... Kenneth Mason, who is now on three months' leave, will be representing Nairobi for the first time at CORT's annual meeting next month.' Don compiled a detailed table of statistics covering the years 1959 to 1964, listing the 82 plays presented at the new theatre, the percentage of capacity in seat sales, together with the total income and expenditure for each year. The bottom line:

Profit before Taxation: 1959 — £7,735; 1964 — *£430.*

The lamentably depleted figure for 1964 was, in part, due to the activities of the Records Clerk who developed a small-scale private enterprise in his office at the theatre.

At one time, both seat sales and club membership fees were operated through the theatre's box office, where two expatriate manageresses handled all monies. At a year-end audit a scam was detected. Henceforth monies received for membership fees must be kept strictly divorced from monies received for theatre ticket sales; thus the Auditor. So 'John' was appointed Members Registration Clerk and, at the insistence of the Auditor, put to work alone to avoid any possible collusion, in a specially partitioned upstairs office. Diligently he entered monies received on the Daily Return sheet. The Auditor was satisfied and John continued undisturbed. When the matter was raised later at a Board meeting it was explained that "... The Clerk had covered his misappropriation of cash by leaving out receipt numbers from the Daily Return sheet. If a check had been carried out on the duplicate of the receipt book against this, the defalcation would have come to light." Before he was suspended from duty, John had misappropriated — at a conservative estimate — more than £1,150.

He got 12 months in a correctional facility, no longer King Georgi's Hoteli — a Kenyan jail. He also got to keep the cash.

At the next AGM Don was able to report some better news: He thought the company was now through a period of two years which he had anticipated would be poor. Membership was gradually mounting again, standing at approximately 4,500. Also, 3,000 more theatre seats had been sold than in the previous year; but expenses were increasing all the time. £6,000 a month was now required merely to survive. They would have to raise seat prices, the first since the theatre had opened in 1958.

"One satisfactory thing," Don reported to his fellow directors, "is that our basic income from membership fees equals what it has always been: roughly £13,000 a year — despite the exodus from Kenya over recent years of so many Club Members."

Mollie wrote to me: 'Although business is gradually improving and the increase of seats to Sh12.50 has made a lot of difference, the whole thing is an incessant worry and, as one gets older, one wonders sometimes whether the game is worth the candle (whatever that may mean). Still, there's nothing else we can do but carry on and hope that sooner or later we will pay a dividend again. Without our salary we would have nothing to live on.'

As far back as 1961 Don had written to Mollie, from his Mombasa Hospital bed. 'We really *must* try to reorganise ourselves and relieve the incessant tension and strain. Our energy is certainly getting sapped, but is it so surprising at 60? Oughtn't we to accept it up to a point? Make plans for alternative arrangements; the gradual relinquishing of our grip on everything connected with the theatre? But we *must* make up our mind to do it *willingly* and happily. I think we should start looking out for someone (maybe two people)...' Now, five years later, their energy was further depleted, set against rising costs and proliferating problems; this would soon lead to a major crisis.

Don arrived in London on June 4, intending to attend a CORT quarterly meeting, see 14 current London productions, interview artists — 'It is a tricky jigsaw puzzle to achieve a) Good balance of plays; (b) Suitable casting; (c) Fitting in with current artists' contracts; (d) Engaging a replacement artist with minimum of expensive overlap of salaries and finding accommodation in the theatre's flats; (e) Consideration of end of schools' terms with (if possible) presentation of entertainment suitable for Club Members' children during the holidays.' He had with him a stack of new theatre brochures designed mainly for tourists. Already about 3,000 a year came to the theatre at Sh22.50 a time. Seat price: Sh12.50. Temporary membership to the club: Sh10. Mollie remained in Nairobi, rehearsing a big role for the July production and designing costumes for the play to follow.

Don installed himself in a small service flat, took the cover from his portable typewriter and set to work. Artists arrived at half-hourly intervals (with or without an appointment — *The Stage* had published the fact that he was in town). The telephone rang incessantly, answered by a self-sacrificing woman friend who volunteered her services. Meanwhile I criss-crossed London searching for items on Mollie's lengthy shopping list which Don had presented to me on arrival, and which grew lengthier with frequent updates from Nairobi.

Despite his busy schedule, Don wasted untold hours typing long, detailed Progress Reports — followed the next day by a further Progress Report and then another. Mollie dashed off a reply: 'I'm going nearly *mad*. None of your letters seems to answer any of mine, and everyone you have so far engaged seem to be coming at the wrong time. I do not, repeat NOT, want a juvenile girl on August 8th, as you should know if you had studied the big sheet with full casting. Also, why TWO leading ladies? Please read that cast list carefully. Don't overburden us with a huge salary list, we can't afford it. It won't make a ha'porth of difference to the membership. It's good *plays* we need. Please take my advice and don't lose your head. God, how I wish I were with you. I'm terrified of what you're going to land us with.'

His visit of 14 days extended to 27, but he made sure to be back in Nairobi for their 46th wedding anniversary on July 3. Mollie, however, was in no mood for romantic anniversaries; she had had to scrap the production planned to follow *Ring Round The Moon* and substitute an Agatha Christie thriller because of what Don had landed her with. Back in his office Don settled once again at his typewriter and produced a report for his Directors. It covered eleven close-typed pages and announced: 'My near-month in England cost a great deal of money.' He concluded: 'But I managed to get Mollie several small items for the DM wardrobe unobtainable in Kenya and such required stage properties as a dozen Chinese lanterns.'

Mollie's nerves were in tatters. She wrote: 'Don, since it seems impossible for us to talk reasonably, can we get a few things straight? I am incapable of thinking any more. We don't want an overlap of leading men. Far too expensive. Having worked out everything so carefully and had it all balled up, I can't take any further responsibility.'

'I awoke this morning with a new and sudden clarity,' Don recorded in his diary in mid-August. 'My misjudgement and proneness to be "carried away" has cost the company a great deal of money. It is more than probable that other certain artists who were engaged by me will have to be returned to UK.'

His emphysema was exacerbated by his continued smoking. 'Still only partly recovered from my worst asthmatical bout yet. Have had to sit upright throughout the night... feeling every moment must be my last — even in this terrible state I long to take a few puffs and have, three times today, tried to do so...'

To ease the administrative load a General Manager was appointed. Faced with recent legislation — PAYE; NSSF; NHIF; Licensing of Plays & Entertainment Tax — he resigned three weeks later, unable to tackle the job. But someone had to tackle it, and both Maules were working long days on separate projects which demanded every ounce of their dangerously lowered stamina.

In an effort to boost income to the theatre, Don was investigating, then implementing a scheme to offer Charter Flights to theatre club members: Nairobi/London/Nairobi.

This involved him in a great many meetings and reams of paperwork. A professional travel agent was a necessary partner, and the approval of the International Air Transport Association had to be obtained. Theatre Club members responded enthusiastically to the excellent value on offer, bookings rolled in and soon Charter Flight 'DM1' was fully booked. The Automobile Association and the Agricultural Society offered flights to their members, and occasionally the DM shared a charter with one or other association to their mutual advantage. In all cases only *bona fide* club members of six months standing might apply.

Soon, however, sharks, smelling a killing, entered the arena, employing phoney back-dated membership cards to non-existent clubs. When the pirates were exposed by IATA, *all* charter flights were closed down. After an interval the pirates were back in business and prospering mightily!

At the time when Don was typing stencils and having thousands of copies run off for members, Mollie, together with Trevor Smith, was making a stage adaptation of Dickens' *A Christmas Carol*.

Trevor composed music for the songs. Next item for Mollie: costumes for 15 children and 15 adults, many of them playing more than one role. Don was cast in three small parts and, much to his irritation, would be called from his office in mid-typing, to attend a rehearsal. Recalling the success of *Oliver!*, he scheduled *Carol* for six weeks. It received an excellent press and enjoyed good business for the first four weeks, but the minute schools reopened in the new year, there was no longer an audience. Towards the end of the sixth pathetic week, Don collapsed. Before this, in mid-January, Mollie told her husband: 'Don, I think I'd better warn you that I'm liable to resign at the Board Meeting this afternoon. Or I shall be forced to point out a few things about the money that is being wasted in this theatre without any increase in efficiency... The office, play library and filing system are in a state of chaos. Various people are engaged to do this, that and the other, but nothing is ever completed... Grandiose schemes are evolved costing God knows what, but the simple, everyday things are never done... Nothing is ever done to alleviate my difficulties.'

The Directors met and covered a lengthy agenda. Mollie remained silent. It was minuted that, with the resignation of the recently appointed General Manager who had been 'unable to tackle the job', it would be 'extremely difficult to obtain someone who could carry out the work of PA. to Mr. Donovan Maule and supervise the accounts and the theatre.'

The following day Don wrote to their doctor: 'My wife and I have been working at tremendous pressure lately, and I feel that she needs your professional advice even more urgently than myself. But her exhausted nerves are in such a state that it is useless my speaking to her about it, or indeed, speaking to her on *any* subject without it leading at once to near hysteria.' He sent a copy to Charles Markham, who responded immediately: 'I am very distressed, although hardly surprised in view of what I have both seen and heard about you both in recent months. I believe quite frankly that the time has come for you both to retire from active work with the theatre on a day to day basis. Why not get Annabel out here as soon as possible and put her in charge? I do not believe that you are protecting either your own or the minority shareholders' interests by thinking that you are the same person who started up in 1949. I don't think that it will work if there are in fact three people doing the job.'

Don sent to me both these letters, adding; 'In essence, I am entirely in accord with his suggestion that Mollie and I should work our way as quickly as possible from running the theatre and that you should take over fully — and I mean 'fully', without interference from us or anybody else. Nothing would delight me more than to have nothing whatever further to do with the DM.'

He asked me to reply to him at the Nairobi Club. He was taking a unilateral decision which excluded Mollie.

A Christmas Carol limped to its pathetic end. Don had collapsed and his doctor insisted on his staying in bed at home. Released from the show, Mollie was put on the train to Mombasa, taking with her the beloved pet poodle, Baggage. The doctor visited Don at home and proclaimed him "completely clapped out" and suffering from very low blood pressure. Four days after this he was hospitalised. What next?

At this juncture, my own life was no bed of roses. I was on tranquillizers prescribed by my London doctor and trying to pull myself up from a traumatic emotional disaster. Very low on self-confidence, I felt incapable of taking on the rocking ship in Nairobi. Another thing: I knew that I would not be allowed to work 'without interference from us'. The minute he felt better, the minute a production pushed up the index on his graph, he would want to be Captain of his own ship again. His statement 'Nothing would delight me more than to have nothing whatever further to do with the DM' was absurd. The DM was the centre of his universe, his sole interest in life — he was a man without hobbies. When we were in Spain the eagerly anticipated news from Nairobi, news of the theatre: Seat sales? Bar income? New members? Total income? made his day. Lack of news shadowed it.

And Mollie? She now knew everything. She had been shown all the correspondence. She was up-to-date. Her sense of betrayal was profound. 'I find it very difficult to write truthfully about Don,' she told me. 'I have been completely loyal to him all the years and never discussed with anyone how absolutely impossible he is to work with... We cannot discuss the smallest matter of business without a row... Life is never on an even keel. He is either completely down with no energy for anything and utterly depressing to live with, or indulging in grandiose schemes like buying the vacant plot next to the theatre and building luxury flats. It would be much more to the point if he stuck to his own job instead of letting everything get out of hand.'

Coming out of hospital after a mere four days, Don drove, alone, the 350 or so miles to Kilifi and joined his wife at Mnarani Club. But 'All was turmoil immediately and the rows began again...'

It takes, as the saying goes, two to tango. It wasn't only the theatre which was rocky. The marriage was in danger, too.

Back in Nairobi, it was to find that the theatre had been broken into the previous night. Tape recorders, a typewriter and bottles of liquor from the bar had been stolen. But far worse was the damage inflicted: wrought-iron grilles wrenched away, coolers in the bar smashed open and every drawer and file system in the box office forced and the contents strewn across the floor, making mincemeat of the club's records. The police gave instructions that nothing was to be touched until the CID sent a photographer.

They waited, but no photographer turned up. 'Box office and bar staff will arrive tomorrow morning to start their day's work to find utter chaos and yet they are not supposed to touch anything!'

Don took to his bed at Riverside Drive, declaring that he could not cope. 'It's an awful thing to have to say, but I'm convinced that Don is not quite sane these days, or shall we say not mentally stable, and the strain of it all is rapidly driving me in the same direction... At the moment life is hell. I only hope Don, won't crack up completely before we can get away from it all.' These bulletins increased my sense of guilt at not coming instantly to the rescue — yet this was not only logistically impossible for me at that time, but would not, I knew by instinct, solve the problem.

News came that Mollie had booked Don on a B.I. boat bound for Durban. 'He will be away at least five weeks and will be unlikely to return to this theatre in an official capacity except to hand over... I must remain to attend the AGM on March 6... The more I think of it the more it seems that you are the logical person to take over...'

Jean Hayes (née Parnell), a loyal friend with a clear-sighted view of events, wrote: 'This theatre has been a great achievement of theirs and it would be a pity to see it pass out of the Maule name and a tragedy if it became a Bingo Hall.'

On the evening of February 28, the *Karanja* sailed from Mombasa. Don wrote in his diary: 'Very hot and very unhappy and completely stupid and "lost".' Mollie wrote to me: 'I reach London 7.15am on Wednesday March 8.'

She stayed with me in my small London flat, which was unsuitable for two women both trying to work out problems.

When the theatre's Directors met on April 24, the Chairman reported: 'Miss Annabel Maule has rejected the idea of coming out... Mr Donovan Maule is obviously not fit to take over his responsibilities...' A week before this, Mollie had travelled down to Mombasa to meet him off the *Europa*. She was deeply shocked at his appearance when he disembarked. Three days later he was, once again, in Nairobi Hospital. He told me: 'I have lost all confidence in every direction.' Endogenous depression causing acute melancholia was diagnosed. 'The doctor states he won't get better until we are entirely free from the theatre with our future settled.'

I agonised over the situation, but knew the solution did not lie in my agreeing to come to Nairobi. In mid-May, Mollie's letter arrived: my heart thumped and suddenly it was hard to breathe. I ripped it open: 'Retirement is OFF! At any rate for the time being. I felt quite sure that as soon as Don was feeling better the knowledge that his great interest in life had gone forever would appal him. He is now on some new tablets which seem to be doing wonders. I have had the feeling in my bones that things would turn out differently. It was my wish all along not to force matters, to 'wait and see'... It was quite obvious that Don's heart was still thoroughly involved and that all that talk of wanting to be free of it all had just been brought about by his illness and general depression ...So long as he doesn't do too much and gets to bed early, he seems to be able to cope, and is busy thinking up schemes for the future, a sure sign that his interest in the theatre isn't dead.'

Just a month after telling me that he had 'lost all confidence in every direction', Don wrote: 'We have the happiest and best team-spirit company possible. James Ward is quite the most useful all-round actor ...My wall-graph is steadily rising.'

Excellent news. But for how long?

One member of the new 'team-spirit' company was Laurie Slade, recently down from Oxford University. He was appointed Assistant Stage Manager and 'to play as cast.' This occurred very soon in Agatha Christie's *The Unexpected Guest*. Nairobi critics were generally lukewarm about the production, but found much favour in Laurie's performance and he scooped the pool. Two productions later, he had risen to the dizzying height of Stage Manager.

Mollie was once again spending long hours in the theatre's wardrobe, designing and making costumes for Sheridan's *The Rivals*. Inevitably this took its toll and she was sent home with a kidney complaint. From her bed a stream of scribbled notes reached the theatre: instructions regarding a flounce here, a button there, the correct coloured stockings...

'The play is gorgeous in every way and mustn't be missed,' wrote the *Kenya Weekly News*. At an extra matinée for schools, the Chief Education Officer, Mr. Kyale Mwenda, told the students: "The number of people who have been able to come to these matinée performances now runs into thousands... It is very fortunate that the DM company chose to make Nairobi its headquarters."

In August came production 203, *Thunder Rock* by Robert Ardrey. The play was panned by the local press and did bad business 'but Donovan Maule making one of his rare appearances on the stage in the part of Captain Joshua, captain of the lost ship, turns in a really fine performance...' — and more of the same.

Don wrote to me: 'I'm enjoying playing Captain Joshua (although to only a handful of audience) now that I at last feel confident in the part. For the first week I was in a state of dithering nerves, feeling that each performance would be my last — ever on this earth!'

In fact, it was to be his last on stage in his own theatre, at the age of 68.

Edward Albee's controversial *Who's Afraid Of Virginia Woolf?* received 'rave' press reviews on the one hand and outcries of indignation on the other; a club member of 17 years wrote: 'I feel I must tell you how disgusted and dismayed I am at the current play. Two acts were enough... too much in fact.'

A lady, not having seen the play, said: 'I hear your present play is revolting, disgusting and obscene in the extreme. I am disappointed that you should have fallen so low and hope it will not happen again.' And another commented: 'I wish to protest most strongly against this terrible play. All the characters are abominable... This play is disgusting.' And: 'We must register our disgust and horror that you should produce such an utterly revolting and often obscene play...' On a post card form Nanyuki: 'You couldn't pay me to see this dreadful gutter play...' and more.

The run of *Virginia Woolf* was extended to accommodate all those wishing to see this disgusting, obscene, horrible, revolting play. 3,169 seats were sold.

'Seldom have we seen so perfect a team of actors and so perfect a direction. This play is definitely a milestone of the theatre, and DM has done it more than justice.' — *Reporter* September 22.

Addressing shareholders at the AGM, Don was able to report that membership had, once again, broken through the stubborn 5,000 barrier. It now stood at 5,246. Shareholders could look forward to a tiny dividend payable in April 1968.

The euphoria of Mollie's letter of May, 'Retirement is OFF!' was short-lived. For the remainder of the year, one or other was away, sick. In and out of hospital — Don, reporting Mollie's latest malady, anaemia and peripheral neuritis, went on: '...it is little wonder that, approaching the age of 70, the physical frame becomes a little worn and exhausted. I personally feel in very grave doubt about the possibility of your taking on the DM with all its ramifications of stress and worry. The main thing needed is for both of us to regain our health. A really loyal and reliable executive assistant... would go a long way to achieve this. But where is he to be found? For you to work *with* ourselves wouldn't last three months. With almost £25,000 at stake it is important to Mollie and me that the DM should continue to flourish. It would be a pity, to say the least, if the DM ended its existence soon after we left it in the hands of others.'

So much for my father's confidence in me.

His letter continued: 'Whereas a few months ago, when I was so very ill, I wanted to retire as soon as possible... now that I feel better, I can contemplate with equanimity a few more years exercising control jointly with Mollie... but if Mollie is seriously ill and she is forced to chuck her hand in — then I would certainly want to do the same.'

They could not accept that, at their age, time was no longer on their side. In the meantime I was to stand by as an understudy.

Jean Hayes reported: 'Mollie has been in a fine state of nerves for so long now, and charges at everything with breakneck speed as always... We get back to the same problem — that theatre has got to be managed by someone else.' Don, on the other hand, continued his fantasy: 'All I personally need is a good PA woman secretary... and all Mollie really needs is a right-hand costume designer and wardrobe mistress with taste and knowledge of period costumes. If these two people could be found, then this aged couple, sick or well, are really the best people *for the DM's future prosperity;* as well as our own happiness... to go on directing its multitudinous affairs for several years yet. Together we have pulled the DM right up to increasing prosperity and got it on a sound economical footing. The ship is sailing full steam ahead — now I want to keep her on course without overloading her with unnecessary extra operational costs.'

Without any move on Don's part, 'extra operational costs' would hit the DM amidship almost immediately. The Immigration Act came into effect on December 8, 1967.

When next the Directors met, it was noted that 'considerable expense would have to be met due to the new Act.' Don was absent from this meeting. Away sick. Mollie told me: 'The new permit restrictions for non-Kenya citizens are affecting our business badly and we are worried to death about it... Don has got over the worst of his malaria but we are both at pretty low par and depressed generally.'

To assess the situation at first hand, I flew to Nairobi shortly before Christmas. I did a lot of dressmaking for Mollie, using the theatre's wardrobe. The weather was glorious throughout. I stayed with friends in Naro Moru. I stayed with Jean Hayes on Crescent Island, Lake Naivasha, and she took me onto the lake in a canoe where we drifted among a flotilla of pelicans. Later, I wrote about this singular and magical experience. The BBC accepted the script and I recorded it for *Woman's Hour.* When I left for London it had been agreed: I would return to the theatre later in the New Year.

I had also studied the gazetted directives of the Immigration Act. The Department of Immigration might not grant a Work Permit without the prior consent of a new official watchdog, the

Kenyanisation of Personnel Bureau.

The theatre employed about 40 people throughout the year. Of this number, approximately half were expatriates: actors, actresses, designers and box office management. For them Class A permits were required, at £25 'for each year of validity or any part thereof.' These were non-transferable.

Don had called the selection of personnel for the DM 'a tricky jig-saw puzzle'; now it became considerably trickier. When an artist in Britain agreed on a stint at the Nairobi theatre, a contract (British Actors' Equity Association's contract for Overseas Engagements) was mailed, in duplicate, to them for their signature, together with approval from the Equity office. The date of travel had to fit in with the schedule of plays. The contract stipulated full salary for the artist from the moment of their arrival in Nairobi. Next: flight schedules on Lufthansa Airlines which, at this time, had a Reciprocal Agreement with the DM (a number of flights in return for East African widespread publicity by the theatre). Details from the artist were required: passport number and — very important — *name* inscribed on passport because many people employed a different stage name (the one on the Equity contract). These were submitted to Kenyanisation (soon to be dubbed Brotherisation) of Personnel Bureau, who forwarded their recommendation to Immigration. When the vital Kenya Entry Permit was received, it was air-mailed to the waiting artist for presentation to Immigration at Nairobi airport, allowing them to proceed to work at the theatre. It was now that the DMs were enlightened in the ways of delays, mislaid files, 'lost' files and further setbacks. The working methods of a repertory theatre, operating year-round without start-up dates and, from time to time, employing people for six months only and possibly needing them at very short notice, were unfamiliar and of no consequence to officers at Kenyanisation or Immigration.

When the Act first came into effect, it was estimated that initially, approximately 50,000 applications for permits would be submitted on behalf of expats already in the country.

Don was no longer in confident mode. 'There is NO real future for the DM Theatre Club... to endeavour to continue a professional repertory company in Nairobi is sheer lunacy... heading rapidly to bankruptcy... In short the entire enterprise is only *just* getting by, by the skin if its eyelids — the new legislation will tear away that eyelid. With all expatriates that remain here having to face the same economic problems can one expect a "luxury" commodity like a theatre to survive?'

1968 marked the theatre's 10th Anniversary, and it was necessary to survive to celebrate the occasion! This was done with Shakespeare's *Twelfth Night* directed by a fervent 'Bardolater': Kenneth Mason. It was a lovely production, and his accompanying 'production', *On Stage,* equalled it. A bumper issue containing a complete catalogue of DM productions to date: 127 of them in the new theatre and a further 88 stretching back to that faraway first attempt at the old Theatre Royal. June 19 was celebrated in style with champagne, and many who were present remembered vividly the evening 10 years earlier, when the Donovan Maule Theatre, with scaffolding still shrouding its exterior, opened its doors.

Don, in better spirits, compiled the box office receipts at the end of *Twelfth Night's* five-week run and amused himself with a letter addressed to 'William Shakespeare Esquire, Late of Stratford-on-Avon. Your Royalty of £283.00 (based on normal scale of 10 per cent) will be converted into nectar — which I feel will be more welcome than depreciated Sterling,'

Physically he was deteriorating. 'My breathlessness and phlegm in early morning (bronchial asthma?) is getting worse every day, especially during this exceptionally cold weather in Kenya... After a hot bath this morning I panicked for want of air, alarming Mollie. But she is right in thinking that "retirement" would probably prove fatal. I hope to keep in the saddle 'til the end.'

By now it had been minuted at a Board Meeting that I would be returning to 'assist them in running the theatre.' The understudy would be nearer at hand.

Not until the end of the year, in December, did I stagger off the overnight flight carrying (as hand baggage) an arm-wrenching electric sewing machine. For some months I had served an apprenticeship at a theatrical costumier in London and the new machine joined two already whirring at the theatre where costumes for *The Boy Friend;* opening in just two weeks, were coming off the production line.

A new Stage Manager arrived in March, replacing Laurie Slade who, regrettably, had left the DM. As my father came into the office, having collected the new man from the airport, I asked him, "Well...?" Don, breathless from the short climb to the first floor, rolled his eyes and murmured "Titania! Queen of the Fairies!"

Titania was full of suggestions. Why didn't we mount a revue? He would simply *adore* to give Nairobi his *Homage to Anton Dolin,* which had enjoyed such *fantastic* success. Why didn't we paint all the dressing rooms in distinctive pastel shades? He pressed typed scripts on us for consideration.

In April, Titania was cast, as an elderly Irish doctor, in *Pink String And Sealing Wax.* On opening night three Maules sat, transfixed, watching an astounding performance. Titania was drunk as a fiddler's bitch. Tense with apprehension, we waited for his scene to end. Titania managed to get off the stage and we gave a collective sigh of relief. But at the curtain call we froze again. Titania reappeared, to acknowledge the applause *("So* kind!!") with extravagant bowing from the waist. With a great flourish he swept the top hat from his head, disturbing the powder used to whiten his hair and, affecting a crooked smile, (Sir Henry Irving) he stood in a haze of talcum powder as it settled gently on the shoulders of his black frock coat.

Titania was on the next available flight back to London. News of his exit brought a flurry of bills: from florists, typing bureaux and grocers, onto my desk — all run up during his short sojourn in Nairobi.

Mollie and Don were preparing for a final overseas leave, leaving me to 'Mind the Shop' in their absence. Priority number one was a replacement for Titania. Don wrote, 'London seems a noisy, vulgar and altogether abominable city. The West End is now a mass of pin-tables and pornographic cinemas and strip-tease joints. Horrible.'

On the point of departure for Munich to collect a new VW from the manufacturers, he announced, 'God — London's Bedlam. Hope (and expect) *never* to see it or UK again!'

Now mobile, they set off in the VW to enjoy a lengthy Continental tour. From Salzburg Mollie told me, 'Where we go and where we stay is actuated purely by chance. This is how things have gone since we left London and nearly all of it has been wrong and nasty.'

Don wrote, 'Until reaching Salzburg this so-called 'holiday' was an unending nerve-strain and the weather mostly terrible — plodding about bitterly cold in pouring rain. Our ten or eleven days in London was worst of all. Mollie: raging toothache. Weather: mostly vile. Self: three days in bed prostrate and the strain of having to see dozens of artists...'

I had very strict instructions to forward, at regular intervals, detailed reports on the theatre: seat sales, members joining/renewing, bar/catering figures, total income...

'A really wonderful week in Salzburg with weather glorious...' had a soothing effect, but 'Weather deteriorating immediately we set off for Innsbruck'. Somewhere along the route they 'spent a night in a hotel like a Neapolitan Ice: magenta-pink walls interspersed with lemon-yellow... I opened the French windows onto a small wrought-iron balcony leading from our rooms, disastrously letting in a terrible stink of drains... Nerve-wracking drive until we reached Lugano... Pelting with rain.' In Lugano they were told of a delightful little inn, high in the Tyrol. Following a long, exhausting drive, they reached it. 'Charming just like 'White Horse Inn', Mollie wrote, but there was no room at the Inn and they drove on — in pouring rain — until Merano, where: 'An unprecedented cold spell for the time of year with wind so biting and the cold so intense...' they were driven into a café for coffee laced with brandy.

They headed South in search of sunshine. 'Having covered 230 miles in search of better weather the rain was pelting down again... and so to bed in the grimmest, most sparsely furnished cubicle of a room — supposed to be a double. One toothglass, one set of inadequate towels, not even a hook on the bathroom door ...Rose and squeezed our way past one another and into the bathroom-loo-shower and watched traffic through pouring rain from a wire-meshed window in our cell... To Ravenna — raining again... The VW's windshield wipers must be nearly worn out, as I am! With all the unpacking, laundering, working out the route to the next place one is going, then repacking — very little time remains to see the place one is momentarily IN! I have a superb collection of police tickets for parking offences in French, German and Italian.'

And so to Florence, where the sun emerged and their hotel was comfortable. The proprietor knew Kenya; he had been a Prisoner of War and had helped build the superb stretch of the road leading down the Escarpment to the Rift Valley. Also: 'Letter from Annabel... Everything appears to be going well at the DM. Club membership now 7,240. If only they *all* came to see the shows!'

On June 24, 1969, Don recorded: 'Well, I made it — three score years and ten! Left Florence in our usual travelling weather: lashing rain and windshield wipers in a frenzy...'

They returned to Lugano and 'decided on a boat trip round the Lake ...Bought *The Sunday Times*. Shocked to read front page headline TOM MBOYA SHOT DEAD IN NAIROBI STREET.'

They booked on a Rhine steamer: Basel to Rotterdam and back again. 'It's a good thing this steamer is so extremely comfortable ,' Mollie reported, 'because the weather is vile and getting worse all the time. Since early morning we have steamed past miles and miles of industrial Germany. Oil refineries belching flames, enormous factories polluting the air with black smoke and such a strong smell of chemicals... rain pelting down incessantly... We try to glimpse a little of the scenery through misted-up windows.'

July 20: 'Landed at Worms and... to Schwetzingen where we had dinner. Safe arrival of the astronauts on the moon was announced and it was champagne on the house!'

Travelling south from Rotterdam, Mollie told me: 'Half a day of beautiful castles and vineyards to four days of heavy industry and smog.' — 'German food and beds and hotels the least attractive of any in Europe,' Don announced. '*And* I dislike their coarse corrugated toilet paper!'

Soon they would be on their way back to Kenya. 'We have had quite enough — more than enough of this holiday. Three months seeking nothing but 'enjoyment' is not to be endured. But the big value gained has been leaving Annabel completely on her own to navigate the DM through all difficulties, without any interference from either of us.'

They were hugely relieved to return to the space and comfort of their Riverside Drive home, which I had filled with flowers. Don immediately settled down to his beloved 'Books' — checking all my figures for errors. The question now: Were they reconciled to retirement? It came as no surprise, just two weeks later, to find a letter on my desk. 'Our three months get-away-from-it-all has rejuvenated us and there is life in the old dogs yet — for another two or three years maybe...'

The understudy retired to the wings while the rejuvenated Boss set about punishing his typewriter, preparing a lengthy report to the Directors.

CHAPTER SEVEN

'The year 1970 will see Don and Mollie's Golden Wedding Anniversary. Their plans are to retire...' *The Sunday Post* headed its piece A DECADE — AND MORE — OF THE DONOVAN MAULE.

'Someone with whom I had lunch last week roared with laughter and said "Oh yes, they've been going to do that for years."'

'I'm 70 now... In July Mollie and I celebrate our Golden Wedding and we shall celebrate here, in the theatre,' Don declared in a South African journal. And long term? 'I think both of us will follow the example of our parents. They died with their greasepaint on. So shall we if I have anything to do with it.'

So, I would have to wait. Meanwhile, of course, I was back on stage: *Little Boxes* by John Bowen. *The Italian Girl* adapted by James Saunders from Iris Murdoch's novel. *Uncle Vanya*...

I was being paid and I had a roof over my head. The previous year the company had bought a block of one-room flats a short distance from the theatre. Previously known as Warman Flats, they stood at the end of Hill Lane, a short, dusty track ending in a cul-de-sac. Neighbouring properties were mostly old Railways staff houses: spacious bungalows-on-stilts. Renamed Hill Lane Flats and redecorated, I was allotted Flat number One at ground level, which allowed me to have potted anthuriums outside my windows. When the rain-drenched VW arrived at Mombasa, shipped from Rotterdam, I went to collect it and now had the use of it. So, what's to complain about...?

The Maule's Golden Anniversary was celebrated in the theatre, but was far from a happy or joyous occasion. On a cold July day a few of us toasted them in champagne, which I had hastily procured earlier. Don was limp and haggard. He had been away from the theatre for three months, a victim of 'Hong Kong flu', which then developed into double pneumonia. Discharged from a long stay in hospital, he had gone to the coast to convalesce.

It was clear he was a sick man. The percentages on his wall chart drooped in sympathy.

Charles Markham wrote to him the following day: 'I honestly believe that with your state of health you are not capable of continuing, nor should you be asked to continue... I feel certain that Annabel is more than capable of running the theatre... After all, that was the original intention when we brought her here from London.'

Still they resisted, but the matter was clinched when, in September, Don suffered yet another debilitating bout of bronchitis and by mid October it was announced in the press that Don and Mollie would retire '..from the day-to-day running of the theatre at the end of the year and leave the administration to their daughter Annabel, who has been taking a very large part of this work of late.'

So, 1970 would be the year my parents would exit from their greatest production: The Donovan Maule Theatre.

Sadly, it would also be the year when its designer, the architect Frederick Wilkinson, died in a tragic accident in the beautiful, treacherous Lake Naivasha. It was the closing of a chapter. Mollie confided to a friend, 'Now that I am used to the idea, the thought of enforced retirement doesn't appal me. 22 years of unremitting labour has left us both pretty tired.'

She had made her personal final bow at the theatre, in *His, Hers and Theirs,* by Hugh and Margaret Williams, playing an eccentric, upper-crust grandmother who was 'fond of a drop'. ("You've absolutely *drowned* this brandy! Top it up, please!")

Don's wall chart continued to look as poorly as he did. The August production was singled out for mention in the *Sunday Nation's* Review of the Theatrical Year: 1970 — 'And in the plum position of carrying off the prize for being overall the worst thing any critic could be obliged to sit through —*She's Done It Again!* at the DM.' From this point the only way to go was UP.

Sleuth! was an entirely new form of thriller by Anthony Shaffer: 'One of the best shows at the Donovan Maule Theatre this year.' — *Sunday Nation*. 'The set was apt and excellent and suitably robust to take the abuse it receives,' — *Sunday Post*.

The timber account made my hair stand on end. A circular staircase curled round a pillar and had to withstand a spectacular fall by the newly arrived actor, James Falkland. *Sleuth!* offered two superb roles and the two James: Ward and Falkland, grabbed them with enthusiasm. The run extended to a further week and the wall chart showed signs of recovery.

In the home stretch, and with the finishing post in sight, Don once again turned to his typewriter. His final report to the Directors covered seven closely typed pages. Clearly set out were the figures for the three previous years. He collated the total income from all sources, down to the last cent retrieved from the coin-operated telephones. The picture was far from rosy. Theatre seat sales had declined steadily and this had a 'domino' effect on programme sales and bar income. He deplored the slack attendance at the opening week of a new production and could only suggest shock tactics such as announcing: Musical Version on Ice of *The Last Supper* with the Original Cast!

His Newsletter number Three in a series of nine, the first written in 1964, ran to 11,000 words. The office duplicator clicked continuously. The mailing list ran into hundreds. 'Mollie and I hope to relax a bit in a new house we are having built among coconut palms at the coast, near Mombasa. The two-and-a-half acre plot at Kisauni rises from a sandy beach and looks out through the Mombasa-Nyali pontoon bridge to the old dhow harbour and further to the Indian Ocean. Mollie is greatly looking forward to being a housewife again... As for myself, I hope — at last — to take up writing once more; planning first to complete my book about the theatre... We are handing over to our daughter as sole managing directress from January 1, 1971... Annabel's economic assignment will not be an easy one. This professional theatre loses, as a theatre, over £5,000 yearly...' While Don spent long hours at his typewriter, Mollie was sorting and packing at Riverside Drive. Much would have to go into storage until the coast house was built.

The final production in 1970 was *East Lynne*. It had long been Don's hope to stage a Victorian melodrama, and what better than the one his mother had toured round the English provinces, in which he himself had played Little Willie?

The plot contained the basic ingredients of villainy, virtue and pathos, an irresistible mix to audiences in those days. Lady Isabel, a penniless aristocrat, marries Archibald Carlyle, a prosperous lawyer living in the country at East Lynne. Meanwhile, Francis Levinson, a complete scoundrel, manages to shift the guilt of a murder he committed on the shoulders of an innocent young gentleman called Richard Hare. He further convinces Lady Isabel that her husband is unfaithful to her with Richard's sister Barbara. Levinson persuades the very gullible Lady Isabel to go off with him. Later he comes into money and a title; as a bold, bad Baronet now 'in funds', he deserts Lady Isabel without marrying her. She is supposed to be killed in a French railway accident and returns to East Lynne as Madame Vine, a French governess. Nobody, not even her husband, recognises her — they only imagine a likeness. She takes charge of her son, Little Willie, who is wasting away. He dies in her arms to soft music and she delivers the line: "Dead! And never called me mother!"

Then, discovered by her husband and amid mutual forgiveness, she too expires. The only happy feature of the conclusion is the exposure and capture of the scoundrel, Levinson.

The production fell short of Don and Mollie's expectations and one Nairobi critic, at least, felt the same: 'Too much burlesque and laughs lose points for *East Lynne*.' — *Sunday Post*.

Don was pounding his typewriter to the last minute. 'I want to hand over to Annabel with everything as tidy and "buttoned-up" as possible.'

On the first Saturday in January 1971 a brand new Renault saloon was delivered, destined to be Don's last car. His first had been bought for £6 in London in 1932, a second-hand square radiator Morris Cowley which he drove away from the stage door of the Royalty Theatre in Dean Street.

Our final morning together in Don's office was both hectic and comic. Urgently we searched through dusty filing cabinets, extracting important documents while overhead, perched on a stepladder, Joseph Gichure re-glued acoustic tiles to the ceiling.

With the Renault packed to the roof, the Maules were finally ready to leave and a small group of us stood on the theatre's front steps to wave them off. Mollie raised her hand in a last farewell before the car turned out of sight, heading for Mombasa and retirement.

The understudy was, finally, "on" — stumping round the theatre like Long John Silver. Because of a slipped cartilage in my left knee the leg was encased in a heavy plaster cast.

My first year flying solo was to hold its quota of incidents: blackmail, arson, armed robbery... But first a coup d'état in neighbouring Uganda. Electric currents of rumour ran through Nairobi on January 25. By seven o'clock that evening the BBC reported that Milton Obote was 'out'. Idi Amin was 'in'. We were thankful to be in Kenya but a postal strike in Britain was delaying urgently awaited play scripts, productions had to be rescheduled and cast-lists altered.

Happily *The Jockey Club Stakes* romped along the normal four weeks, extending, in the home stretch, to a fifth and a good box office finish. A couple of flops followed, during which a somewhat clumsy attempt was made to blackmail me.

At Hill Lane flats, tenants were moving out while others moved in and I had written, 'If you need any assistance with your stuff I dare say we can find some slaves to help you.' My letter was deliberately retrieved from the garbage and the word 'slaves' taken literally. I received anonymous letters and threatening phone calls, followed by a visit from the manager of a motel at Westlands, a German, who told me that he had "overheard" some of his regular customers mention my name and "Threaten to make plenty of trouble for me... expose me to MPs, Cabinet Ministers, the Press..."

Shortly after this I received a peremptory note to attend the motel at Westlands where 'some definite news awaited me.' The manager told me he knew the main figure in the business: a Seychellois prominent in a Trade Union. He assured me that they intended to "Blow the matter wide open to the press... in Parliament..."

Seychellois was just the clue I needed. It led directly to a Seychelloise employee, accommodated at Hill Lane flats, whom I had recently dismissed for unacceptable behaviour. This was her revenge. The German came to the crux. "Of course, there is a way out of it all." I could *buy* back the incriminating letter and keep the whole thing quiet. He sat gazing at me with pale blue eyes. I played it cool. "I'm astonished that they have waited so long before informing the press, Parliament, or anyone else who cares to listen."

I suggested that they carry out their intentions without further delay. I added that I had, of course, already informed the police about the letters and phone calls.

Within half an hour I was back at the theatre rehearsing Katherine in *The Taming Of The Shrew*. I heard nothing further from the German or the Seychellois.

Shakespeare's comedy opened in May at a special Caltex-sponsored matinée. Students from 10 schools — 270 of them — packed tight the auditorium, augmented by the VIP Guest of Honour, the Vice President Mr. Daniel arap Moi and his large entourage.

Every matinée performance of *The Shrew* was packed with students, but nearing the end of the run I noticed that no boy from Starehe had attended. I extended an invitation and, the following week, received most charming letters of thanks. 'This was a grand occasion for all of us,' wrote George Omollo.

Illness of a cast member led to a hasty replacement. On this occasion Nigel Slade came to the rescue at extremely short notice. This wasn't his first appearance at the DM. The poor man had suffered in the previous year's egregious *She's Done It Again!*

I flew to Mombasa to celebrate Don's birthday on June 24 and more important, to discuss a recent development. On June 11 the new Chairman of the Board, G.B. Shields, had written to my parents, copying the letter to me, regarding '...the possibility of an offer for your DM shares from James Falkland... A group of Nairobi businessmen... were aware of the rumour in town that the DM was in financial difficulties. This presumably arises from our 1970 accounts which certainly gave little grounds for optimism, and continued to reflect the generally downward trend in profitability. In addition your own valedictory letter did not reverse this, and I think it was fair comment on your part that a British repertory theatre in an African Republic was something of an anachronism. This "Group" thought otherwise. Falkland was undoubtedly behind their enthusiasm... I heard of all sorts of ambitious suggestions for greatly increasing the profitability of the DM Theatre "in other hands"... I pointed out that whereas last year's accounts were gloomy, our half year's figures to last March were of quite a different order... On the other hand, I had been aware that Annabel had found the first few months of sole management extremely trying, and both Charles [Markham, the previous Chairman and still a Director] and I had been afraid that she would run herself right into the ground if things went on much longer with ultimate collapse of both Annabel and the theatre...'

I had been attending Nairobi hospital early every morning for therapy both to my knee and a painful shoulder. The letter continued: 'Most importantly, her shoulder has responded to treatment, whether medical or mental I don't know but would guess that the improved climate within the theatre has been largely responsible for reducing worry ...She is full of enthusiasm for the future. Which brings me back to Falkland/local group intentions. 1 do not know how serious these intentions are; but assuming they are positive, then the action could take this form: Falkland makes you an offer for the whole of your (and your joint) shareholding. If you sell he gets something over 40%; he then... makes a similar offer to the larger shareholders around Kenya (I am aware that he has obtained a list of these from the Registrars): if sufficient accept, the new group get more than 50% and can immediately take over control of the DM Co. Ltd. with such changes on the Board as they wish... As a Board we have no intention whatever of contemplating a sale but of course a commercial take-over is something that no Board can do anything about other than to offer advice to shareholders. So the future hinges on your intentions if Falkland approaches you.'

Falkland, as he was known to almost everyone, attempted to set up a meeting with Don and Mollie in May, driving to the coast at the end of the opening week of *The Taming Of The Shrew;* but the Maules were living in rented premises without a telephone. The only point of contact was Mombasa Club where Falkland's note was not received before his return to Nairobi. He now wrote to Don suggesting a meeting at the end of June.

Bertie Shield's letter continued: 'Any decision in this matter is for you alone: you have built up a business which has been highly successful; your pension depends on its continuing to be so and I would not like to guess at the situation in say five years from now, work permits alone become less easy, costs increase (despite the encouraging reduction in present accounts) while revenue cannot be expected to rise much more... You must therefore think of your own future (coupled with Annabel's) and if you receive a thumping good offer you might be unwise to reject it even if the end result is a complete change in ownership and character of the DM Theatre as we know it now... Annabel quoted some remarks from your recent letter to her and you mentioned a dividend from the theatre on this year's results. I will strive to achieve this for your sake; but I would think 10% most improbable. And we have had a report that £4,000 must be spent in the next year or two on renewing our electrics, so that provision will have to be made for this.'

In fact Mollie and Don were very 'strapped for cash' at this time. On June 2 Mollie told me, 'The house has now reached roof level! It has advanced so rapidly in the last six weeks... The size of it really frightens me... It looks enormous! The size of the Albert Hall.' They were growing concerned about how to pay for Chateau Maule. If a 'thumping good offer' for their big shareholding was made, their financial problems would be solved.

On the other hand I, also a shareholder, was fiercely resistant to any take-over of the Donovan Maule Theatre.

All For Mary; in which Falkland was playing, opened on June 23 and he drove to Mombasa the following weekend. The meeting took place, a pleasant social evening developed. No offer, thumping or otherwise, was made. Business was not discussed. The Maules were bewildered.

In the event, Falkland would leave the DM in mid-August to set up his own organisation.

Before it was revealed what form this would take, the DM Theatre received a visit from armed robbers. *A Boston Story;* a gentle, charming adaptation of a Henry James novel, was running its not particularly successful course on the evening of August 5 when five armed thugs stormed into the Club during the interval. A doughty *memsahib,* sipping her G & T, was ordered to *"Lala chini mama!"* The Colonel's lady would have none of this nonsense and remained just where she was, which unnerved the robber who joined his colleagues engaged in backing James Githua, the head barman, to the rear of the bar, threatening him with a *simi,* while one of their number prepared to make off with the newly installed Sweda cash register.

The weight of the machine almost overcame him as he stumbled and staggered up the two shallow steps to the foyer, then out and down further steps to the pavement and the getaway vehicle.

No one was hurt in the incident and the pathetically little cash in the machine came as very poor reward for the trouble the robbers had taken. Their 'timing' had been lamentable. Falkland's timing, however, was spot on. In a press release dated August 11, headed. Theatrical Enterprises (Kenya) Ltd., it was revealed that 'James Falkland... has launched out under his own banner... The Company intends to act as a theatrical consultancy in décor, lighting design and installation, play production and backstage techniques, and in teaching speech and drama. The Company's first assignment will be designing the lighting for Theatre Group's forthcoming production of *Call Me Madam* at the National Theatre this September... and it is also probable that his talents will be employed in the City Players' Christmas production... He hopes that his new Company will contribute... to the growing interest and development of theatre in Kenya.'

Without office premises of his own, he made use of the lounge at the DM where a pay-phone was conveniently at hand.

He would be missed at the theatre. Falkland was a superb stage director and lighting designer. His replacement was not in the same league. In fact, he and his wife, engaged as an actress, would not remain long at the DM.

Rehearsals were under way for a farce: *Move Over Mrs. Markham.* Kenneth came to the office, bristling with indignation. The previous day he had asked the stage management to record a sound effect. This had not been done and Kenneth demanded to know why. He was told to "Do the fucking job yourself."

'The funniest of them all... The laughs come fast and furious.' — 'Best cure for the blues that I can think of... The DM is to be congratulated on presenting this farce at the same time as it's being shown in London.' — 'It's a non-stop laugh... it just cannot fail... see it you should.' And see it they did! The HOUSE FULL boards were located, dusted off and remained on near-permanent display. The four-week run extended to five, with me replacing a guest artist ear-marked for *Call Me Madam*. Toward the end of the fifth week patrons were still clamouring for seats. Kenneth and I made the snap decision to extend the run further. This involved some fast work rejigging all our press ads and I was churning out fresh stuff at the typewriter in the office when the door burst open while simultaneously the stage director's wife burst into tears. "I'm on the verge of a nervous breakdown..." she sobbed. "It's the overwork. I can't cope with long runs." Overwork?! Long runs?!! To date she had been dismal in *A Boston Story* and was now on stage, in a small but important role, in *Markham*. A member of the company had christened her "007 — Guaranteed to kill anything: other people's laughs and performances!"

She was unique in her misery. I wrote to Mombasa: 'The sheer gales of laughter from capacity houses acts like the most wonderful drug on us all. It is a super experience.'

Don replied, 'What a wonderful finishing post to the DM's financial year *Move Over Mrs. Markham* provides.' She certainly did! She allowed me to put in hand the vital replacement of electrical equipment. Before she ended, however, there was a small problem: the company's leading lady, playing Mrs. Markham and rehearsing for the play to follow, was arrested at Embakasi Airport in the wee small hours — 'Drunk and Disorderly'. She was released on bond (the cash being delivered by the theatre's office messenger) and returned in time for the matinée that day. The hearing of her case was set for November.

At the end of October my parents moved into Chateau Maule. The waiting period had not been easy. Since March they had been living in 'The Parrot Cage' situated near their plot, which allowed them to keep an eye on the building process.

'A small rondavel facing inland on Tudor Creek, the house is incredibly hideous, built all the wrong way round and as hot as hell,' Mollie told me. 'It doesn't get a breath of breeze even though there is a gale blowing everywhere else. *But* — and this is why we've taken it — it has a large lock-up garage and we are risking having our furniture sent down in the hope that we'll get it all in somehow. The house itself is very sparsely furnished. The second bedroom is like the sliver of an orange and only has room for a bed and a chair and is quite airless. The only veranda which faces the creek and should be a delightful spot in which to have meals and be used as a sitting room, is minute and wired in like a parrot cage. The round sitting room faces the wrong way. In fact, it's a bastard but it's a roof over our heads.' A month later Don deplored, 'The builders haven't even started on our house yet. Life seems pretty senseless and arid partly I suppose because just a month ago I stopped smoking. Certainly that, combined with sea-level, has greatly eased my breathing, but I have not adjusted to having absolutely nothing to do, and — what is worse — no desire to try. It's a tremendous relief to be rid of all the worries of the DM Theatre but at the same time one is left with no purpose in life. Perhaps when the builders begin on our new house I shall pull out of this terrifying, stupefying inertia...'

Sweltering under the *mabati* roof and without any help, Mollie declared: 'Living here is like rehearsing for a Laurel and Hardy film. Nothing works. Doors, of which there are (believe it or not) *fifteen,* either stick fast or hit you in the nose. All taps leak, some come off in your hand, or — if you don't stop turning at exactly the right time, refuse to turn off at all. To produce any sort of a meal on the inadequate little cooker requires mental and physical gymnastics. None of my casseroles are small enough to go into the tiny oven; the grill never gets hot and the quick hotplate is out of alignment so that only a pan with a very small base will balance on it. I'm already sick to death of housework and cooking. Did I ever really say I was looking forward to being a housewife again? I must have been mad.' In May: 'The rains are here with a vengeance. This horrid little house is just bearable when the weather is good and we can live out of doors, but when it rains...! Living at the coast isn't all sun and coconuts. This house is, apparently, the joke of the district. Nobody can live in it...'

After eight uncomfortable months they were now on the point

of moving out. Chateau Maule offered space and comfort and all Mod Cons, but 'one terrible snag we've discovered: fruit bats which we never see must be somewhere around in the garden in large numbers and their excrement is appearing in the form of large yellow-brown splodges all over my beautiful gleaming walls!'

'The joy of retirement is that it gives one time to work! Uninterruptedly, satisfyingly, doing the things one *wants* to do. These at the moment consist of boring holes in walls with my electric drill, fixing rawl-plugs, hanging pictures, mirrors and brackets for ornaments... But perhaps the most relaxing and satisfying joy of all is PAINT! Chairs, tables, standard lamps, table lamps, wrought-iron work... oh, a thousand and one things become in danger of getting painted anew once the amateur enthusiast sets out his array of brushes, paints, turps and rags.' Don's new-found zest extended to a work bench with carpenter's vice in a workshop where 'I can hang up my splendid array of tools and then make myself a nest of drawers for nails, screws, hinges, etc. etc. What has probably NOT escaped your notice is that my delight in doing things physical is largely because it is such a splendid excuse for putting off again and again what I know I should be trying to do. I refer, of course, to making a start on the Mémoirs.'

He had squandered nearly a year. Uncomfortable as it was, the Parrot Cage had provided 'The biggest bedroom ...allotted to Don both to sleep and, I hope, work in,' Mollie told me. Instead, he had succumbed to 'no purpose in life' and bored inertia. True, the need to visit the Club for mail and the town for shopping (yesterday's milk sour, today's not yet arrived and, a short time later, sold out) took time. There were also appointments with the architect at the site. Mollie's inability to drive demanded Don's services as chauffeur and prevented him from settling to long hours of concentration.

Furnished, fixtured, settled in at Chateau Maule, Don turned to his typewriter on January 1, 1972 in the perfect surroundings of his large bedroom-study with its custom-made desk flanking a big picture window. Newsletter number FOUR: 'My bedroom is provided with louvered double doors that lead onto a small veranda facing NNW. A short flight of steps leads down into the garden and in another 80 yards I reach the water's edge. After my pre-dawn dip I return to my private veranda for my early morning cuppa.'

A great veranda ran the entire length of the house where 'we can take our ease and watch the almost continuous activity: in the distance big freighters and Goliath tankers glide under pilot towards Kilindini Docks. Nearer, one of the small fleet of cement-carrying ships belonging to Bamburi Cement Company arrives, accompanied by a puffing tugboat. On the landward side, behind the house, where I sometimes take a tottering walk with Baggage, a colourful feather-mop of a coucal flutters untidily across my path to disappear into some bush beneath the palms.'

He made it sound idyllic. To me, the previous November: 'On the whole I believe my damnable asthma is a little easier at sea level but only very little. The effort demanded to go down to the sea from my veranda, for instance, however slowly and full of pauses and gentle deep breathing, sets up such a strain on my lungs that any good a few sedate breaststrokes may do, is more than obliterated by the heart and lung strain of tottering back to the house.'

The newsletter was completed and despatched. The Mémoirs were put on hold.

On Christmas day I flew to Mombasa and saw Chateau Maule for the first time. There were lovely views of sunlit water framed by Arabesque arches and slender coconut palms waved their topknots in the breeze. Mollie's flair for home-making was everywhere apparent and her work in the garden, begun the moment the plot was cleared when she started a nursery of cuttings, was showing signs of progress. Under the age-old mango trees, where the soil was rich humus and the shade encouraged growth, she planted cool green creepers and ferns. Bougainvillea fronted the veranda facing out to sea while potted plants stood on the patio at the entrance to the house. A trio of 'royal' palms stood sentinel in the drive.

The administrator of the Theatre Royal at Windsor, John Counsell and his wife, stayed at Jadini while John wrote *Play Direction — A practical viewpoint*. In January the Maules drove the Counsells to Nairobi where they attended a performance of *Canterbury Tales* at the Donovan Maule Theatre. A greatly downsized version of the big, noisy, choreographed London production, this had opened on December 22. It had been a hassle: scripts posted surface mail by an inattentive secretary in London, reached us on the morning of opening day. We had reproduced from the Master script. Instead of a piano score we were sent an entire set of band parts for a sizeable orchestra.

James Ward, cast in a large role and directing, went sick with jaundice half-way through rehearsals. Kenneth Mason, also cast, as well as producing *On Stage,* was up to his eyes, so I took over the show. Ward's doctor cautioned us to get Gamma Globulin injections. Obediently, a series of bottoms were presented for puncturing prior to rehearsals the following morning. The theatre's accountant was away with a bout of malaria and Joseph Gichure suddenly had to visit the Kinangop to settle a *shauri kidogo* involving a piece of land which he had bought from some rogue currently in police custody. In the wardrobe department hessian and *americani*, velvet and satin submitted to scissors and sewing machines. I concluded a hastily typed letter to Mombasa: 'No time for more — I must now sew rosebuds onto pink ribbon for Damion's cod-piece.'

'A bawdy hit... lovely stuff' — 'I cannot remember looking forward to a DM production with such enthusiasm, and I have not been disappointed except in one unavoidable particular, the absence of James Ward, whom I hoped to see being himself as the rumbustious miller ...Whatever else may be in your Christmas stocking make sure that there are tickets for the DM as this is something not to be missed.' — 'As predicted in this column *Canterbury Tales* has been extended until January 29, 1972.'

I claimed the cost of the expensive Gamma Globulin jabs on the theatre's medical insurance policy. My claim was repudiated with some arcane gobbledygook!

I had survived my first year in the 'Hot Seat', as Bertie Shields dubbed it. Oh, yes... the touch of arson! A few days after the armed robbery, during the run of *A Boston Story,* on a Monday with no performance, it was discovered that the scenery behind the elegant fireplace had been set alight, causing some damage. Strangely, the fire once lit and allowed to burn, had also been deliberately extinguished and when the mischief was discovered, at about 9 o'clock, the area was cold. The CID was called and came the following morning to take statements and photographs. The matter remained an unsolved mystery.

Home again following their safari to Nairobi, Don recorded: 'A lazy, unsatisfying day — breathing painful and could not (or rather hadn't sufficient will power) to snap out of it and do some work — that far too long postponed book about the theatre for instance... "Time" is *not* on my side as a would-be writer. If I am to write, well or ill, the avoidance of making a start will achieve neither!'

All too soon he was, yet again, struck down with bronchitis. 'He has been quite ill for the past week,' Mollie reported at the end of March. The benign coast climate could change with astounding speed. 'It rains and rains with sudden gusty squalls that blow us almost out of the house. The near-hurricane force of horizontal rain sweeps us rushing off the veranda but comfort and shelter cannot be found inside the house either. The sliding doors from veranda to living room should never have been louvered.'

Glass doors were fixed to another entrance where elegant wrought-iron-work allowed a freshening breeze to sweep flower arrangements to the ground. The fireplace, an unusual feature in a coast house, was never again lighted after choking smoke engulfed the sitting room at the first attempt.

'The doctor has changed the treatment for the third time and there is certainly now an improvement.' But from this moment a portable cylinder of oxygen was to hand at all times. It was now that the residents of Ras Kisauni Road got wind of the fact that their peaceful, rural surroundings faced destruction. A new bridge, linking Mombasa Island to the North mainland would thrust its six-lane highway through their gentle backwater. 'Mollie and I attended the Inquiry at the Lands Office re compensation for the probable loss of a portion of our Kisauni plot.' In July: 'The Government has bought Nyali Estate and the rates have been increased.' Mollie added, 'Don is very bad today. His breathing is getting worse. The howling monsoon has nearly blown itself out. We are thrown about like leaves in a gale, catching objects as they fly past.' Then all too soon, in August: 'Don has been very ill with bronchitis... each of these bouts leaves him little weaker.'

At the company's AGM held in April 1972, the Chairman reported, 'The accounts for the financial year ended 30th September 1971... are very good with a pre-tax profit of more than £10,000 which is £7,600 better than the previous year and the best for several years past... This satisfactory result is only to a small extent due to increased revenue and is largely consequent on reduced expenditure in many different directions... Theatre Club income rose by £3,000... while expenditure fell by £7,000... The continued existence of the theatre depends entirely on the extent to which the members use it, and present usage is just not adequate to guarantee its permanency in the face of rising costs... only about half the number of full members make use of their theatre. Turning to the current year, it is unlikely that last year's profit will be repeated. Costs rise inexorably for reasons over which we have no control, while heavy unusual expenditure will be incurred shortly in the renovation of the auditorium carpeting... There are no further economies available to us to combat rising costs and your Directors have therefore reluctantly decided to increase the price of seats by Sh2.50, the first increase since 1966. The never-ending search for suitable plays and the continuous recruiting of new artists from overseas (the chagrin and expense when the occasional one turns out to be a pig-in-a-poke and has to be quickly returned), together with the day-to-day administration of a complex business, is a very great strain.' The good news was that the company would be paying a tiny dividend.

With this my parents were able to settle all outstanding costs of Chateau Maule. Don calculated, 'The new house will, I think, cost just under £15,000 in all (this includes legal charges and purchase of plot: £3,000) and we have managed to pay for it CASH DOWN — no mortgage or overdraft — but will have cleared ourselves of all investments.' In fact the final figure for Chateau Maule came to more than £15,000.

In June, on the day before Don's 73th birthday, Edward Rodwell's *Coast Causerie* column in the *East African Standard* reported, 'My wife and I were taking a drink before lunch in the new house of Donovan and Mollie Maule. We sat on the veranda looking toward Nyali Bridge and Mombasa Old Town, the whole vista providing an incomparable view... Mollie and Donovan Maule have chosen one of the beauty spots of the coast; their home and the appointments are all that one would wish. The library, silver, leather, old prints, polished woodwork. Don's study overlooking the harbour. Mollie's room in splendid taste and the shaded veranda all mirror civilities of more gracious times. What a curious thing it is that these good people who have spent their lifetime in earnest pretence have never wavered from their own dream of a real house. On the stage they have fashioned a thousand rooms, verandas, kitchens, from medieval, through Regency, Victorian to modern styles, preparing the scene to convince an audience of the authenticity of the setting.

'Yet here they were, living in a house, again of their own design, as graceful as any you would ever see on the stage, except that the doors lead to other rooms... A striking feature of the veranda is the furniture. We sat on straight-backed chairs fashioned with much skill by an ironworker. The curlicues of the rounded metal attracted my attention. The seats and armrests were of a light leather. And when I asked where the chairs and the table to match had been made Mollie said they had been ordered from Mtwapa prison.'

The Chairman's warning '...it is unlikely that last year's profit will be repeated. Costs rise inexorably for reasons over which we have no control' was prescient. British Actors' Equity Association was pressing me to come into line with the new 'Minimum Salary' recently negotiated for their members employed by repertory theatres in the UK. I pointed out the very different circumstances at the DM where no subsidies of any kind were received, set against repertories in Britain which were substantially funded from a number of sources. Further, at the DM artists were housed on the premises at very low rents and provided with clean bed-linen and towels weekly. And then too, at this time, the cost of living in Kenya was noticeably lower than in Britain.

Equity accepted none of this reasoning and the correspondence continued. On hearing Equity's terms, Don was shocked. 'A minimum salary for an ASM straight out of school and her contract to read – Assist with stage management *only* — no appearances on stage or even being asked to understudy! Well, well — things have certainly changed since my touring days as Business Manager/Stage Manager/Principal Comedian — all combined and in sole charge of The Girl And The Drug company for Arthur Gibbons, who paid me the fully adequate salary of seven pounds a week.' He was recalling 1919, immediately following 'demob' from the Army when he had found employment quickly. Later on circumstances changed and there were hard times.

In Nairobi, rehearsing for the next production, a sound effect was needed: 'Fierce barking by a large dog.'

A friend of mine had recently acquired a young Irish woolfhound. "He'll bark at anything, but to make sure I'll bring a tortoise. He goes mad when he sees a tortoise."

"Have you got a tortoise?"

"No. I'll borrow one from the Snake Park."

We set up a microphone at the side of the stage, tested it for level and all was ready for the arrival of the aptly-named "Donovan" accompanied by the tortoise (duly signed-for against its safe return) resting in a cardboard box surrounded by fresh lettuce leaves. "Donovan", the size of a Shetland pony, was introduced to me. Curling his lip in a goofy smile, he leaned against my hip, nearly sending me to the ground, at the same moment loosing a stream of warm piss over my feet. "He likes you!" exclaimed his infatuated owner. We prepared for "Donovan's" fierce bark, but nothing happened. He just stood there, a distracted look in his eyes, gazing through the open dock doors at the pretty little cupola atop County Hall.

We closed the dock doors and directed his attention to the tortoise, slowly munching its way through a lettuce leaf. "Donovan's" muzzle approached the head, which was swiftly withdrawn. Puzzled, he investigated the other end, with the same result. The tortoise, removed from its box and its lettuce, tentatively stretched a wrinkled neck to test the air. "Look, Donovan. A tortoise!"."Donovan" looked but remained mute and the tortoise withdrew once more. In the dimly-lit silence of the stage, a movement under the sink caught his attention: a MOUSE? A mouse might provoke a bark! We pressed RECORD. But nothing happened.

An hour later we conceded defeat. The tortoise, now permanently withdrawn among the sheltering lettuce leaves following its ordeal and "Donovan", still wearing his goofy grin (a hound unlikely ever to make the charts), were removed from the theatre. Ten minutes later we had our sound effect. A cast member produced 'fierce barking by a large dog' without any problem.

Johnny Belinda, a drama verging on melodrama, focussed on two central characters: a deaf-mute girl and the sympathetic doctor who teaches her sign language, thereby opening up her world. These roles were beautifully played by Nadine Hanwell and James Ward. The production received a 'rave' press and many letters of appreciation from the few who came to see the play. Pitifully few.

I did not, however, regret my decision to do it. At a Saturday matinée 20 young children, sponsored by the Kenya Society for Deaf Children, occupied seats — at Sh3 each — in Rows A and B.

'They will *never* forget that play. They understood it all — especially the sign language. They all identified with Belinda and the boys fell in love with her immediately. They didn't believe me when I said she could hear and speak, but were convinced she was one of them and James Ward was actually a teacher of the deaf. They knew it was a play, in that they realised that it was a story and the baby was not real, but Belinda and her teacher were completely real to them. It made their day... *Johnny Belinda* was beautifully done and I think deserved better support from the extraordinary Nairobi public than it has had.'

'It's different to anything we have seen here for years. *Virtue In Danger* is the naughtiest and campiest show in town.' — *Sunday Nation,* December 1972. How, I wondered, would the extraordinary Nairobi public react? The play-with-music embraced a gallery of characters both sympathetic and outrageous. Sir Novelty Fashion has recently bought himself a peerage. "Well, 'tis ten thousand pound well spent, stap me vitals!"

Known now as LORD Foppington, he is a vain and egregious ass. James Ward gloried in the role! The setting: 'London & the Country.' Horrified, Foppington declares, "A man of my delicate breeding cannot consummate in a country bed among BUGS!" — The period: '1697.' A world of powdered wigs, lace cuffs and cravats, silk stockings, knee breeches and swords, fur muffs, fans and 'beauty spots'.

By a stroke of wonderful good luck Gary Dahms, the head cutter at Glyndebourne Opera House, came to our assistance. He was in Kenya on a 'working holiday'. The huge workload spilled out from the wardrobe into the adjoining office where bolts of *americani* were flung over any flat surface and Gary set about cutting the heavy skirts for the men's coats and waistcoats. He planned to stencil designs onto the fabric, followed by spray-paint to simulate the elaborate embroidery and lace overlays for which we had neither the time nor the money.

The cast listed 20 speaking characters with 'Footmen, Servants, Sedan-chair Carriers And Pages' over and above that.

Periwigs and perukes were contrived and constructed from bleached sisal. Hula hoops wound with damp sisal, the groundwork for curls and ringlets, were set to dry in the sun on the flat roof of the theatre.

In the workshop under the stage, battlements and boudoirs, country mansions and coffee houses were under way. So, too, was Lord Foppington's sedan-chair. It came up to be used at a preliminary technical rehearsal.

Jimmy, superb in towering peruke, stepped in and seated himself. For and aft sedan-chair carriers grasped the poles and tried to lift M'lord as he fluttered a delicate lace handkerchief from the tiny curtained window. The contraption, made of solid timber, gave a lurch but remained rooted, centre-stage. Jimmy waved 'Good-bye!' again and the carriers, bracing themselves for one tremendous, synchronised, Herculean effort, succeeded in lifting him an inch from the ground then head for the wings on a shuffling, staggering, groaning zig-zag course before collapsing.

The sedan-chair was returned to the workshop for serious weight reduction. At every free moment the girls in the company gave Gary a hand in the wardrobe. As opening night drew closer the tension mounted.

One afternoon a young man appeared at the wardrobe door. He wished to hire a Santa Claus outfit. Six heads were raised and six pairs of eyes fixed on him. Before he could speak he was asked, "Can you sew?" Over a three-day period, prior to opening on December 20, a series of chaotic technical rehearsals, cancelled or postponed photo-calls and inchoate dress rehearsals occupied the hours until the moment when the first night audience arrived.

It crossed my mind to emigrate.

CHAPTER EIGHT

Newsletter Number FIVE. 'For a full year we have just whiled away time in our new house, enjoying it. Healthwise, both of us have had intermittent illness... It was sheer madness, of course, to spend over a hundred pounds having a carpenter's workshop built and buying all those expensive tools. About three weeks ago I felt a sudden urge to grasp the nettle and really make a start on my long-planned book... At the moment a near-exhausted Annabel is staying with us over Christmas. She flew down from Nairobi yesterday: Christmas Eve, having launched her production of *Virtue In Danger* which, I am happy to say, has got rave reviews...'

On my brief visits to Chateau Maule I spent much of my time sleeping. When conscious I sat on the veranda reading plays. We devoured 12 or 13 a year. I might read 10 or more scripts before finding one that was suitable and castable.

Vervet monkeys infested the big mango trees. When fruit hung there they would pluck one, bite into it then, in a prodigal manner, fling it away and move onto the next. Baggage's fury at the intrusion of these creatures into his territory knew no bounds. He would bark himself silly and leap into the air in futile attempts to reach them. The monkeys bared their teeth and chattered at him, finally presenting their Wedgwood-blue behinds in an insolent gesture of dismissal.

Secure in the knowledge that it was *their* territory, they made use of hanging creepers to swing from the mango trees onto the tiled roof: rolling and tumbling, scampering to the other side where they would leap into the shelter of the great wild fig tree and stare in defiance at anyone, human or canine, seated below. Occasionally, an upside-down vervet face could be glimpsed peering directly into a bedroom, curious to know what went on in there. Fruit left unguarded anywhere in the house would attract a slim, furry arm making a lightning snatch. They were intrusive, rude, destructive, impertinent, thieving and always with further babies in the troupe. They were also very entertaining.

Back on duty I was attending a hearing at City Hall. The Nairobi City Council had decided to 'adopt' St John's Gate and County Lane and tarmac both areas. The DM and its neighbours, St. John's, the Red Cross and the Boy Scouts, would bear a proportion of the cost. Already we were paying rates. If the NCC wanted to adopt small roads, why couldn't it support them? The DM would have to pay £1,400, godammit!

The lighting equipment had reached £5,000 and soon would come the expense of re-carpeting the auditorium.

Bertie Shields produced his annual Chairman's Report: 'During the year subscriptions from membership remained constant while Box Office revenue showed a welcome improvement of £4,600 due to a combination of slightly increased attendance... and to an increase in seat prices midway through the year. Operating expenditure was however up by £3,400 for the usual reasons. The Club Bar is a constant source of anxiety. Bar income showed a substantial decline, the consequence of price control on beer, while expenses inevitably rose. For several years we have enjoyed a reciprocal arrangement with Lufthansa whereby they provided free air travel for actors and actresses in return for free advertising. This agreement was arbitrarily terminated by the airline in March and we are now obliged to find the full cost for all air travel; since few artists stay more than six months this will build up into heavy outlay, and indeed it could ultimately cripple the theatre.'

I was directing *The Government Inspector;* presented mainly for the benefit of schools, while workmen were busy in the auditorium ripping up existing carpet before laying new. Six guest artists, able to rehearse only at limited times, created further problems. Each evening the auditorium had to be made ready for an audience.

Each morning the resident company rehearsed with an ASM 'reading in' for missing characters. Out front I would be startled by the sudden appearance of a head above the seat in front of me. Leaping to my feet, intent on checking the sight-line from a different angle, I might fall over a workman on his knees unrolling grey haircord.

Then Sub-con explained that they had underestimated. A further 303 square feet of haircord were required...

All early performances were crammed with students at Sh5 per head. At the only interval a tumultuous surge would burst through the double doors from the auditorium and scatter: to the toilets, to the bar. 15 minutes later, with bells ringing continuously, only a proportion was back inside. Where was the rest? I checked outside the building. Girls (it was almost exclusively girls), flushed and breathless, were hurrying back from a nearby fast food outlet clutching greasy packets of hot chips reeking of vinegar; their intention being to devour these when back in their seats, discarding greasy paper round and about my £800-worth of new carpeting.

As they scurried up the front steps I relieved them of the offending items. A wail went up: "Our chips!"

"They will be right here," I assured them, "on this counter. You can collect them at the end of the play." Word of the *kali mzungu bibi* ran along the grapevine. Packets were concealed inside blouses and bloomers in an attempt to smuggle them into the auditorium. The unnatural bulges, the smell: hot fat and vinegar, betrayed them and the contraband was confiscated. The interval extended to half an hour before we were able to go ahead with Act II. I then filled a bucket with hot water, grabbed a mop and undertook a clean-up operation in the Ladies. Chip-patrol had to be maintained throughout the run. I was aided by Njoroge Waibu, a bar steward, who acted with the utmost decorum.

From the time when I became M.D. — January 1971 — G.B. Shields had been the Chairman of the Board. He had been of great help to me: giving wise counsel on a variety of issues even as he himself became acquainted with the extraordinary, sometimes bizarre problems which arose when operating monthly repertory. Now, in July 1973, he wished to step down as Chairman while remaining on the Board as a director. At the time, he was of the opinion that we should begin to make plans for the closure, in the immediate future, of the Donovan Maule Theatre. The figures told it all: against ever-rising costs and difficulties: work permits getting harder and harder to obtain, the time could not be far off, he opined, when only losses would be shown, and he considered it prudent to wind up the operation before this occurred.

Writing from Mombasa, Don enquired: 'The real question is, can the set-up as a whole continue as it has done in the past?' Two years earlier, he had pointed out: 'It is the running of professional repertory with Equity artists that is getting more and more economically impossible.'

Despite Shields' clear reasoning, the incoming Chairman was opposed to the suggestion of closure and wished to struggle on, arguing that one really successful production could turn the tide. Another *Move Over Mrs. Markham,* for instance.

There was another reason for carrying on, the new Chairman insisted. In just two months, in September, the Donovan Maule Players would be completing 25 years of continuous production. This, surely, was something to celebrate?

The new Chairman was me — so the matter was settled.

I had a play in mind: *A Short History Of The English People* by Frank Harvey — author of *Saloon Bar,* production number 4, April 1948 at the Theatre Royal.

Kenneth described *Short History* as 'An experimental play in that the on-stage time covered one day in the life of the Bowers, but the off-stage time spanned several centuries of English history.' The Middle Ages to the Ground Nut Scheme. The author's theme was: 'History is people. The long threads of his tapestry — the warp of History — crossed by the weft of people, embodied by the Bowers family in their small tied cottage in Kent.'

'It is a most courageous undertaking on your part and I salute you,' the author wrote to me. It would have been a less stressful undertaking if 1973 was not developing into a Vintage Year for pigs-in-pokes... The cast listed Mother and Father Bowers, a son and daughter — the daughter's boyfriend and a neighbour.

Two new actors arrived fom London, already cast as father and son. Daughter would be a pretty young actress who had been with us several months, a well-covered *ingénue* on arrival, she had expanded somewhat. When dressed in muslin as the May Queen, she resembled nothing so much as a tethered barrage balloon.

Mother Bowers, a guest artist perfect in both looks and personality, had difficulty retaining her lines, her mind preoccupied with the antics of her family, variously engaged in adultery, rolling cars and abusing drugs. Father Bowers, the new man, was superb when 'on top of it' and fully concentrated. Unhappily this only occurred a fraction of one per cent of the 39 weeks of his contract, which he insisted on fulfilling.

Only Jimmy Ward could not be faulted as Walter Carter, the Bowers' neighbour, a cobbler by trade. 'His subtle matchings of delivery, stance and reactions, as he progressed fom Non-conformist to potential Tolpuddle Martyr and thence to Marxist trade union shop steward, were a delight and theatre of the highest order.' — *Daily Nation*.

Kenneth's anniversary *On Stage* reflected Frank Harvey's theme: listing plays presented by the DM Players' 25 years alongside world events of the same period. At his request Mollie contributed some memories of the early days in the little Studio. 'Many club members will remember our lantern hanging over the pavement on Government Road, marking the entrance to our theatre. The lantern's side panels of frosted glass bore the Donovan Maule Players' insignia painted in red. One night, during Kenya's Emergency, two slightly tipsy Lancashire Fusiliers, wandering along Government Road, spotted what they took to be a red light. Heavy boots clattered joyfully up stone stairs. "How much?" our box office receptionist was asked. "Reduced prices for Forces. Five Shillings."

"Eee! That's cheap. Right. We'll 'ave a bash."

The Maules came up from Mombasa to be VIP guests at the opening on September 12, but only Mollie attended; Don was in Nairobi Hospital, overcome by Nairobi's altitude. Two days later I drove them both straight back to Chateau Maule. Two months after this Don was again in hospital in Mombasa, gravely ill with double pneumonia.

Later — some time later, Mollie wrote, 'The day came when the Matron asked me with assumed casualness: "Could you stay here for lunch?" I said I could. "Could you stay through the night?" My heart went cold. "Do you mean he's sinking?" I asked. There followed three nights sitting at Don's bedside. Everyone expected Don to die. He looked like death. I tried to prepare myself without success.' From Nairobi I telephoned every night: Chateau Maule or the hospital, trying to make contact for news. I had to get *My Fat Friend* on stage on Wednesday November 14. Kenneth took me to the airport for the first flight the next morning.

At the hospital I too was convinced my father was dying. It was only a matter of time.

My plans for the theatre would have to be changed. Noel Coward's *Hay Fever* was about to start rehearsals with Kenneth directing and myself in a large leading role. Clearly this was now impossible. I could not leave Mollie alone and unable to drive in Mombasa.

The routine of living had dissolved. Each day merged into the next as we waited. 'The future loomed darkly ahead. Then, due to the efforts of a brilliant African doctor lately trained in America and Edinburgh — and brave enough to use the most drastic and desperate treatment, kill or cure — Don pulled through, and slowly, recovered.'

Before this I had returned to Nairobi. Kenneth had put Dorothy (Dee) Gibbs into my role in *Hay Fever*. I took over Clara, there being nobody else available. Every night I telephoned Mombasa and received the same answer: "No change".

Not until Mollie's birthday, November 24, was there a positive sign of recovery.

There was other good news *My Fat Friend* was the success I so badly needed to help the theatre's finances.

'Came home after a month in hospital. Naturally very weak and exhausted but mercifully recovered from far *too* near "Death's Door". Mollie marvellous and patient with me after a ghastly month of anxiety for her.' Don's diary. She told me: 'He ate a splendid lunch. We stayed up until 11pm and then he went to bed and fell immediately asleep. Now he is busy doing his accounts and getting everything in order. Baggage was overjoyed to see Don and feels his world is normal again.'

Baggage could now see Don with only one eye. He had been blinded in the other by a spitting cobra. Mollie's ghastly month of anxiety had been worse than Don could know. Leaving Baggage attached by his lead to the heavy wrought-iron table on the veranda he had been a sitting target for the snake, which had usurped his basket and spat at him when he growled. Soon after this Bags had a fit. 'It was the most unnerving experience I've ever had in my life really quite terrible...' She was unable to make contact with the vet, she was alone and immobile and the beloved pet poodle needed help.

'I haven't told Don anything about it. I don't want to worry him. He is walking without help — slowly of course — and his breathing seems better than formerly. He's so happy to be home and is particularly cheerful. Isn't it wonderful?'

Mollie's last letter of 1973 told me, 'Daddy is feeling wonderfully well today and felt no strain in the manic traffic of Mombasa. His appetite is still good and healthy — asking eagerly: "What's for lunch?"'

Don reported: 'Bills for medical expenses, both human and canine, will exceed £1,000 over the past twelve months.'

The *Sunday Nation* headed its Round-up-of-Year's-Theatre, WHERE HAVE ALL THE AUDIENCES GONE? 'On the professional scene, James Ward has achieved heights of acting greatness that should help draw them in in 1974... The Donovan Maule Theatre deserves far more support than it has been getting.'

Jimmy and I were a useful team on stage. We enjoyed working together and in 1974 I found three plays which offered us good roles. *Murder Mistaken* in January, *Lloyd George Knew My Father* in March and *In Praise Of Love* in August. But there was a snag: I was 12 years older than he. In the case of *Murder Mistaken* this was correct as Jimmy's role was that of a vicious Teddy Boy who ensnared older women, planning to murder them for their money. I was the older woman who turned out to be as smart as he was.

'The scenes between James Ward and Annabel Maule are professional theatre at its best with the actors deep in character. Miss Maule's high pitched laughter and occasional bottom scratching and hitch of the skirt left an enthusiastic first night audience in no doubt as to the character of this brassy dame.' — the *Standard*.

Lloyd George Knew My Father had us both as Senior Citizens in their 70s but we enjoyed playing General Sir William Boothroyd and Lady Sheila Boothroyd, both of them a little dotty in their separate ways. 'TEARS OF LAUGHTER ALL THE WAY... Annabel Maule and James Ward made a perfect pair of aristocratic oldies.'

Jimmy had gallantly vacated a hospital bed to appear in *Lloyd George* and was still very shaky, entirely appropriate for doddery old Sir William, but it was abundantly clear that he must be allowed a respite after a string of leading roles.

Without him, I was left with a few pigs-in-pokes and, Oh God! a further consignment on the way.

First I needed a replacement for the stage designer. I advertised in *The Stage* and received several responses, but before I had time to sift through these and make a choice, I was surprised in my office by a young man applying for the post. He had bought himself the cheapest package holiday to Kenya and here he was: ahead of all applicants. I asked him to design the play to follow *Lloyd George*.

On a Sunday morning, after four weeks playing Lady Boothroyd with one more week to go, I collected a pile of mail from the main post office, took it to the theatre, unlocked my office and settled to some quiet, uninterrupted work. While I was totting up authors' royalties, I was surprised by a thump on the door. There stood the designer flanked by two Special Branch police officers. He had spent the previous night in the cells at Central Police Station. He had gone to the Kenya Cinema the previous evening and failed to stand up for the National Anthem.

Following an hour of questions and answers in my office, I was instructed to appear at Central to record a statement. I was the culprit's employer.

He was due to appear in court the next day, Monday. My desk was piled high, so I sent my assistant to hold a watching brief. She returned at lunchtime with the reassuring news that the case would be heard at 2.15 and there would be no problem if he pleaded "guilty" and paid the fine.

At 3.30 she was back in the office, visibly upset. He had pleaded "not guilty" and gone further by being rude to the Magistrate. He was now back in police cells. I contacted the British High Commission. The second secretary persuaded the supine-at-the-anthem-offender to reconsider and stop making a fool of himself. "Fined 300 shillings, or 60 days in jail." The accused paid the fine (advanced by the theatre) and left Kenya shortly thereafter. The Special Branch officers told me they suspected he was in possession of illegal drugs. I expressed surprise. "You can smell it!" they told me, implying I should readily recognise this tell-tale clue. Not being a trained sniffer dog I had no idea what smell to sniff for and did not consider it part of my job.

I wanted only to be rid of the whole tiresome business and obtain a talented, upstanding, drug-free stage designer. A frisson ran through the theatre. Rumour had it that the police planned a raid on the flats. Some furtive thespians hurriedly disposed of whatever substances they might be harbouring and put on squeaky-clean faces. The 'raid' never occurred.

There still remained other unsuitable, uncastable elements. One, making his début in *Lloyd George,* quickly proved to be a disaster. The *Daily Nation* concluded its review '...the rest of the cast are unbelievable.' By mutual consent he left us to pursue some 'hippie' trail, leaving unpaid rent and taking with him a quantity of utensils from his Hill Lane flat as well as the keys. A.N. Other, eagerly accepting my offer of a contract, arrived as a replacement. Another error on my part. Soon he informed me that his wife (there had been no mention of any wife) would be arriving; that he intended to house her on the theatre's premises; and further he wished me to offer her a contract. She duly arrived and turned out to be a much better bet than her husband. Presently both departed, heading for South Africa, which was illegal at this time.

Two And Two Make Sex, a title guaranteed to bring-'em-in, quickly had the House Full boards on display. The set, a split-level, two different locations affair by the newly-arrived designer, was great. Scenes changed, smooth as silk, from one location to another indicated by lighting. Simon Wambua Mutisya, until recently an assistant carpenter and tabs-man, was now chief electrician, Joseph Gichure having left us. When congratulated on his splendid cross-fades between Holland Park and Highgate which had contributed greatly to the success of the evening, Simon told me, "I was keen... I was so KEEN!"

R.D. (Kay) Francis, theatre correspondent for *The Standard* for the past four years and, prior to that, the *Kenya Weekly News,* was leaving Kenya. He was replaced at *The Standard* by Nigel Slade. 'I urge you to see *In Praise Of Love* which in this, my first review of a DM production, I cannot praise too highly. The Donovan Maule is at its very best.' Despite uniformly good reviews, Rattigan's piece failed to reach 50% of capacity. Dealing as it did with a woman

The Donovan Maule Theatre.

Donovan Maule at his desk in THE DONOVAN MAULE THEATRE

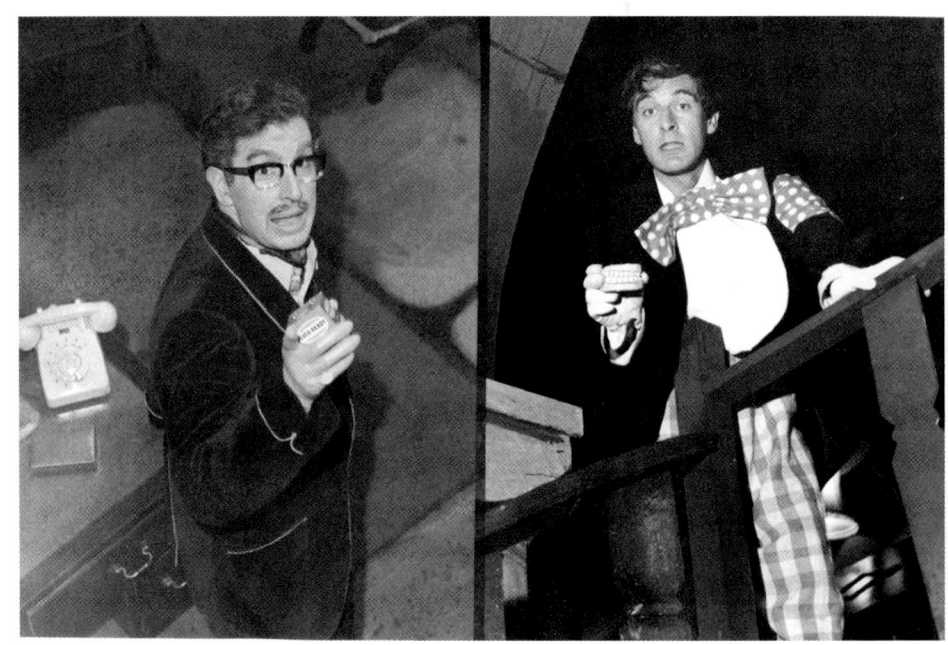

The Two James: Ward (left) and Falkland (right) in *Sleuth* at the Donovan Maule Theatre September/October 1970.

Mollie Donovan Maule in her last appearance at the Donovan Maule Theatre, as Lydia in *His, Hers & Theirs*, production no. 236, January 1970.

The TEAM: Annabel Maule and James Ward together in *Murder Mistaken*, 1974.

Annabel Maule and James Ward in *Lloyd George Knew My Father*, March 1974.

Annabel Maule and James Ward again: *In Praise Of Love*, August 1974.

Crown Matrimonial: Production no. 300, June 1975. From left - Sarah Twist as Alice, Duchess of Gloucester; Elizabeth Lynne as Mary, Princess Royal; Richard Hamer as King Edward VIII; Annabel Maule as Queen Mary; James Ward as the Duke of York; and Angela Ellis as Elizabeth, Duchess of York.

Annabel Maule in the office of the Donovan Maule Theatre, circa 1978.

Donovan Maule on the veranda of the Kisauni, Mombasa home, after retiring from the theatre.

Equus by Peter Shaffer in Frith Banbury's production at the DM Theatre, September 1978.

James Ward as Henry II and Annabel Maule as Eleanor of Aquitaine in *The Lion In Winter* by James Goldman. September 1978 - the 30th Anniversary of the Donovan Maule Players.

The stage of the DM Theatre in 1986; an impromptu setting for *Mother Courage*.

suffering from leukaemia, Nairobi theatregoers, wanting only a 'good laugh', were scared off.

Replacements for pigs-in-pokes arrived shortly before *In Praise of Love* ended. From the airport I collected an actor and a director, the latter to 'play as cast' if required. We had been without a director for too long and the work-load on Kenneth, Jimmy and myself; each one of us undertaking other chores, was considerable. I had received glowing references on behalf of the director, newly trained and consequently inexperienced, but — it would seem — just what we needed.

The new arrivals watched *In Praise Of Love* that very evening. The director's first assignment would be a thriller, still packing them in at London's Haymarket Theatre. All too soon disturbing rumours reached me regarding his rehearsals. Unhappy actors; slow progress. I extended the current production for a further week merely to create extra rehearsal time. The thriller opened, received tepid reviews and box office takings were dismal.

The director came to tell me that he was sleeping badly and losing weight. I sent him to my doctor who prescribed tranquillisers and Mogadon. His second production opened in mid-November to a minuscule audience and a very poor press. I was informed, by a company member, that he had received — on the very morning of opening night — the news that his 18-month-old son had died of a tumour on the brain. This was not all. There had been an earlier tragedy when his young wife died of leukaemia. It was with anguish that we recalled him watching *In Praise Of Love* on the evening of his arrival in Kenya. Sympathy washed through the theatre like an incoming tide.

Kenneth would direct the next show, *Doctor In The House,* and the unhappy widower would play a role for which, physically, he was perfect. Soon Kenneth came to tell me that his rehearsals were badly stalled. If the gentleman came down from his theatre flat he was so drugged that work was impossible.

Next he was admitted to hospital and from there I received his written resignation and request to be flown back to the UK as soon as possible. I made all the necessary arrangements. The same afternoon he withdrew his resignation. He wanted to stay. He wanted to play in *Doctor In The House* (opening six days later). He wished to know what play would follow...

I wrote back: I was sorry but his resignation (the second one made, then withdrawn) had been accepted. Travel arrangements had been confirmed. Kenneth would be playing the role in *Doctor.* Six days after this, strapped to a stretcher and heavily sedated, the poor man was taken by ambulance to the airport. Accompanying him was a doctor clutching a box brimming with syringes and drugs. Immediately he had delivered his patient into secure hands in London he would fly back to Nairobi. To accommodate the stretcher the space of two passenger seats was required. Thus: four air passages on a scheduled EA Airways flight were charged to the theatre. Further accounts from the hospital and the woman psychiatrist who had treated him reached me after the departure. Her report of 'A personality disorder... As it was not possible to detain him in hospital in Nairobi without his consent nor manage him satisfactorily in a general ward... I recommended that he should be transferred to the UK for psychiatrist treatment. He stated he felt depressed as his wife had died 18 months previously from acute leukaemia and four weeks previously his son had died of a brain tumour. He continually requested discharge because he wanted to continue with his performance in the current production at the theatre and on December 14 he discharged himself contrary to advice. A few hours later he was readmitted under the influence of alcohol, having again attempted suicide. He was extremely uncooperative and would not disclose any personal details of his family in the UK but I subsequently managed to trace his parents who stated that the facts presented to us were complete fabrication.'

The suicide attempts; overdoses and an attempt at wrist-slashing with a broken beer bottle and which he himself in a subsequent letter to me, vehemently denied, had taken place at the theatre;

each and every one orchestrated to fail. But 'four suicide attempts' provided the grounds on which the insurance company repudiated my claim.

The cost to the struggling DM Theatre was considerable. During the days when he was in and out of Nairobi Hospital, the company car, the VW Beetle, ran a shuttle service to and from the hospital ferrying members of the company: self-appointed counsellors, therapists and part-time psychiatrists, all eager to give advice, offer opinions and, this above all, voice condemnation of the inhuman management's insistence that his resignation had been accepted and his presence in Kenya was no longer required.

Sufficient damage had been inflicted on the finances of the theatre, the morale of the company and my own nervous system.

Kenneth's production of *Doctor In The House* — the combined age of the three young medical students at its centre reached one hundred and four years — was just what we needed for the Christmas season.

'The funniest show of 1974. I chuckled all the way home.'

'I confidently prescribe *Doctor In The House* as a perfect antidote for the blues...'

'A completely revitalised, swinging, professional cast kept the First Night audience in the aisles with unabated laughter from beginning to end. A show which will remain one of my favourites.'

'What better way to end the dreary 1974 than laughing one's sides sick. My favourite way of seeing the old year out and the New Year in is in going to the New Year's Eve performance and staying on for the lively party that goes on into the wee small hours in the lounge bar afterwards.'

'Annabel has kept the theatre going and out of the red virtually single-handed and by scraping and saving, often to the anger and agony of those around her' — *Sunday Nation*.

The effort to keep down costs while trying to maintain some standards was unremitting. The 'anger and agony' occurred when

I vetoed costly purchases which I considered unnecessary. Each set designer wished to give full rein to his or her creative imagination at the management's expense. Soon it would all be demolished and the bill for 'rubbish removal' would be on my desk. Why, I would ask, were so many kilos of nails ordered for each new set-up? Locally manufactured nails, the only ones available to us, were so poor that huge wastage occurred. There was also the quantity regularly filtered out of the theatre to be employed on private enterprise. Bolts of *americani,* purchased for use by both stage and wardrobe and kept locked up in a wardrobe annex would suddenly, unaccountably, be found reduced to a mere yard or two.

I would ask: How? Why? How much? I was not popular. When I read of the excesses perpetrated by Artistic Directors at heavily subsidised theatre companies in Britain, I would foam at the mouth, fall down and bite the threadbare carpet. I could have run the DM for a month, maybe even longer, on the money spent to get John Gabriel Borkman's custom-made boots to squeak convincingly as he paced; unseen by the audience; overhead in the production at the Old Vic Theatre in January 1975. This was British tax-payers' money — lots of it — being squandered on an offstage sound effect!

But 1975 developed as a year blessedly free of pigs-in-pokes. On a few occasions during the time that I occupied the Hot Seat, a golden surprise came my way.

In 1972 a tall and luscious blonde sashayed into the office asking for employment. Jacqueline Delhaye's first appearance was in *No Sex Please, We're British.* She stayed with us for a year, giving many splendid performances; one of them entirely on roller-skates!

Angela Keen came from her home in Elburgon to be an assistant stage manager. She carried out her duties for 18 productions and was sorely missed when, eventually, she decided to spend time travelling in Europe.

In mid 1974 I was buzzed by the box office: there was a young man in the foyer wishing to speak to me. I found a boy of maybe 16, going on 17 with an endearing smile, curly air and the biggest hands and feet imaginable. His passport stated he was 22. He told me he was walking around the world — which explained the feet — and he had just arrived from India. I took him on.

Christopher Garland worked as an ASM for a year. He could turn his hand to a multitude of jobs and was a sunny, cheerful presence in our midst, willing to undertake any chore.

While in Nairobi, he took flying lessons and obtained his licence before, finally, walking away from us. A few years later, I heard he had married. Some girl hit lucky there, in my opinion.

It was Chris who solved the Mystery of the Missing Toilet Rolls. Several spare rolls of toilet paper would be placed in the Ladies and would disappear in no time at all. It was concluded they were being smuggled out of the theatre, but no bulging ladies were spotted by the receptionist in the nearby box office. Still the toilet rolls vanished; dozens of them. Just vanished.

Returning from an errand in town one hot, slumbering afternoon, Chris parked the VW in St John's Gate and was startled to observe toilet rolls flying out of an open window. These were skillfully fielded by an accomplice who sped off and was out of sight within seconds. Presently the bowler, unencumbered, emerged from the Ladies and walked sedately out of the theatre. We had been the suppliers to two enterprising ladies working in the Private Sector.

Halfway through the year, in June, production number 300 was staged. *Crown Matrimonial* by Royce Ryton, dealt with the 'Abdication Crisis' which occurred in England in 1936 when King Edward VIII abdicated the throne in favour of marrying a twice-divorced American woman. The cast listed six members of the Royal Family. The setting was Queen Mary's private sitting room at Marlborough House.

Queen Mary, widow of George V and the unmotherly mother of the unwilling King, was the main focus of the play. A long and tiring role. To achieve the correct 'upholstered' look of the regal bosom and hips, I padded — foam rubber sandwiched between layers of *americani* stretched from neck to hip. Over this constricting corset went a variety of more or less elaborate costumes together with a quantity of jewels, but it was the wig, made especially for me in London by Wig Creations, that achieved the transformation.

In fact I had, many years previously, met the real Queen Mary. I was presented to her when she attended a matinée of *His Excellency*. She sat in the Royal Box at the Piccadilly Theatre, stiff-backed and gracious, and I noted her delicate shell-pink skin and witnessed an unexpected flash of humour. On learning that I had served in the Women's Royal Naval Service during the war, she remarked, "Very different from all this," gesturing in the direction of the stage.

Her whole life had been dedicated to 'duty'. Personal wishes or desires must all be sublimated to duty, and this uncompromising attitude was at the centre of her relationship with her son. David, as he was known in the family circle, did abdicate. His brother Bertie became King George VI while Edward VIII became the Duke of Windsor and his American wife the Duchess of Windsor.

Kenneth's production was a big success, extending to a fifth week of Full Houses, but it exhausted me. As I sat under the stage lights, stiff-backed on a beautiful chair made especially for us by Leonard Moore, 'Fine Furniture Makers', I could feel sweat breaking out under the wig; feel it breaking out between my shoulder blades; feel it tricking down my back. At the moments when I was offstage it was merely to struggle out of one costume and into another before the Queen's next entrance. Wherever possible, I had sewn jewels to the fabric, to save time. And all the while I was aware that the padding was growing damper.

When, at the end of the evening, I was released from the unlovely garment, I hooked it at the back of my dressing room door, where it hung limp and clammy. Each Sunday I would launder it, in readiness for the following Tuesday performance. The strange, headless torso hanging in the garden at Hill Lane made a surprising sight.

Chris Garland was on the book for this production and made

occasional comments on the running sheet for each performance. At number 27 he wrote, 'Only another week and *you* can abdicate!' On Friday July 11, at performance number 32: 'Two more to go and 12 changes!'

The splendid box office income — topping £5,000 — was swiftly and brutally annihilated by the two following productions. The mournful minutes of a Directors' meeting stated: 'In the month of August the takings had been only £5,000 estimated to be the worst ever.' This was income from all sources — while expenses rose and rose...

A Touch of Spring by Samuel Taylor helped a bit. 'A sparkling gem of a play' — Kenneth Watene, writing for the *Sunday Nation*, and 'Portrayal of true professional work.' — Seth Adagala, now correspondent for *The Standard*.

Set in a Grand Suite in an old-fashioned Grand Hotel in Rome, it was a romantic love story. Jimmy Ward enjoyed himself as an amoral Roman 'fixer' of overwhelming charm and scant ethics while Kenneth offered a perfect little cameo of a geriatric waiter who arrived with Room Service.

Kenneth had acquired Violetta, a spanking purple bicycle, and for many years could be seen riding round Nairobi until such time as the traffic in town became so undisciplined and murderous that he was forced to forgo this mode of transport.

Adagala declared: 'The theatre season (August to December) that has just ended has been a most satisfying one.'

The year 1975 saw the emergence of several extraordinary talents. Steve Mwenesi appeared as Dedan Kimathi in the play of the same name written by Kenneth Watene. John Okumu (the 'Sibi' came later) was seen as Starbuck in *The Rainmaker* at the National Theatre. In fact, John had won laurels two years before this, playing Shakespeare's Romeo.

Francis Imbuga's *Betrayal in The City* had its first production at the National Theatre under the direction of Tirus Gathwe.

Touching on audience apathy (all too familiar to us), Seth

Adagala had continued: 'Here was wholesome African entertainment staged by Africans for Africans, but no audience... It is hoped that in the new year Kenyans will do even better in developing their own theatre... It is to be sincerely hoped, too, that Kenyan audiences will resolve to support their theatre.'

CHAPTER NINE

Chateau Maule had been the focus of attention for thieves. Eight or more robberies left the Maules without curtains, cushions, bedspreads, blankets, pictures, transistor radios or tape recorders. Antique brass and copperware, binoculars, small side tables, an electric iron — together with laundry — all had been removed.

Maule's Folly, the well-equipped but never-used carpenter's workshop, had long since been relieved of all equipment. Instead, travel bags and suitcases were stored there. Not any more. Mollie found the place empty. It happened that I witnessed one of these raids.

On a flying visit to Mombasa (except that, on this occasion, I chose to travel via M.P.S. — the Mombasa Peugeot Service — barrelling all the way to the Manor Hotel) I woke up at about one in the morning to find a tall figure testing the sliding window, no further than two feet from my pillow. Unable to unfasten the catch, the figure moved off along the veranda.

Whipping out of bed I opened the bedroom door a crack. Three or four figures were approaching Mollie's bedroom window. Gathering a lungful of humid air I yelled "MOLLIE!!!"

One of the men turned and, with arms raised above his head, started back toward me, gibbering as he advanced. I locked the door and struggled into a bathrobe, while maintaining as much noise as possible. Presently light flooded the veranda. I peered out again. The thieves were gone, possibly to a getaway canoe waiting on the dark water of the creek at the bottom of the garden.

I had come to Chateau Maule for a few days' rest following the intense session of pigs-in-pokes culminating in the stretcher-case evacuation. But it was not to be!

Soon after my arrival, Mollie went sick with pleurisy and the cook departed on his annual leave. I took over housekeeping and cooking, but quickly developed a high fever. My virus presented a threat to Don, so I rattled back to Nairobi. At the theatre I found the accountant was in hospital.

Don's health had remained reasonably good throughout 1974. 'Nothing but good news about Don,' Mollie told me in February. 'He is now much better than before his illness. Twice last week he went bathing...' Three months later: 'Daddy is in wonderful health at the moment and eating as he's never eaten for years. The only snag is the ever-increasing weight...'

In mid-year he began work, compiling notes for his History of the DM Players — a ground-plan on which to build — but by September he lamented, 'The book I never get down to writing.'

In 1975 it was Mollie who required nursing. 'I've got shingles! Of all the silly-sounding, childish ailments to attack me in my 76th year...'

Don wrote, 'I need not tell you how completely dislocated life here has been for the past three weeks with Mollie so ill...'

His next report declared: ' "LIFE" really is a four-letter word, isn't it? Can't think why anybody continues to put up with it...' Mollie's recovery was slow but, at last, 'I'm much better and able to work normally at any gardening or household chore.'

"What's on next at the DM?"
"*The Importance of Being Earnest.*"
"Oh! I've seen that. Don't want to see it again!"

Oscar Wilde's 'trivial comedy for serious people' ranked now as a 'classic' and students from a Preparatory School attended a matinée. Committing their impressions to paper was part of the deal.

'I liked how the lights went out very slowly... I liked the dresses... The best act was when Cecily gave Gwendolen the cake when she asked for bread and butter... I liked all the old fashioned dresses, I wish I had them... I enjoyed the play very much and the actors were very good. Thank you for letting us in... I liked the first act best especially the furniture... I liked Mama's costume, she was funny... I thought the last scene was the funniest when they turned out to be brothers...'

A couple of slightly older students took the matter more seriously. 'The Donovan Maule Theatre is a nice theatre because the walls had got a nice pattern. The play started with the inside of a nice house and the butler who was called Lane was setting out the cucumber sandwiches. A bit later on in the play Algernon ate all the cucumber sandwiches and his aunt Lady Bracknell asks him where the sandwiches are and the butler says, "There were no cucumbers in the market, sir. Not even for ready money." There was a lot of backchat and then it was the interval.'

The famous 'interview' scene between Bracknell and John Worthing *'backchat'?* I was outraged!

Another review, written with great care: 'Yesterday evening I roared down to my Mum's car and exchanged my suitcase for a picnic basket. In the basket were four lettuce and marmite sandwiches, three sausages, seven apricots, lots of raisins, one flapjack, two toffees and a thermos of milk.'

There followed detailed accounts of travel arrangements, traffic hold-ups and arrival at the theatre: 'On our left were the bathrooms and on our right was the bar...' At last came a mention of the performance: 'What I liked about the play was when Ernest kept on telling Algy off all the time. I thought Gwendolen was a perfect nuisance and how Ernest loved her at all I cannot imagine. In the second interval we had a drink. I had a lemonade which cost me Sh1.55. At the end of the play the curtain went up and down three times ...On the way home I ate the last of my supper. I really enjoyed the Donovan Maule.'

Here, surely, was a conscientious catering manageress in the making.

In January 1976 James Falkland was appointed Director of the Kenya Cultural Centre and Administrator of the National Theatre.

This caused instant uproar. The Writer's Association of Kenya, Ngugi wa Thiong'o and Okot p'Bitek among the members, protested: 'He may be a good administrator but we fail to see how his background can help him direct theatrical movements in this country... we fail to see how the appointment of a foreigner will help in our return to the sources of the African Cultural being. Only a Kenyan African director, supported by a largely Kenyan Governing Council of the Kenya Cultural Centre... can liberate our Theatre.' The Governing Council listed 11 members, only two being expatriates. Okot p'Bitek was a member.

Without question Falkland was a good Administrator — better, in fact, than any previous incumbent. The 23-year-old National Theatre was in dire need of a little tender, loving care.

He set up an Appeal Fund with a target of £11,000 to be used, in the first instance, to reseat the dilapidated auditorium. To raise the necessary funds he mounted a series of Harambee productions. He created the *KNT Newsletter,* which gave details of upcoming productions and concerts by all drama and music groups — the DM Theatre included.

While angry letters of protest continued to splutter in the press, Falkland got on with the job. The new seats were fixed in January 1977. The foyer was also refurbished and some light bulbs fixed, thereby giving the place a more welcoming aspect. By October Falkland was gone. A near-audible sigh of relief went up and the KNT was allowed to relapse into its previous dust-collecting, malfunctioning torpor.

On the other side of town we struggled on. *Rosencrantz And Guildenstern Are Dead,* Tom Stoppard's funny, teasing, word-juggling piece, where two characters on the margin of Hamlet's world try to figure out what the hell is going on, had long been a favourite of mine. There are 'roles-to-die-for', even the non-speaking extras get to demonstrate a number of play-acting 'Deaths', offering opportunities for outrageous overacting.

Stoppard acknowledged, 'These two guys, who in Shakespeare's context don't really know what they are doing. The little they are told is mainly lies, and there is no reason to suppose that they ever find out why they are killed.' The day after opening I wrote to Mombasa: 'The lighting rehearsal took nearly all day — there are 25 cues, some quite difficult; but the problem is lack of *bulbs!* There is only one supplier and he's out of stock 50% of the time. One is not allowed to import direct. So the splendid equipment I installed cannot be used to its full potential due to lack of *bulbs!*'

A note reached me from the Director of the United States Cultural Centre: '*R&G* is magnificent — we've seen it twice in the States, but your production had more impact — better acting and smoother flow.'

There were further letters, excellent press reviews and, above all, *audiences!*

The DM, six years younger than the National Theatre, had been in constant use for 18 years. On its flat roof laundry was hung to dry. Several memorable parties had been thrown up there. Bodies, oiled for bronzing, had been spread-eagled up there. The occasional, tumultuous hubbub outside the Parliament Building had been observed from up there. Now, the wear and tear had become apparent: rain found its way into the auditorium in May 1976, when some patching-up took place, but clearly more extensive repairs were needed. A firm of 'roofing experts' was called in.

Rehearsals for The *Dame of Sark,* at the end of August, were rendered near impossible due to the deafening noise as the 'experts' stripped away the roof over our heads. At five o'clock they departed, leaving the stage area open to the skies. The heavens opened soon after their departure. The evening's performance was cancelled. The stage crew worked throughout the night. The stage director stripped all wires from both sound and lighting equipment and, where possible, moved it to a dry area upstage. Using polythene sheeting to shroud conduits and sockets, he managed to keep as many as possible dry. His assistants swept rainwater out through the dock doors and tried to rig a tarpaulin over the gaping hole above. Telephone calls to the 'roofing experts' led nowhere. Instead I typed a detailed two-page report and had it delivered to their office. Two weeks passed before a couple of representatives called at the theatre to deny any responsibility for negligence. 14 months later, on the point of being hauled into court, they decided to settle out of it: paying a small sum in damages.

In January 1977 James Ward and I were once again together on stage. Ben Travers called his play *The Bed Before Yesterday*, 'A period comedy'. He set it in the 1930s. A London critic wrote, 'In his 90th year, Mr. Travers casts off the shackles of censorship and embraces the permissive society with a joy worthy of an adolescent.'

Alma Millet is a ferocious harridan of a rich widow. Victor Keene is a meek gentleman of slender means. Alma is lonely for companionship and makes Victor an offer he cannot refuse.

Alma was raped on her honeymoon a couple of decades earlier and wants nothing to do with obnoxious S.E.X.

Victor wants nothing more than a quiet life, regular meals and an opportunity to watch cricket. They get married.

Alma hears a few disclosures from a woman of somewhat loose morals which set her thinking. Has she, in fact, been missing something good? She persuades poor, gentle, out-of-practice Victor to try It. Miraculously Victor triumphs. Alma is a changed woman: passionate... insatiable!

What roles for Annabel Maule and James Ward!

'These two, as the formidably frigid Alma and the mild-mannered, anxious to please Victor, give what may very possibly be their best performances to date. Which is saying something. Both are on stage throughout the play and perform as if Ben Travers had written the parts with them in mind.' — the *Standard* January 7.

I wrote to my parents: 'The last three weeks have been so hectic and so horrible that I don't wish to dwell on them. We open tonight and I am more insecure, worried and entirely without any confidence or even knowledge of what line I am taking with Alma ...If we "die" I shouldn't be at all surprised.'

The next letter reported, 'It wasn't until the second performance yesterday — Friday (with 126 in the house) that we really got the comedy 'pacing' right and felt a bit more optimistic... The audience adored it and it went like a bomb and I felt a bit less ashamed of the performance.'

A young actor in the company had been urging me to give him a production. I gave him *Bed...* and wished I hadn't.

It was the audiences at the early performances who taught us where the sudden gear-changes occurred in the script which had been bugging us throughout a strenuous but unproductive rehearsal period.

Carole Channing, the American star, who played Alma on a tour of Florida, declared, 'If you play it verbatim, it's like translating from the Chinese.'

The Bed Before Yesterday developed into a crowd-puller.

The Blessed St. Alan (Ayckbourn) — Patron Saint of theatre managers, manifested himself with *The Norman Conquests*, three full-length plays using the same cast of six characters. This boon could occupy the DM stage for 12 glorious weeks and allow me to take overseas leave.

I scanned the shipping page of the *Daily Nation* and hit on a small Greek cargo ship, the *Hellenic Glory*, which carried a few passengers, due in Mombasa on March 23 where she would 'Load for Suez, Instanbul, Salonika, Piraeus, Patras, Venice and Trieste.'

I booked passage from Mombasa to Venice, from where I would fly back to Nairobi.

Soon after reaching Chateau Maule my parents, one after the other, went sick and took to their respective beds. I catered, prepared invalid trays, shopped, collected prescriptions from the chemist and waited for the *Glory* to bear me away. This didn't occur until 28 days later. Eight days out from Mombasa we reached Suez and there we stopped, mostly at anchorage among a flotilla of ships, for a further 16 yawning days, gazing at the barren, sun-scorched hills of the Arabian Desert on one side and the Sinai on the other; waiting for the pilot to take us through the Canal.

Nine weeks after my departure from Nairobi the *Glory* was slowly approaching Piraeus, her home port. The fabled Aegean Sea was littered with débris: plastic containers, bottles, polythene bags, assorted rubbish... the dross of human existence. I had now overstayed my leave and proposed to cut short the trip and fly back to Kenya. This plan was firmly opposed by both Kenneth and Jimmy, engaged in operating the DM most ably.

The moment the *Glory* berthed in Piraeus the crew disappeared. I was left on board with only a lonely watchman at the gangway. Hot water ceased. So, too, the services of a cabin steward, erratic even at the best of times.

Dockyards are not holiday resorts. Cranes, derricks, containers, rail-tracks, pallets, metal, oil, rust. *Glory* floated a lengthy walk from the dock-gates. A bus ride took me to the terminus in Piraeus, and from there a train took me to Athens.

I learned to ride Greek buses. Athens to Delphi: three and a half-hours of hairpin bends and hair-raising driving in a vehicle innocent of shock-absorbers. My neighbour, an elderly Greek in striped trousers, black jacket, and black hat, fingering his worry beads, wished me *"Bon voyage"* as the driver leapt into his seat, let in the clutch and we lurched away. Racing past goliath tour buses (AIR-CONDITIONED-TELEVISION), we streaked up Mount Parnassus. From my window no road was visible, only a sheer drop of Apollo only knew how many metres with the Gulf of Corinth glinting in the distance. I put my trust in my neighbour's worry beads. Another memorable bus trip: I was returning to the *Glory* one evening following a long day in Athens.

A crowd waited at the terminus for the rare number five bus. When it arrived it was full already, but as many of us as possible pushed on board, thrusting our way into the throng jamming the standing room area. Bodies pressed one against the other in a solid mass. The doors closed, squeezing us into further intimacy and off we went. I became aware of a warm pressure on my trouser-clad backside and thought nothing of it until certain motions of a thumb left me in no doubt that I was being well and truly goosed. Not a hope of moving away — impossible to move at all. I clutched at an open window and instantly my hand was pinioned by a large, warmly pulsating mitt. Struggling to find drachmas for the fare and to locate my stop, I was thrown off balance. A strong thigh was jammed between my legs and before I could right myself a recognisable erection was thrust at my behind. Still pinioned to the window on one side I reached for the bell on the other, then wrenching myself away from the clutches of the Travelling Seducer, I pushed and shoved my way ("So sorry... Please excuse...") to the exit and out of the bus. It was the wrong halt. I was left with a long trudge to the dock gates. Who, I wondered, would be his next victim? Surely not the tiny, black-clad Greek granny wedged between the swaying mass of humanity remaining on the bus? Was this a normal occurrence on after-dark buses in Greece? Was the Travelling Seducer a season-ticket holder?

I was back on stage in mid-August in William Douglas Home's *The Queen's Highland Servant*. Jimmy grew an authentic beard to play John Brown. I, on the other hand, was in no way transformed into the ageing Queen Victoria. The wig ordered from London failed to arrive. The show was a long one: three acts with 12 scenes set in a trio of Royal sitting rooms at Balmoral, Osborne and Windsor. The action spanned 22 years.

The padding used in *Crown Matrimonial* was hugely expanded. The order of dressing was: 1. Black tights; 2. The padding; 3. A quantity of petticoats; and 4. A variety of costumes — always, of course, black. When fixed into this fortress I found it hard to move and harder still to breathe. There were a scant 30 minutes between the two performances on Saturday with, of course, a costume change back to the start of the play. Tough on the stage crew too: three scene changes per show. The cast listed 11 male characters.

Kenneth made a fine Benjamin Disraeli and Laurie Slade returned to the DM stage to play Dr. Randall Davidson in the final scene. In September I wrote to Mombasa, 'I shall, of course, not be sorry to see the last of old Queen Vic and her endless words and emotion and padding and hot, constricting costumes... On Saturday nights we don't come down until long after midnight!'

The minute the next show, *Rat Trap,* opened, I travelled to Mombasa. *Rat Trap* dealt with five villains breaking into a bank vault. It was a financial disaster! "What can you expect?" asked the Italian Ambassador. "There are no pretty girls in it!"

The surroundings as I approached Chateau Maule were unrecognisable. At the start of the year work on the new bridge, the one that would replace Nyali pontoon bridge, had begun. Don charted progress: 'JANUARY 25 Road construction company began work today.'

And the day following, 'Neighbour's servant quarters demolished.' Mollie reported: 'They are busy cutting down our trees. The sound of axes is pure Cherry Orchard — last Act. All very sad.' At the end of February Don wrote, 'It is still swelteringly hot here and with Ras Kisauni Road looking like one of those photographs of World War I: Battlefield on the Somme after preliminary bombardment. When the rains break the bulldozers and giant mechanical diggers will have their caterpillar tracks completely submerged in mud and God knows how our Renault will manage... The despoliation of our lovely surroundings is horrible. All the trees, bushes and undergrowth has almost entirely disappeared. One consolation, now that the old feeding grounds of birds such as coucals have been demolished, they are seeking sanctuary in our garden.'

During the time, in March, when I waited for the arrival — and the delayed departure — of the *Hellenic Glory;* I had witnessed some of this. A slice of our garden had gone, the approach to the house was from a different direction. Power cuts were frequent. The air was full of noise and dust.

Now, in September, Don's forecast regarding the effect of rain on the construction work proved correct; all the heavy earth-moving machinery round Ras Kisauni was grounded. The air was filled with the continual slurp of suction pumps. The approach road became ever more difficult to negotiate or even to locate. The Renault slithered and skidded in the quagmire. Often it required pushing, or even lifting entirely, out of the sea of mud. The rain continued in torrents.

I had come to Mombasa to check on Mollie who was in hospital for an operation. She was in a room not far from the one occupied by Don in 1973. The same veranda ran the length of the ward with the same incomparable view of the Indian Ocean as it creamed across the reef and curled into the old Dhow Harbour. It was almost possible to see Chateau Maule from here. Any crow, on a direct flight, would cover the distance in moments. It was a different matter for Don, visiting the hospital twice a day, with lengthy queues at either end of the old Nyali bridge. The drive could take 45 minutes, or more, in either direction.

Torrential rain continued for weeks, raising the humidity which exacerbated his breathlessness. He told me, "It's like trying to breathe through a wet flannel."

Mollie came home from the hospital and almost immediately was confined to bed there with 'flu and bronchitis. Up and about again, Don reported: 'Mollie had a sudden very bad dizziness during luncheon. So bad, she had to be assisted by Musa and myself to her bed.'

These attacks were to recur with distressing and later, disastrous consequences. However at her 80th birthday party, in late November, she appeared in a new evening dress looking marvellous and enjoyed the small gathering of friends. Don wrote to her: '57 years ago I bombarded you with love letters imploring you to marry me... My life began on July 3rd 1920. Now, at 78 years of age that ardent boy of barely 21 is unable to write a proper love letter. All I am trying to say is Thank God for you and all you have always meant to me. All I want is for us to remain together until the end...'

In Nairobi, I was starting work on the next production and about to cope-with-a-pig-in-a-poke. The actor was absent from a morning rehearsal and the A.S.M. went up to his flat, returning soon with the news that he was incapably drunk. I recast the role and completed the paperwork connected with his return to the UK: flight booking, cancellation of his just-received work permit, tax clearance, medical insurance etc. That same evening I was called to the telephone. "This is the Hotel Intercontinental. One of your employees is dead drunk on our premises. Please make arrangements to have him removed." He was 25 years old. His sojourn in Kenya lasted just 14 days. Meanwhile, British Actors' Equity was insistent that I pay the latest minimum wage: £60 a week loaded with 'away from home' allowances.

A second P-in-a-P had been with us since January. He had failed to make a good impression on audiences. Rather the contrary. In July he came to tell me he was bored... He had not been offered any good roles... He wanted to leave...

Concealing my delight, I accepted his resignation. One hour later he was back in the office, withdrawing it.

The heavy rains at the end of 1977 were not confined to the coast. Nairobi was just as wet.

Driving to the airport for my flight to Mombasa to spend Christmas at Chateau Maule, I passed abandoned cars wallowing in the rising flood. Pedestrians with shoes, briefcases and handbags held over their heads waded through swirling water, struggling to reach home.

My trip was unplanned — just a last-minute decision. I was lucky to get a seat on the evening flight and had, that afternoon, dashed into a Nairobi store to fill a carrier bag with a multitude of small items. I had one other, more valuable gift: a Parker pen intended for Mollie. Don maintained a small array of pens, neatly ranged along the left-hand breast pocket of his safari suit. At his desk he favoured a real, old-fashioned fountain pen filled with real, old-fashioned ink. An anguished note in a diary lamented: 'Mislaid my precious fountain pen and am most distressed about it.' Thankfully, the very next day, came: 'Pen found!'

Mollie, on the other hand, maintained no pens. She would pick up the nearest ball-point and start scribbling. Pens succumbed and expired under her grasp, leaving their last drop of ink as a messy blob on the page. Another victim would continue the narrative until, all pens spent, she would resort to a pencil for the final paragraphs. Her letters could prove real puzzles to decipher as she dashed, at a slope, across the pages.

As well as the carrier-bagful, I had a large American cheesecake encased in a flimsy carton and if it was to arrive in one piece, it had to be balanced — flat — on the palm of the hand.

Delayed by the waterlogged drive to the airport, my flight had been called. I dashed through pouring rain to the aircraft; the steps at the rear were on the point of being withdrawn. "Wait for me!!" I shouted into the dripping darkness. The cabin crew member peered out, muttering something under his breath, but allowed me to board. With hair drizzling cold rainwater down my face, I sat nursing the cheesecake. My parents collected me at an hour long past their habitual bedtime and it was with relief that we reached home and I deposited the cheesecake, intact, in the refrigerator.

On Sunday morning, Christmas Day, we sat on the veranda facing the creek where the water was still and glassy. The rain had stopped and a pale, hesitant sun emerged.

The Christmas 'stocking' was a big success. Nothing was gift-wrapped but out came throat pastilles, hair conditioner, needles and thread, buttons, memo-pads, kitchen tongs, plant food, soap, yeast tablets for Baggage... Then finally came the Parker pen. "Oh, splendid!" Don exclaimed, and immediately added it to his breast pocket. I had to be firm: "It's for *Mollie*." I witnessed him handing it over. Thereafter her letters to me were a great deal easier to read. But not for long. Either Don misappropriated it, or it got lost, and we were back to feeble ball-points who just weren't up to it.

Visitors arrived. Benny Wielandt brought his young wife and little daughter to wish us Happy Christmas.

Benny, Danish, was at this time setting up the Mombasa Industrial Training Centre. He had entered Don's life the previous October, arriving at the house to offer him a game of chess in answer to a slip of paper found in Chess Manuals in the library at the British Council. Don had given his contact and asked for players. Several turned up, Benny among them, and he would prove to be a Gift from God as time went on.

On January 1, Don made his initial entry in a new diary: 'I begin the year by counting our blessings.'

It would be the last occasion on which he had blessings to count. 1978 was to develop into a year of change for both the Republic of Kenya and the Maules.

CHAPTER TEN

'REPERTORY — A permanent company established in a theatre building and appearing in the same play for one to three weeks, to distinguish such a theatre from the theatre housing touring companies for a week only, or from a London theatre where a run may last for years.'

-The Oxford Companion to the Theatre.

' "Repertory" is a euphemism for "churning" which is just what the DM, night in and night out have been doing for exactly 30 years...' — Nigel Slade, June 1978. Slade returned to the *Standard* at the start of the year and to date we had churned out: *The Sunshine Boys; Scarlet Ribbon; Confusions; Pygmalion; Hands Across The Sea; The Browning Version; The Hot Tiara;* and, in June, *Sleeping It Off.*

Hindle Wakes was in preparation to celebrate the 70th anniversary of the 'repertory' system, pioneered by a lady named Annie Horniman. She had sponsored several new playwrights, among them Stanley Houghton. Set in Lancashire, *Hindle Wakes* centres on a working girl: a mill-hand, who resists pressure to do the "done thing" and marry her seducer, the son of a rich man. "You're a man and I was your little fancy. Well, I'm a woman and you were my little fancy," says Fanny Hawthorn. Her parents are appalled. The boy's parents are amazed. The audience in 1912 was delighted. This was something new: the first stirrings of Women's Lib and the revolt against parental authority.

Our production received wonderful reviews and did distressingly bad business. Writing to Mombasa, I groaned: '...the latest discovery made by the designer is paint in *aerosol* cans. Can after can is used and this as well as ordinary paint, timber, *americani*, glue, masking tape, nails, screws, upholstery tacks, dyes, fittings to make gaslights, rubber castors for the truck for scene 1, etc... etc... AND ETC... It kills me when I have 30 people in front at Sh30 a head...'

'On Wednesday April 5th, at 8.46pm, an earth tremor rumbled through vast areas of Kenya. And people were shaken. Some terrified.' — *Sunday Nation.*

On Wednesday April 5th, at 9pm, the first performance of *Pygmalion* was due at the Donovan Maule. Some people were, indeed, shaken while others were terrified. At the very first quiver the box office receptionist fled, screaming, into the street. "Keep calm! Pull yourself together!" I admonished her as she sped past me. Drinkers at the bar wasted no time in following her example and her screams now mingled with the wails of car alarms set off by the turbulence. Behind my back, in the Ladies, ceramic tiles crashed to the ground. A party sat in front of the picture window fronting Parliament Road, their drinks on a table in front of them. A rumble akin to that of a famished elephant could be heard and the picture window shattered. A slice of glass, the size of a guillotine blade, stood poised above the neck of one woman. I stood petrified. It skimmed past her and fell at her feet, splintering into shards. Chairs slid this way and that across the small, polished dance floor.

The shaking subsided. The noise abated. No one had been hurt. I conjectured that George Bernard Shaw had turned in his grave but, despite this, his play would be seen at the theatre and the curtain rose a little after 9 o'clock.

The production garnered an exceptionally high number of non-theatre club members, the 24-hour variety, totalling 854; due, I imagine, to the name G.B. Shaw. But it wasn't always so — *Candida* had done appallingly and *Arms And The Man* not much better. A Kenyan family came to *Pygmalion:* father, mother and six children, the youngest no more than four. How bored and bewildered he must have been; all that talk, talk, talk — where was the action? Nevertheless, he sat quietly until the end when his mother announced, "That was very good. Now, let's go."

Reporting to Mombasa the previous year I had concluded, 'Well, that's it. Nothing much has changed in fact! Dramas, personality clashes... the hard workers working as hard as ever; the malingerers malingering, and: next year our 30th anniversary, would you believe? What to do then, I wonder?'

In Kenneth's *On Stage* issue in May 1978, came the announcement:

'The management extends a cordial invitation to all Founder Members of the DM Theatre Club to be guests at the First Night of the play chosen to mark the Thirtieth Anniversary, *The Lion In Winter*, which takes place on Wednesday September 20 1978. Will any Founder Member still around — and there must be many of the gallant 343 — please get in touch.'

The indifferent box office returns for *Hindle Wakes* had been grievously disappointing but I had high hopes for the play to follow, due in August, before the anniversary production.

Peter Shaffer's *Equus* had opened in London five years earlier. '*Equus* is sensationally good; it is based on a direct confrontation between reason and instinct. It suggests that though organised faith is usually based on neurosis, a life without some form of worship or belief is ultimately barren. It deals with the psychiatric exploration of a hideous crime. A 17-year-old boy has blinded six horses with a metal spike; and we watch as the doctor patiently pieces together the evidence that will explain this act of cruelty.'

James Ward would play the psychiatrist. The director would be Frith Banbury, one of England's most prestigious directors with an awesome list of credits. I had been in his very first London production, *Dark Summer* in 1947.

I could not, of course, afford Frith's normal fee or even anything approaching it. I offered air travel, accommodation in a flat at Hill

Lane and petrol for a hire car.

Frith arrived on July 19.

His production of *Equus* was superb. He had stimulated the company and widened all our horizons. He would not be able to attend the first night. A fresh assignment awaited him. His flight to the UK would be airborne at the moment the curtain at the DM rose on Wednesday August 23; but like a well-prepared soufflé, he had brought his production to the point where it needed only to be taken from the oven and brought, triumphantly, to the table.

At midday on Tuesday, I was called to the telephone and told the President was dead.

Jomo Kenyatta, the founding Father of the Nation, had died at State House, Mombasa. His age was uncertain: 'Born somewhere between 1890 and 1895.' As the news spread the city became a ghost town. Shops, offices, cinemas, theatres closed. A silent grief fell upon the streets as they emptied of cars and pedestrians. All life slowed or came to a standstill as people retired to their homes to grieve and await further news.

This was slow in coming. There was no guiding protocol for the death of the President of Kenya. Kenyatta was the first. A declaration told us the State Funeral would take place on August 31.

Equus opened at the Friday matinée on September 1. There were pitifully few in the house. All my press ads, had been submerged in full-page, black-bordered messages of condolence. Newspapers were not losing any business, that was certain.

To his credit, Mugambi Karanja, writing for the *Daily Nation,* was there. '*Equus,* the compelling play on psychiatric exploration has brought what must be the first complete nude scene to the Nairobi stage...' Other, delayed reviews announced, '*EQUUS* TRIUMPHS AT DM.'; '*EQUUS* at the DM WILL LEAVE YOU BREATHLESS.'

During the nine days when the theatre had remained closed, we had in fact been at work backstage, behind drawn curtains. Frith's soufflé was kept airborne with the occasional run-through while rehearsals for *The Lion In Winter* continued.

The following week, when Nairobi slowly returned to normal, *Equus* took off like a rocket with queues at the box office and the telephone ringing continuously. This was the success, so badly needed, I had hoped for. Alas, *Equus* had to close after only 18 performances. No extension was possible. Two contracts came to an end, leaving us minus important cast members and the anniversary date, September 20, had to stand.

The invitation to Founder Members had been repeated in every issue of *On Stage* since May. Bookings by members — Founder or otherwise — were filling the seating plan with special requests: "Our usual first night seats"; "Near the stage, please, and next to Mr. and Mrs. XXXXX"; "Next to the exit..."

James Goldman's play *The Lion In Winter* has to do with internecine manoeuvres among the Plantagenets as they prowl suspiciously round one another in a chilly Chinon Castle at Christmas 1183. Known historical facts formed the basis of the plot but the dialogue, in a mode of hip American, suited neither the period nor the characters.

In my research I learned that Eleanor of Aquitaine's dresses 'Were made of Samite, a rich medieval silk fabric with a warp, each thread of which was of six strands. Her embroideries were picked out in pearls set in gold. Her bandinella was of linen and her cloaks were of wool dyed with indigo. The seams of her clothes were concealed with strands of pearls and she wore the most refined jewels, veils and other accessories.' Yes, well, Nairobi theatre-goers would have to settle for something less. Castles and crowns — even fake, theatrical ones — are costly.

At the start of opening week messages and cards began to arrive. 'Congratulations on reaching 30!' There followed cables and flowers and then Mollie, the V.I.P. guest who, at 80, arrived from Mombasa via M.P.S. She settled into the nearby Hotel Intercontinental in accommodation I had arranged with flowers and fruit to welcome her. Don's ruined lungs would not allow him to come to Nairobi. Baggage was delighted to have Don's undivided attention and Don enjoyed 'My favourite corned beef for lunch but not like good old pre-World War One Machonachies!'

Kenneth's anniversary issue of *On Stage* ran to 47 pages and was a masterpiece of research. It listed the 340 productions to date. It offered potted biographies of all three Maules. It included an eye-opening article about Eleanor of Aquitaine which, had I read it prior to opening night, might have hugely influenced my playing of the role. There were photographs in plenty. It was a real 'souvenir' issue.

My own research had unearthed some equally eye-opening information. The very first audited Balance Sheet covering April 1948 to September 30, 1949 (17 months) showed:

Total Income	K£2,081.68
Total Expenses	K£ 635.16

The last audited Balance Sheet before production number 341, the anniversary play, October 1, 1976 to September 30, 1977 (12 months) showed:

Total Income	K£65,280.00
Total Expenses	K£62,305.00

On Wednesday night the curtain rose at 9.03 and came down at 11.35. A party followed in the bar lounge. Old friends were reunited; old productions were recalled; other anniversaries remembered.

Three members of the cast of *The Guinea Pig* were present: Mollie, Fred Hutton and Sir Ernest Vasey. It was a night thick with nostalgia.

I noted, '...truly alarming run-in to the première of this production — NO designer; design by a student who couldn't paint. Two assistant stage managers *playing* in the show. Cancelled dress rehearsal... However — all went well.'

The Maules and their theatre received a great deal of publicity, both locally and in Britain. On September 15 *The Standard* featured a double page spread compiled by Nigel Slade. He had gone down to the coast to interview and photograph the Maules. Later, after we had opened, the *Daily Nation* spread an Anniversary Supplement over four pages crowned with the theatre's insignia: the masks of comedy and tragedy tied together with the initials D and M standing for Donovan Maule, or, Don and Mollie.

She had spent three nights in the city, lapped in the luxury of her hotel room. She had been fêted, wined and dined and enjoyed an orgy of shopping. From her balcony she had a clear view of the newly-built mausoleum where Jomo Kenyatta had been laid to rest.

Before preparing for the matinée on Friday I saw her safely into the M.P.S. taxi that would return her to Mombasa. In her handbag was Kenneth's bumper *On Stage* as well as copies of press clips.

Don recorded, 'To bed shortly before midnight suffering from a surfeit of publicity which doesn't seem real at all. Did we really do all that? Life's a rum go!'

To date 1978 had run reasonably smooth for them. 'Our days are happy but monotonous,' Don told me in April. 'Almost a study in Still Life.' In June he started on a new inhaler. From the start of 1975 he had used Ventolin and told me, 'The spray (just one puff in the morning with early morning tea) still provides the most miraculous relief which lasts pretty well all day!' But, as time went on, 'just one puff' proved insufficient. Mid-1978 he reported, 'There is a Becotide in the affairs of man, which taken at the flood... leads to oodles of long-lost mental energy... My doctor suggested it as an additional inhalant with Ventolin. At last, after shying off it for years I am getting down to writing my Mémoirs, and, if Becotide holds out, am hoping to get the book completed well before the new road and Nyali-Mombasa bridge are. The contractors never allowed for our freak downpour of almost continuous rain. It has let up a little now, but we still get sudden storms and gusts of very cold wind.'

Now, the trio was reunited at Chateau Maule and Don was working, which, as Mollie knew, 'gives him a renewed interest in life' while Baggage was happy to have his people safely back together on his territory. He had been their treasured child since 1965. Beloved beyond all riches and in return he gave uncritical, unconditional love and companionship. This state of affairs suited all three admirably.

They had, indeed, Done All That, but there was a time when the strain had almost destroyed them: In 1967 when Don wished to 'Quit the DM instantly and forever'; when Jean Hayes told me, 'Mollie has been in a fine state of nerves for so long now'; when Don had been shipped to South Africa to recuperate; when Mollie had come to London to discuss the matter of my taking over the management of their theatre. She had, one evening alone in my flat, written to her husband:

'I've waited until I had time and quiet and I hope the capacity to write to you on a very emotional subject — no other than our future life together. You are not going to like this letter but things in it have got to be said. I hope you are feeling better mentally and physically to be able to read it without getting too upset. After nearly four weeks complete rest I hope you will be able to "take it." '

She could not know that her husband was in no way rested or improved. Quite the contrary.

Her letter continued, 'Now, firstly, I know you love me in your own selfish, self-centred way. I had hoped that over the years you would grow more considerate and less selfish, but this isn't the case. You wound me so unbearably at times that I could curl up and die... You yourself veer between your moods of arrogant self-confidence when you play (live?) the big business tycoon... brooking no interference or criticism from me and the other extreme when you need me to boost your waning morale and retreat into illness as a means of escape. I don't mean by this that the illness is imaginary, I know it isn't, but it is a mental rather than a physical illness. But whichever end of the scale you are living you take it out on me in the form of reproaches...

'How are we to continue our life together in the future when I won't be able to anaesthetise myself with work? I know that you think that when we are free of the constant worry of the theatre everything will be different and we will live in the spirit of sweet reasonableness. I don't believe that. Although I realise we can't go on working in the theatre forever and I would love to have a little less worry and anxiety. A little less responsibility — I also know my life will be horribly empty without the interest which has been my whole life for so many years.' She then touched on Don's ill-judged, frantic letters to me with the instruction to address my reply to the club. 'The final betrayal of sending everything to Annabel hoping that she would accept the offer and the whole thing would be a *fait accompli* before I knew anything about it, that you could do a thing like that to me, after all our years of close partnership! I am still astounded that you could have done such a thing and please don't try and tell me it was to save me worry! Our whole future lives were at stake and I wasn't told what was happening...'

Her letter reached Durban where Don was in a doctor's care. He attempted a reply: 'At the moment I am so shattered and devastated that I don't know what to write. I realise the fundamental truth of all you say...' Her letter, a lengthy one, concluded, 'Even if you don't change at all, I will never think of leaving you. Although I am so very often terribly unhappy living with you I should be more unhappy living without you. After 47 years our lives are inextricably bound up with each other and I'm afraid we've got to put up with each other until the end.'

Don returned from South Africa after an absence of seven weeks, 'The most wretched time of my life', unhappy and ill. It was Mollie's resistance to retirement from the theatre which they had created that prolonged and exacerbated the misery.

Only when the decision was taken out of their hands; when Don's deteriorating health caused Charles Markham to take a firm hand; when finally they drove away, in a new Renault saloon, heading for Mombasa on January 2, 1971, was their 'future life together' assured.

Don made a diary entry: '...the longer we are married the more we seem to grow into each other and are content, July 3, 1920 until December 31, 1973 — 55½ years. What God-sent luck.'

Another: 'Mollie and I continue to live our lives in almost perfect surroundings in companionable peace.'

And his letter to her on her 80th birthday: '... All I am trying to say is Thank God for you and all you have meant to me ...All I want is for us to remain together until the end.'

And after reading *On Stage* and the press clips Mollie had brought back following the 30th anniversary of their theatre: 'Did we really do all that? Life's a rum go!'

Soon though, dreadfully soon, all this would change.

Henry Plantagenet and Eleanor of Aquitaine were still bickering at one another in mid-October. I had scheduled a five-week run; a big mistake in the circumstances. The play was not popular and now Jimmy and I were exhausted. On October 19 my father telephoned. "At last! I've been trying to get you for the last 48 hours. Mollie is in hospital."

Three days earlier she had fallen when shopping at a supermarket; not the famous OMEE's — another one, where she had tripped over a carelessly discarded carton. Her left kneecap had been shattered. An operation to remove it had been successful.

'There is nothing to worry about!' she wrote, 'But what bad luck. I'm not the sort of person who breaks her bones. With all my frenzied dashing about in the theatre and cutting lumps out of my legs, I've never broken a bone. There's always a first time for everything.'

I was particularly harassed by problems at the theatre at that moment. This was just another piece of bad news. Her next letter assured me, 'Don't worry about me. I'm doing fine and feel remarkably well.' Then, 'I'm completely out of plaster. My actual health is excellent, better than normal. No giddy attacks; no exhaustion except learning to get about on crutches and going through exercises to strengthen my thigh muscles. I leave here for home on Wednesday morning...'

A friend wrote, 'I called into the hospital to see your mother. Sitting in an armchair, beautifully made up, she looked so young and gay and rested and is to go home today.'

Don reported, 'She is out of plaster, but unable to move without two strong people assisting her, who must then continue assisting her while she tries to use crutches... far stronger than I am able to provide.'

Back at Chateau Maule she wrote of Baggage's delight. 'He blossomed and settled happily on the stool my injured leg rested on. It was like old times.'

The following day Don recorded, 'Shortly before 6pm I was reading on the veranda when I heard a loud cry from Mollie, from her bathroom. She had fainted, striking her head on the W.C. seat (breaking it!) and was lying on the floor, bleeding from head and recently repaired knee...' She lay wedged in her small bathroom. Anybody trying to open the door caused her further agony.

Back in hospital she was X-rayed and stitched up. On November 3 Don reported, 'Mollie looking wonderful and feeling fine.' She wrote, 'Poor Baggage was just pining away with being left so long on his own. It was quite pathetic, during the short time I was home he was so happy; but oh, for such a short time.'

Ten days later she was back home with plaster still supporting the back of her leg. 'The hospital staff tell her to take this off and try to do without, but Mollie is afraid to do this,' Don told me. 'She *just* manages to get about with the borrowed Zimmer walking frame... At 8.45pm I was on the veranda, a short sharp yelp came from Bags, lying under the table beside me. Then the poor darling's heart stopped beating and his tongue fell out sideways in death...'

> 'When sorrows come, they come not single spies,
> But in battalions.'

From this time nothing would ever again be merry at Chateau Maule. In a hard-to-decipher scrawl Mollie told me, 'I've lost all sense of time and can't remember if things occurred during my first or second stay in hospital. So much strain has been put on my arthritic arm and hand that writing is a great strain.' Don calculated, 'It is almost seven and a half weeks since Mollie's fall in a supermarket; and it seems like a lifetime ago! She goes up. She goes down. She had another terrifying giddy attack only two days ago — luckily she was sitting in her chair at the veranda table — so didn't fall.'

I wasn't able to travel to Mombasa. Eleanor of Aquitaine had relinquished her iron grip; now I was in the exhausting, tenacious coils of Amanda Wingfield in *The Glass Menagerie*. The theatre was spawning problems on a daily basis. Nigel Slade told the *Standard* readers: 'Tennessee Williams comes as yet another in the impressive list of fine playwrights presented by the DM this year, Shaw, Shaffer, Rattigan, Coward, Feydeau, Ayckbourn, Simon ... what other body here could stage all these? Indeed where could the like be done in independent Africa? As I've often said, Nairobi is very lucky.' In fact, Nairobi didn't give a damn.

The treadmill of operating the DM Theatre Club became steadily more arduous and more costly. The Government and Nairobi City Council were skilled in the business of extracting the cash required to pay their ever-more bloated workforce.

Withholding Tax payable on Authors' Royalties necessitated a great deal of paperwork and consequent delays at Central Bank of Kenya followed by the theatre's bank, which led to protests from authors' agents.

The theatre's box office was managed by two ladies working a shift system, but in reality three ladies were required. One lady would be absent on her two-month fully paid maternity leave. When the new mother returned, lady number two would absent herself on her fully paid annual leave. When she returned to work, pregnant, lady number one went on fully paid sick leave. All too soon lady number two went on *her* fully-paid maternity leave while lady number three was now asking for fully paid annual leave...

Mandatory Licences covered Snack Bar or Eating House; Liquor; Theatre Canopy; Neon Sign; Recorded Music; and, for each production, Stage Play. If these were to be obtained without argument or delays, bribes were solicited. As I would not pay bribes I faced arguments and delays.

Forms and questionnaires came flying from Government Departments.

Page after page of questions, only a few of which I could answer. 'Stocks & Goods on hand'; 'Income expected in the 4th Quarter of the Year'; 'Employees'; this one I could answer. Initially I had handed on one such questionnaire to my accountant. Prior to signing it I ran my eye over her entries and was dismayed to see that all the expatriates: actors, actresses, designers, all on British Actors' Equity contracts, all on Class "A" Work Permits had been placed in the category of 'Semi-skilled Workers'. Henceforth I thought it wise to complete such forms myself.

From the beginning of December it was no longer possible to remit money to banks overseas. This caught the DM's London account with only a minimal credit balance. Shortly after this, on Jamhuri Day, the newly-installed President announced that all employers were required to take on a further 10% of their existing workforce.

This measure, the fourth of its kind since independence in 1963, was designed to alleviate the rising rate of unemployment, which continued to rise due to the uncontrolled birth rate.

From London came a further blow. British Actors' Equity declared, 'The salary you are offering our Members is below the minimum salary which is now current in this country. Indeed our claim for the new contracts which come into operation in November of this year is for a minimum salary of £70 per week... For this reason you must understand that it is impossible for us to approve a contract that is below that current in this country. We shall not of course instruct our Members that they may not work for you but that if they do they will be without the protection afforded by this Association.' Equity's letter was dated September 20, 1978; the very day when the DM celebrated its 30th anniversary. 'There will be no question of our taking into membership any Artist or A.S.M. engaged by yourself and the weeks worked at the Donovan Maule Theatre will not count in any way towards full membership of the Association. I serve notice that the agreement between British Actors' Equity Association and the Donovan Maule Theatre is no longer in force.' Thus ended a bond of 27 years. It was Equity's refusal to acknowledge the different circumstances of an unsubsidised repertory company in Kenya when compared with heavily funded theatres in Britain that sounded the death knell of the DM.

At this time Equity was a closed-shop union. Possession of the Equity 'card' was essential for anybody seeking employment in the UK. Youngsters fresh out from Drama School (or, it sometimes seemed, Remand Home) were eager to work the stipulated number of weeks for a professional theatre company that would vouch for them, thereby helping them on their way to acquiring their 'card'. If the work was in Sunny Kenya, so much the better.

There had never been any lack of applicants; files bulged with letters, CVs and photographs from young, and not-so-young, hopefuls.

At this moment the DM company was in a state of transition. Some artists were leaving, the stage management was inadequate and we had been without a designer since August. I had, at last, arranged a replacement for this position and booked a flight. The new man would arrive at the start of the New Year. One problem, at least, was solved. In mid-December *The Glass Menagerie* came to its miserable end. I saw the following production launched then flew to Mombasa, arriving on December 22; exactly three months since I had last seen Mollie, waving to her as the M.P.S. taxi drew away from the Hotel Intercontinental. Don met me at the airport. His mood was subdued. On the drive home he told me I would find my mother in bed. She had, yet again, slipped and fallen in her bathroom.

As I came into her bedroom her arms shot up in a gesture of yearning distress. I enfolded her in an embrace and could sense her desolation, her wretchedness, her urgent need to be rescued from her situation.

She was tiny and frail and piteous.

Following four days of catering, cooking and emptying bedpans I returned to Nairobi to face the next body-blow.

A directive from the Kenya Government made the purchase of tickets for air travel in Kenyan currency subject to approval from Central Bank of Kenya. A "fee" of K£100 must accompany each application. In the case of incoming expatriates a Work Permit must also accompany the application. This had the effect of making it impossible for me to fly anyone into Kenya and more difficult, and costly, to fly anyone out. There was no problem if payment was made in hard currency, but I had no hard currency. The restriction sounded the second death knell for the already invalid DM.

The theatre's charter was 'To afford members facilities for seeing a maximum number of professionally produced plays throughout the year.'

How was this to be done?

At that moment with the help, once again, of the Blessed St. Alan. *Bedroom Farce* would be the first production of 1979. But to follow? The company would dwindle further still when the Ayckbourn play ended in February and two or three people left.

I couldn't meet Equity's terms. It wasn't possible to obtain the necessary Class "A" Work Permit for an artist before their arrival in Kenya, so it wasn't possible to apply to Central Bank for permission to buy them an air ticket. It was Catch 22.

'Good Luck to the Donovan Maule in 1979 in their unremitting efforts to divert our thoughts to other directions than the realism of everyday life.' — *Sunday Nation,* January.

The new designer arrived on January 3 and the following day

we held the first production conference for *Bedroom Farce*. I noted: 'Set designer is going to be *very difficult!*' This was an understatement. We had a Monster-P-in-a-Poke in our midst.

Within hours he was busy stirring up trouble among the remnants of the resident company. His instant distaste for the DM Theatre and, more selectively, the Managing Director, was palpable. The plays we did, the manner in which we did them, the whole tone of the Theatre Club caused such withering contempt, such sneering ridicule that the very least we should do was quietly to curl up and cease, without demur, to exist.

'If the DM continues to maintain such a high standard 1979 should be a bumper year for the company. *Bedroom Farce* is a splendid start to the new season...' — *Sunday Nation.*

Unhappily the 'high standard' was not maintained. Next came *Gigi* (the play, not the musical version), which I could *just* manage to cast with the help of one guest artist — Dorothy Gibbs — and casting myself.

The director Jimmy Ward, the stage manager and I endured production conferences with Monster-Pig at which prolonged argument and plain abuse was handed out. Finally, on a Sunday in February, Jimmy set eyes on the scenery for Colette's middle-class Parisian living-room, circa 1900. He told me, "Our worst fears are confirmed — the set is quite horrendous." Encountering the designer on the point of leaving the theatre, Jimmy requested a repaint.

"Certainly not!" was the rejoinder.

"Then will you please stay away from the set?"

"But of course!"

Several members of the cast, together with the stage crew, now set to work. Suddenly there was a great 'company feeling'. There was sufficient paint, at a cost of more than K£100 over and above the two bolts of *americani* he had ordered, for them to effect the alterations needed. By Monday midday things looked a lot better. The afternoon was spent hanging curtains, sewing on trimmings and polishing furniture. We were ready for the photo call on schedule.

That morning, Monster-P had received my letter of dismissal and I awaited his response. This duly arrived: demands for compensation. A hastily convened meeting was held at our lawyer's office. The demands were downsized and settled. The necessary paperwork, accompanied by the K£100 fee, was forwarded to Central Bank and their approval was anxiously awaited. If, for any reason, permission was withheld, we would be stuck with him...

He departed on February 16 taking with him, or in some other way abandoning, the whole set of keys including the 'master' to every door in the theatre. We had returned to the situation of six weeks earlier: we were without a designer.

Gigi opened on St. Valentine's Day but this Saint did not exert the same magic as the Blessed St. Alan. Reviews were mixed with the single exception of Dee Gibbs, playing Great Aunt Alicia, who drew warm praise. Dee had been seen so many times on the DM stage. She stepped in, at appallingly short notice, to play Lady Bracknell in *The Importance Of Being Earnest* in 1965 when Gwen Alban collapsed. She was a delightful Prioress in *Canterbury Tales* at Christmas 1970 and together with James Ward she had created a great comedy-duo in *Dead Easy* in 1973. As Lady Kitty in *The Circle* she scored again. It was always a pleasure to have Dee in a show. She was affectionate and warm-hearted and audiences loved her.

My most immediate problem was how to cast the next play. Two further departures when *Gigi* ended reduced the company to anorexia.

Jimmy solved the problem. *Rattle of A Simple Man* was basically a two-hander with a third character in a small role. Jimmy directed, played the third character and designed the set, which was constructed by Tim Ngui, the theatre's head carpenter. The play opened on March 14 but Dee was not among the first-night audience. She had died in hospital the previous Monday — the result of a road accident.

She and Bill, her husband, had gone *'bundu-bashing'* as they named it, on the Sunday after *Gigi* closed. While travelling in the Kedong side of the Ngong Hills, a Safari Rally vehicle, on a test drive, came round a blind corner at high speed, braked on the murram surface and skidded, causing a head-on collision.

I had accompanied the Gibbs' on numberless Sunday excursions, exploring anywhere within a day's drive of Nairobi. A waterfall we came across in the Aberdares was named Maule's Falls. We bathed in the pool at its foot, gasping with shock when the cold, clear mountain water washed over our sun-warmed skins and laughing at the sight of Bill's safari hat floating away on the surface when he submerged. The air was like chilled wine and we were intoxicated with the beauty and tranquillity of our surroundings.

I had been with them on the safari to the Kinangop and Sasumua Dam. We had stopped en route for a cold beer, sitting on a grassy knoll overlooking the Rift Valley. Lake Naivasha glinted below and Africa stretched away, immense in the sunshine. I glanced at Dee. She was intent, gazing at the view, imprinting it on her mind. She embraced life with so much joy and fervour, radiating her pleasure to those around her. A week later she was dead.

I had not only lost a friend, I had also lost an actress.

More and more, maintaining the DM resembled training a dysfunctional camel. If one portion of the beast was up and running, other sections remained clamped.

I now made the discovery that the General Manager, a key figure in the main office, was suspect. Vital daily paperwork was delayed or overlooked. All the Petty Cash floats were plundered. Beer ordered from our distributors never reached the theatre. His frequent personal cheques, drawn for cash, were dishonoured. Each and every day disclosed further misdemeanours. I called in the CID.

With his departure more and yet more irregularities came to light. A drawer in his desk was found brimming with work-sheets claiming overtime payments due to the bar and catering staff

I set about checking these: they dated back for months, payment was dreadfully overdue. Presently I grew suspicious. I consulted a calendar and found that overtime pay was being claimed for drudgery performed on days when the theatre never opened: Sundays and public holidays and (most negligent of all) the lengthy period of mourning for the late President. It became clear that fictitious claims were routine.

A blatantly racist representative from the Union, a Mr. Kariuki, stormed into my office, abusive and threatening, demanding that I pay immediately and in full. I insisted on checking the figures while Mr. Kariuki fumed and protested. I prepared more accurate figures while still allowing for many bogus hours. Mr. Kariuki grew choleric. He would arrive, unannounced, shouting accusations and insults. An elaborate "Court of Enquiry" was convened attended by the Union's shop steward (the Cook) and the secretary (the Electrician) in the glowering presence of Mr. Kariuki.

Meticulously I proved the accuracy of my figures; so meticulously that the Cook and the Electrician, embarrassed, urged me to reach the end of the shameful matter. But I would not 'cut to cues'. "This day — you see by this calendar — was a Sunday; and this day was Jamhuri Day. The theatre was not open..."

Reduced to smouldering silence, Mr. Kariuki witnessed while payments were made and the meeting was closed. Due to the Cook's absence from the kitchen, lunch in the Club lounge was somewhat delayed.

Following their letter of September 1978, Equity made known their ruling in the weekly trade paper, *The Stage,* in November.
DONOVAN MAULE THEATRE NAIROBI
'There is no longer any agreement between Equity and this theatre. Members should be aware that they are working without the protection of Equity, and further that such employment will not be considered as professional experience for the purposes of Full Membership.'

Then, in April 1979 they repeated their warning. This prompted the resignation of an actor halfway through rehearsals for the next production. There now remained only Five Green Bottles...

The Killing Of Sister George required a cast of four women. If I played "George" and invited a guest artist to complete the cast, we could mount one further production. At a break in rehearsal I read Equity's latest bulletin in *The Stage:*

THE DONOVAN MAULE THEATRE NAIROBI

'Members are instructed not to accept engagements at this theatre. Full details from Equity office.'

I wrote immediately to Equity and so, too, did our lawyers. Neither of us received a response.

This, coupled with the cost of Work Permits (raised by 600%) was the final knock-out blow. There was no future for the Donovan Maule as a professional repertory company.

Since early in the year this had been common knowledge around Nairobi. The Chairman of the Nairobi City Players came to see me. He was furnished with all the information he asked for and departed. I heard nothing further.

The livelihood of many people was at stake. Would-be purchasers of the valuable plot came sniffing round, looking for a bargain, not interested in theatre.

The Killing of Sister George opened in mid-May; a poor choice on my part. A letter to the Editor of the *Standard* enquired, 'Really, I mean to say, do we really want to spend an evening watching two lesbians?' Ten days later Nigel Slade called to return a play-script he had borrowed. I told him the sale of the theatre to a bargain-hunter was imminent. He urged me to allow him to contact Falkland. When James telephoned I told him the asking price, K£105,000, and that he had just 48 hours to raise the money.

Falkland got the theatre he wanted and Slade got the front page 'scoop' *he* wanted: the news broke in the *Standard* on June 1, Madaraka Day, 1979. Nigel quoted me: 'Conditions, including recently introduced regulations, make it impossible for the present format to continue.'

At the matinée that day I stood in the wings waiting to make my first entrance as Sister George. To my right the murmur of the audience penetrated the thick blue velvet curtains. On my left the sweep of the cyclorama gleamed white. We had spent the Easter weekend repainting it, not getting to bed until 3am each morning. How many times had the cyc been painted? With medieval castles, with Alpine chalets, with rooftop, with skyscrapers, with rustic cottages, with landscapes, with seascapes, with clouds, with trees...

So many plays, so many personalities, so many talents, so many workers. Soon I would no longer be any part of all this. No longer would it be my concern if fag-ends and half-empty coffee mugs, abandoned when the morning's rehearsal broke, remained uncollected by an unobservant A.S.M. If the working lights were left burning throughout a 'long' weekend, when everyone made off to the coast or upcountry, that would not be my business. If a dressing room had been left unlocked with consequent thefts of valuables, I would not be there to hear the complaint. I would no longer be there at all.

The red WARNING light put the tabs-man in the O.P. corner on the alert. Then came the green, followed by the swish of the heavy house curtains as they rose. I squared my shoulders and strode onstage as June Buckridge — star of a long-running radio soap centred on a hymn-singing District Nurse: Sister George.

It was my last role at the DM and, unfortunately, far from being one of my best.

CHAPTER ELEVEN

'Mollie's daily routine, since she fell and broke her kneecap, has been — and still is — pretty grim', Don recorded in January 1979. 'Waking after an almost sleepless night; arthritis in her arm and shoulder plus stabbing pains in her knee, she waits for the dawn and Musa to bring tea at 6am. I try to comfort her but am so breathless and disabled myself... The intricate business of getting Mollie washed, emptying slops, conveying a multitude of small necessities hither and thither and finally rolling up rugs and getting Mollie into wheelchair and fixed up with footstool cushions etc. on the veranda, is exhausting.'

Several old Persian rugs were scattered across the highly polished tiled floors of Chateau Maule. On my first visit following her accident I said, "Those rugs will have to come up."

Don retorted, "She'll never stand for that!" Nor would she! I had myself confiscated the rugs before departure, but back they came, their curling edges and knotted fringes an accident waiting to happen.

In early March Mollie wrote, 'I've got a very difficult decision to make. It seems something vital was broken during one of my falls and that I ought to have another operation. Even then I may never be able to walk quite normally. I have heard this from the physiotherapist who talked to the surgeon. Meantime I get deafer and deafer. Old age has descended on me so rapidly and I haven't become acclimatised.'

Once again she was taken to Mombasa Hospital. Don took the opportunity to install a non-slip mat in her bathroom. She was home toward the end of March, but a month later she told me, 'The last operation wasn't a success, or if it was, I buggered it up by slipping again. You've no idea how easy it is to slip when you've got one completely unsteady leg...'

She made no mention of the fact that she had spurned the non-slip mat and ordered it removed on her return from hospital. Two days later she had fallen again.

Don's quality of the life that remained to him was being swiftly eroded. A diary entry begged, 'Oh for the return of sanity and *peace* if only that of the grave or the crematorium.'

In an attempt to distance himself from his shattered domestic surroundings he turned once more to his Mémoirs, endeavouring to recall and record a world of touring the 'Smalls' with Miss Lydia Donovan, his actress-manageress mother in *East Lynne*. Remembering his first encounter with the actor who was his real father, a meeting made by appointment, at an A.B.C. teashop in Regent's Street.

"What would you like?" asked his father. "Poached egg on toast, please. And tea." Then, as the waitress approached, "Might I have two eggs?"

The tours of *Peter Pan* sent out by a management that ran to the luxury of a wardrobe mistress who set out freshly laundered pyjamas for 'John' in the dressing room on Monday and Wednesday in every town... But presently his concentration would be cut short by a plaintive cry from the veranda: "Don!" Painfully, breathing hard, he would go to her. "I think I'll go back to bed... "

She never became 'acclimatised' to the old age that had come upon her so suddenly. Her personal world had suffered such a drastic reversal that, at her advanced age, she was unable to handle it. Perpetual fatigue and lassitude plunged her into profound depression. The indignity of needing help to the bathroom (a weak bladder and uncertain bowels made the visits ever more frequent) was unendurable but had to be endured.

The excellent suggestion that a lady of 'meagre means' should live in to act as housekeeper and general 'help' was swept aside as unacceptable.

Her erratic letters to me became more and more difficult to puzzle out as faint, shaky writing fell away to the side of the page and words were repeated or omitted altogether.

Unable to hear, unable to write, unable to walk, she knew she could no longer be of use.

Chateau Maule had become Bleak House.

Sister George was finally killed off on June 9, at which point I would have liked to hand over the theatre to James Falkland but he particularly wanted the shortest possible interval between my administration and his to avoid the theatre going 'dark'. This meant one further production.

"We could do a revival of *Why Not Stay For Breakfast?*", Jimmy Ward told me. "Cut those two tiny roles of hippies — they'll never be missed. I'll play George. Kenneth directs..."

Through the traumatic months I had received unstinting support from Jimmy. A tower of strength with an unquenchable sense of humour, he had kept me going and kept me laughing against all odds.

And — for this final production, number 350 — Kenneth wrote his final *On Stage, The Magazine Programme of the Donovan Maule Theatre Club*. He had been its Editor and sole contributor and never missed a deadline. The final issue, number 12 in Volume 23, brought the record to a neat and masterly close.

I had wished to bring the Maule administration to an end without fuss — just extinguish the lights and hand over the keys to Falkland. *Why Not Stay For Breakfast?*, a tepid little comedy, opened to a tepid reception and continued on its tepid way toward July 7, thus allowing me to work out terminal benefits for the staff; inform the Labour Department; the Union; the Federation of Kenya Employers; the Hotelkeepers' Association and anyone else who had to know. I was kept busy. Presently I got wind of the fact that theatre-goers were urgent to attend on Saturday July 7. The house was booked. Fully booked. Overbooked.

In the same manner in which the auditorium had overflowed on June 17 1958, at the opening of the newly-built theatre, so now, 21 years later, theatre-goers wished to attend at the Wake.

Some kind of ceremony was being planned by a few enthusiasts. The matter was out of my hands which allowed me to address the pile of paper on my desk until news came from Mombasa: The aged parents planned to attend on July 7. Mollie, nearly 82, couldn't walk. Don, over 80, couldn't breathe. The prospect was appalling.

Don wrote, 'Now, don't put a damper on any of this. On the contrary, I hope you may be pleased.'

My diary entry for that Saturday in July 1979 reported 'Weather VILE. Cold, raining and very, very dark.'

A small detachment of volunteers: Kenneth Mason, Nigel Slade and James Falkland extracted the two invalids from the overnight train... 'after a ghastlty nightmare journey...'

They were ferried to Nairobi Club where I arrived at 9.30 after borrowing from the theatre's wardrobe an armful of warm clothing, to find them in a crepuscular ground floor room where daylight barely penetrated.

A minuscule electric fire glowed sullenly in a corner. Don was lying in bed, fully clothed, his oxygen cylinder nearby, trying to get his circulation moving once more. Mollie, ashen and gaunt, fumbled at a chest of drawers, readying herself for a visit to Invalid Equipment.

After lunch I left them tucked-up in bed hugging hot water bottles, having administered sleeping pills. Falkland promised to bring them to the theatre at 11 that night.

They were seated on a *chaise-longue* set in front of the now closed box office; bundled up in wool and fur, a warm rug over their knees when the audience emerged from the auditorium.

There were congratulations and commiserations. Programmes were signed, tears were shed, cameras were clicked, gifts were presented and speeches made. Finally, when all the "Thank yous" and "Goodbyes" had been said, the founders of the DM Theatre, near collapse, were returned — in the rain — to the Nairobi Club.

I still had work to do. Over 30 years of non-stop theatre productions had accumulated a daunting mountain of paper alone. Day after day I read the contents of bulging files, discarding what seemed redundant, retaining anything relevant as the basis of the Donovan Maule Theatre Archives. Carton after carton would be filled and loaded into the ageing, ailing Holden station wagon.

At Hill Lane, a flat two doors away from my own, was now the office of Annabel Maule Limited. Joseph, the gardener/caretaker, helped me unload. Immediately, I would return to the theatre for the next shipment. Stuff squeezed into Flat 3 soon reached to the ceiling yet more — much more — remained to be evacuated from the theatre.

Every production had been photographed and a selection of these pictures displayed in large, glazed frames hung on all available wall space. John, the office messenger, loaded the Holden and we set off. The big car bucked and snarled as we crept, at one-snail-power, up Haile Selassie Avenue. Reaching the Jex Blake Memorial garden, where the road is at its steepest, the Holden came to a grinding halt, the engine stalled and the vehicle began to roll back downhill. John hurriedly set rocks behind the rear wheels. Together we removed photo frames from the grossly overloaded station wagon, setting each one on the lumpy grass verge. Large heavy frames designed to hang upright, did not take kindly to the uneven terrain and the tinkle of breaking glass became the *leitmotiv* of our labour. John set off at a run for Hill Lane, returning with Joseph. The Holden's load now reduced by half, Joseph and I gingerly essayed the remainder of the distance, leaving John to watch over the roadside exhibition. Speedily as we could, we unloaded and returned, making a hazardous U-turn between the ever-busy traffic on Haile Selassie. *The Lady's Not For Burning* — 1950. *Bell, Book and Candle* — 1952. *The Happiest Days Of Your Life* — 1954. *Hedda Gabler* — 1958. *Dry Rot* — 1960. *The School For Scandal* — 1962. Passers-by gathered to view this strange business. *The Merchant Of Venice* — 1964. *Saint*

Joan — 1966. It was raining now. *Twelfth Night* — 1968. *The Taming Of The Shrew* — 1971. *Crown Matrimonial* — 1975. 'Slowly by slowly', every frame reached Flat 3 and filled the remaining space.

At a well attended Extraordinary General Meeting of the DM Theatre Limited, held on Friday July 13 — the last to be held in the theatre's auditorium, the shareholders ratified the sale of the Theatre and received the glad tidings that for each Sh20 share they held, they would receive Sh19 in cash, while retaining a Sh1 share in Annabel Maule Limited. The change of name had been made to avoid confusion. Only the theatre building had been sold to the new owners. Hill Lane flats, together with further assets, were now owned by the shareholders of A.M. Limited.

On the Monday following the meeting I handed over to James Falkland the keys to the theatre.

Don was delighted with the course of events. For more than a year he had been urging me to 'get-out-from-under.' Now, he would receive payment for his large shareholding and the future of the DM Theatre, whether for better or worse, was out of the Maules' hands.

Back at Bleak House following a second 'Nightmare journey with nobody to meet us', he was 'Still feeling groggy physically, but raring and taring to get back to my book.' Unfortunately, he failed to do so. The visit to Nairobi left them further enfeebled.

Some time before, they had made the grave mistake of dismissing Musa, the cook/houseman, claiming he was becoming 'difficult' and 'dictatorial.' With his departure the domestic routine slid steadily downhill. Don fulminated: 'John a bloody awful cook. Without supervision the kitchen, catering and culinary arrangements in this house have been a shambles for months.' John was only one in a series of replacements for Musa. With the departure of each temporary incumbent it was discovered that bottles of whisky, linen sheets and assorted groceries had also departed.

An advertisement in the *Standard* offered the guest-room with bathroom en suite, plus 'board' in return for the services of a 'Supervisor/Housekeeper.' A lady moved in, announcing that Jesus had told her to look after the Maules. A week later Jesus told her to move out. Religious tracts typed on slips of paper were found inserted between the pages of a great many books at Bleak House. A cookery book yielded 'Grease a 12" flan tin "0 Lord! My Master!! Enable me to occupy myself in thy name only" and bake in a moderate oven.'

A handsome Englishman took her place. Modestly he admitted that he had, just recently, come into a title and an inheritance which, unaccountably, he had yet to receive. He filled the refrigerator with joints of meat, gave the Cook-of-the-moment a few instructions and left the house. Badly cooked, large meat meals came to the table, followed by even larger accounts from the butcher.

So, too, did a string of young Africans, carefully skirting the side of the house, to visit 'Sir' in the guest wing. Following his departure came the news that he had absconded with the staff wages from a nearby Golf Club.

Bearing glowing references (as an *ayah*) a house-girl arrived. She understood no English, knew nothing of cooking and ran away when assaulted by the current Cook. The police took away the assailant and the Maules were once more without indoor staff.

Mollie's lovingly nurtured garden fell into neglect. No longer were great arrangements of cool green leaves and ferns in well-polished brass or copper containers adorning the dining room. She could no longer get out to her fernery in the shade of the great, spreading mango trees. From her chair on the veranda she surveyed her surroundings and grew increasingly irritated. There was so much to be done: watering, cutting back, tying up... Where was Charles, the gardener?

Charles, who understood and spoke some English, was in Mombasa, taken there by Don to help with the shopping. This had become a near-daily routine and Charles found it hugely preferable to slashing grass and sweeping up leaves. It offered opportunities for gossip in the shops. It afforded him an up-to-the-minute observation of the vibrant life of Mombasa town. Above all, it distanced him from the recurring commands, made in a querulous voice, by a *kali memsahib*. This was the life!

Don's impatience grew as he waited at the wheel of the car, under a blazing sun, while a parking meter ticked away the minutes. Outside Mombasa's great municipal market his attention was drawn to an inscription on the cast-iron pillar at the entrance — 'John Lysaght Limited, Bristol, 1914.'

1914 — the outbreak of World War One and the cancellation of another tour of *Peter Pan* in which he was going to play a better role. Instead, he joined the Army; the London Scottish, but not for long. The Army discovered he was underage, discharged him and he was soon an actor again — available to replace the volunteers as they were sent to France. Then at the age of 18, the Army recalled him, not to the London Scottish, instead the 24th Northants claimed him and retained him until a diary entry in red-inked capitals announced: DEMOBBED AT CRYSTAL PALACE ON WED. JANUARY 15 1919. A tapping at the car window roused him. "No limes today *bwana*." Charles was seating himself with a brimming *kikapu*. "Also spinach not good. We have *sukuma wiki*." *Sukuma wiki* was much favoured by Charles.

Congestion on the overworked old Nyali Bridge grew worse daily. The drive home was slowed to a walking pace. Mollie was all anxious agitation. "What have you been doing? Why are you so late? I've been worried to death. Lunch will be late!"

Don asked for a cold beer and sank into his chair on the veranda. "Where's Charles? I want him to tie-up the hoya..."

Charles, having unloaded the car and handed over to the cook, was now safely in his quarters, out of earshot.

'If *only*,' Don wrote, 'Mollie would keep out of the kitchen and cease fussing!'

When would he be able to find the time, the solitude, the concentration to return to his Mémoirs? 'It takes all one's energy and contrivance to get through each day,' he told me. To his diary he divulged, 'Life with poor, inarticulate Mollie is so inexpressibly dull, damp and deadening.' And then: 'October 16 1979: A year ago today Mollie had her disastrous fall over a carton left in the aisle of the supermarket — which has blighted both our lives and so far, cost well over two and a half thousand pounds. Hid rejected calliper away in the guest room wardrobe to avoid Mollie seeing the damned thing.' A few days later he wrote, 'Ours is a vast expanse of hopeless boredom and aridity that seemingly can only be terminated by death.'

In December I spent a week at Bleak House. At the rear of a cockroach-infested kitchen cupboard, I came upon a quantity of broken china and glass: the legacy of many breakages by a succession of domestics. I bought glue and repaired what I could. For the remainder I instructed Charles to dig a large pit in the garden where I conducted a decent burial. There was a multitude of other small jobs to be done before I returned to Nairobi for Christmas.

At Bleak House Don was suddenly impelled to his typewriter — where he shot off another of his Newsletters — number 7 in the series. 'Christmas Day, and this is probably the last newsletter I shall be able to write ...The domestic arrangements of our house remain, alas, a rather hit or miss affair. Mollie, unable to use the calliper specially made for her, has to have someone with her when using the aluminium elbow crutch; even then she can barely toddle a dozen yards before exhaustion sets in — mainly due to arthritis. Our Christmas dinner consisted of some slices of rather tough cold lamb and a salad with watercress. Servantless, it was a terrific effort for Mollie and myself to get to the kitchen refrigerator. Unless a housekeeper-caterer-cum-companion can soon be found to control the servants and help look after us, I fear that on Public Holidays we will become reduced to nibbling a cold sausage without the niceties of table mats, china and cutlery which we haven't the strength to transport.'

The newsletter ran to four pages of single-space typescript and his typewriter, having shed its cover after many months, now lay waiting to be of further service. In early 1980 I was told, 'I am keeping on with my reminiscences, and it's the only thing that keeps me more or less sane — although it's bloody hard work!'

Overriding his anxiety regarding Mollie and the lack of efficient 'stage management' in his once-perfect home, Don was increasingly exasperated at the delay in receiving the money due to him, the major shareholder, from the sale of the theatre.

Why the delay?

The new owners, Theatre Arts '80 Limited, were tardy in the first place. The purchase price was not received until three months after they had taken possession. Surely now, he thought, he would receive his cash. 'The money has been paid by the purchasers,' his Christmas newsletter announced, 'but has got clogged in the turgid pipelines of Excess Profits Assessors, Solicitors, Accountants and Uncle Tom Cobley — so the Maules are still awaiting payment.'

The 'clogged pipelines' were quite other than those he named, but no less 'turgid'. We had to make an application to the High Court of Kenya for permission to reduce capital in the company.

This required sworn Affidavits and the listing of Creditors and Debtors, causing hold-up number 1. A Chamber summons was set for November 1. My lawyer and I attended, but the Registry had failed to list the summons. A fresh date was fixed for later the same month when the Application was approved. Certified copies of the Order now had to be forwarded by the Court Registry so that we could register them at the Companies Registry — hold up number 2. This took until mid-December and with Christmas looming, no further action could be taken. Hold-up number 3. Not until mid-January did the Certificates reach the Company Secretaries with a covering note from our lawyer: 'You must now be in a position to pay out Sh19 in the £ to the Registered Members.'

Don anticipated: Any day now! But hold-up number 4 occurred while the Secretaries set about sifting through the register of shareholders. Only those resident in Kenya with a known contact address could benefit at this moment. In mid-February I collected from the bank three fat cheque books of 200 counterfoils each. These I delivered to the Secretaries who completed the vouchers — hold-up number 5. The cheque books came back to me for my signature and I tried to reduce hold-up number 6 with a prolonged signing session which produced writer's cramp. The cheques were now returned to the Secretaries for mailing. March 7, 1980 had been proclaimed C.R. DAY — Capital Repayment Day — but at the very last minute, Central Bank caused a further delay. Not until March 14 were the cheques mailed. The Resolution had been approved at the E.G.M. on July 13, the previous year. While waiting, a few elderly shareholders had died.

So now I was left with the simple business of running Annabel Maule Limited? Far from it! Loose ends still attached to the 'old' DM Theatre flapped and tugged at me for many months to come. Membership fees received by 'us' had to be computed from the time the new management took over and returned to 'them'. Bar stock at mid-July was calculated and the value refunded to 'us'. Deposits with a number of suppliers had to be recalled. Monies *long* overdue from advertisers in *On Stage* had to be pursued with vigour with, unhappily, only partial success. If *On Stage* was no longer being published, recalcitrant debtors reasoned they could abandon their previous commitments. Suddenly, mysteriously, a communication from the Income Tax Department demanded:

FOREIGN ENTERTAINERS

'I shall be pleased to have the following information in relation to each of the years 1976, 1977 and 1978:

i. Name of entertainer; and,

ii. Gross amount of payment made to every entertainer.'

I was the Chairman, CEO, secretary, accountant and office messenger of Annabel Maule Limited and quite the most time-consuming and tiring of these roles was that of office messenger.

Researching the details for the Tax Department's request regarding Foreign Entertainers took many tedious hours' work in my role as Accountant. Trying to trace the large number of unknown shareholders in Donovan Maule Theatre Limited was yet another chore which continued for a great many years. They had scattered to all corners of the globe: Australia, Canada, Scotland, Spain, Hong Kong... In my role as office messenger I stood in line at the bank, delivered cheques and letters to offices in Nairobi and collected mail from the main Post Office. As accountant I wrote up the company's books in readiness for the auditors at the end of our financial year. As secretary I typed letters and filed copies. As CEO I had little to do beyond trying to exercise control over 10 one-room flats where the tenants broke lavatory bowls — *twice* by the same tenant — caused floods when a water tap was left open in their absence and performed brilliant exits leaving unpaid rent and accounts for electricity. Above all they never, ever informed me of their intention to vacate. Instead I would observe a stranger coming and going while rent payments were enveloped and slipped under the office door to side-step awkward questions. Flat number Two, right between the one I occupied and the Annabel Maule Limited office, was used as a lunch-time knocking shop with great finesse and surprising speed. When the loquat trees in the garden were heavy with fruit they were made heavier still by hordes of nimble little thieves from the neighbouring Kenya Railways staff houses. I didn't mind them picking the fruit; what I minded was the damage they inflicted on the trees.

Income to the Company accrued solely from rents received plus interest on some deposits. At every meeting of the Board of Directors the 'Future of the Company' headed the agenda but failed to be resolved. A professional assessment reported: 'Following the disposal of its theatre club business, Annabel Maule Limited is left with a small undertaking and much too many shareholders, so that the administrative costs are greatly excessive relative to the income.' Just so. Fees raised by our Company Secretaries swallowed what little remained after paying tax and the auditors.

When time allowed, I turned my attention to the Donovan Maule Theatre Archives. Flimsy copies of letters, sepia-coloured and nibbled to delicate lace by voracious insects, were painstakingly pasted to fresh, firm sheets of paper; their curling margins coaxed into alignment with the aid of tweezers and knife-point. I even brought the ironing board into the office and ironed out wrinkles and creases. Press-clipping files had been maintained throughout the years but now needed further attention. I incorporated into each production photographs and other relevant details thereby enlarging the file and pushing out the following productions into yet more files. When the work was completed it totalled 53 fat volumes.

Shelves were set up in one portion of the recently vacated DM Theatre furniture store at Hill Lane. There I set out my handiwork, each file neatly labelled: Date. Prod. Number. Play Title.

Number ONE — Middle East. Kenya. School of Dramatic Art. Production number 1: *The Guinea Pig,* September 13, 1948. Theatre Royal.

Number 53 — May 1979 *The Killing Of Sister George* (Revival) SALE OF THE THEATRE... Final Production number 350...

When spotted in town, going about my office messenger duties, I was invariably asked, "What are you doing with yourself these days?"

When Don finally received the Redemption of Capital due to him he speedily tied up nearly the whole amount in equities on the Nairobi stock market, thereby increasing his portfolio. At the same time Annabel Maule Limited stopped paying him his monthly pension which it could ill afford, being tax-free to the recipients but tax-burdened to the company, and from this instant Don was convinced that the wolf was permanently baying at his door.

They had no insurance to alleviate the ongoing and ever-mounting medical costs, and the irregular income from dividends made the shadow of the workhouse forever loom in Don's imagination.

Soon the sight of letters from Mombasa filled me with dread. The perpetual litany of woe: 'Wretched — Ill — Chemist's bills — Leaking roof — Telephone out of order — Overdrawn at the Bank — Shortages — Hard up — Ill — Wretched' made miserable reading. The distress was abated at the end of April 1980 when Elizabeth McConnell, whom I had met in Nairobi, came to Bleak House to look after them. Mollie told me, 'Elizabeth is a darling.' She even gave Don a good game of chess in the evenings. A degree of peace and quiet descended on the scene at the coast. Not for long, however. Two months later Elizabeth had left to fulfil a long-standing promise to render succour elsewhere.

Before dawn on the morning of June 23 I set off in the valiant little VW heading for Malindi. This was the break due to me from the moment I ceased working at the theatre but somehow, I had been kept busy until now. The next day would be my father's birthday and I planned to return to Mombasa and surprise the aged parents.

My diary records: 'Weather still and overcast. Parents, unhappily, likewise.'

Onlookers might wonder why I didn't take on the job of housekeeper and companion.

'Lizzie Borden took an axe and gave her mother forty whacks. When she saw what she had done, she gave her father forty-one.'

I wished to avoid a repetition of this at Bleak House.

In August, in the pouring rain, the svelte new Japanese-built Nyali Bridge was ceremoniously opened by the President.

'Our peaceful, NO-THROUGH-WAY, dead-end country lane, alive with colourful butterflies and birds, where Baggage and I used to walk in the days Baggage was alive and I was still capable of a slow and gentle totter, is now a six-lane motorway with toll-gate proclaiming:

"Foot passengers, bicycles and rickshaws free. Private cars Sh1 single toll..." So, though Nyali and Kisauni (both on the North coast) now have a post office, there is no chemist, supermarket, bank or any shop worth using. Practically all shopping has to be done on the island of Mombasa adding two shillings bridge tolls to the ever-spiralling cost of living. My eyesight and general inability makes it dangerous for me to drive and soon I shall no longer be able to do so. Mollie, alas! can seldom leave her bed. We have acquired a wheelchair, on loan, but it isn't entirely satisfactory. It quite exhausts me to write a letter, do the shopping etc. Have to leave now with Charles, for fishmonger, market, Omees, bank etc. It usually takes about three hours from 9am to 12 noon each day.'

At midnight on September 30,1980 the old Nyali bridge would close after nearly 50 years of continuous service. A pontoon bridge, which stretched across 1,300 feet of creek water, it had also to make allowance for the rise and fall of the tides. The work had been completed in 20 months and the Governor, Sir Joseph Byrne, performed the opening ceremony on August 8 1931. In its early days it carried fewer than 100 vehicles a day. By 1980 it was carrying 9,000.

I would play Lady Byrne in the film *Out Of Africa;* the little scene toward the end of the movie, focussed on the meeting between Karen Blixen and the newly-arrived Governor and his lady. The script outlines the setting:

'273 EXT. GOVERNOR'S RESIDENCE — WIDE — DAY — 273'

'An afternoon reception on the lawn. A long reception line after which there are buffet tables, bar.'

Nairobi School, deserted during the Easter vacation, was given a lick of paint and 'gussied-up' to stand in for Government House. Arriving at 6.30am on April 26 1985, I located my dressing room, one of the sports changing rooms, cement-floored and, at that early hour, distinctly chilly. A great number of us shed our jeans and sweaters and donned the 'best party frocks' already chosen and fitted at an earlier wardrobe call. My costume was glorious: fine silk and lace of palest cream in the style of 1931 was topped off with a hat down to my eyebrows. Thus attired, I presented myself to Milena Canonero, the costume designer. She looked me up and down, whipped off the hat and replaced it with a lovely wide-brimmed creation of swathed and folded silk trimmed with a great, sweeping feather.

Following a further appraisal she reached to a rail of costumes and selected a pale, lightweight, raw silk coat lined with chocolate-coloured silk. Each of its buttons was a small masterpiece of workmanship. This was authentic stuff; possibly from a famous Parisian *couturier* of the period. Gloves of supple kid completed the outfit. The script gave me two lines which together totalled nine words, only one of which reached two syllables! Nothing too strenuous.

By 5.30 that day the scene was in the can and the multitude at Nairobi School — stars, feature players, bit players and extras — were dismissed. "A good day's work!" shouted Sydney Pollack, the director.

I had certainly enjoyed it.

Late in 1980 Don underwent treatment for cataract, '...a harrowing and somewhat nasty business, as well as being very expensive. Elizabeth drove me to Christ's Lighthouse and we arrived exactly at 7am.' Mrs. McConnell had been and gone from Bleak House more than once since her first visit in April. Thankfully she was on hand at this crucial moment.

'Throughout the operation I remained more or less fully conscious, and to keep my mind off things repeated silently *The Walrus & the Carpenter* — all of it — several times. The prick of the needle for local anaesthetic was extremely painful but I knew it was essential I must not move a hair's breadth while the operation took place. The persistent silent repetition of the *Walrus & the Carpenter* did the trick. Elizabeth remained in the op. theatre and watched — which she said afterwards was pretty harrowing. Well, to cut an absurd story short, Eliz took me to Christ's Lighthouse again two days later. The bandages were taken off and Dr. Grist announced "Perfect". Eliz has to take me there again tomorrow. Have left little room to mention Mollie. Her condition is much the same — in bed nearly all day, with an hour before lunch in a wheelchair and again an hour in wheelchair watching the sunset.'

This letter, typed with scarcely any errors a mere three days after the operation, greatly encouraged me. Its mood of cheerful resignation struck me as admirable and I wasted no time in sending my congratulations together with my cheque to help with 'the damnable expense'. The nonsense poems of Lewis Carroll had always been favourites with Don. Excerpts from *The Hunting of the Snark* or *You are Old Father William* might be quoted if he was in a sanguine frame of mind.

Unhappily this occurred very rarely now. Anxiety for his wife overshadowed all his days. 'Mollie fell again last night. Am getting a special commode made for her bedside. This will have a sturdy post which Mollie can grip with her unarthritic *left* hand and so (it is hoped) a bum-slide can be safely accomplished. Cost: enormous, but what the hell! I want M's last few years (or maybe only months) made as pleasant for her as possible.'

Shortly before Christmas he took possession of this piece of joinery but it was reported to be 'A very unsatisfactory job. The invalid table has had to be cut down and it is *still* unsatisfactory; but after so many promises of delivery, numerous measurements and drawings by "experts" I accepted the bloody thing. Had I been 20 years younger, I could easily have made a better job at less than half the cost. Ah, well!' This was no idle boast. Had he not, with the help of friends, built a mini-theatre in 1949?

No longer did he maintain contact with a desk diary. 'Too expensive to buy and tedious to write... *and* read!' Entries in pocket diaries which I forwarded from Nairobi registered nothing more than the number of inhalations made and tablets swallowed every 24 hours. They were a sad reflection of his diary for 1956 which listed only the agonisingly slow growth of shareholders in the proposed Donovan Maule Theatre Limited.

Robberies at Bleak House had, once more, become frequent. Pole-fishers lifted from the dressing table near his bedroom window his wallet containing freshly-drawn cash for wages, together with both car and house keys. Locks throughout the house were changed shortly before the stolen keys were found abandoned in the garden.

Mollie now required a full-time, live-in *ayah* and accommodation for a third employee was built; yet another 'Damnable expense!'

The search for the ideal housekeeper/companion continued. Elizabeth had travelled to India. Don admitted the job held little allure. 'We need Florence Nightingale combined with the Virgin Mary; Mollie, alas, grows weaker and weaker every day.'

In July they had been married for 60 years and Don, in his Newsletter number 9 (the final one) dated November 1980, declared: 'The great thing is that, at all costs, we hope never to have to stop living in our own beautiful house and home.' Writing to me, his misery and despair were more evident. April 14, 1981: 'I feel I am living in limbo, too worried and distracted to attempt a proper letter.' And, just two days after this, 'Mollie says daily she doesn't want to go on living.' Shortly before his birthday in June he reported, 'Emphysema getting worse. Now almost blind I cannot even reply to letters properly or do household accounts.'

His last remaining pleasure (with the possible exception of a few tots of whisky in the evening) was now denied to him: compiling figures beneath a series of headings, in his neat small handwriting, thereby *proving* that the cost of living was rising ineluctably.

In July I paid them a visit, an exhausting and anguishing experience. I shopped for a few luxuries: flowers, fillet steak, wine... At lunch I wheeled Mollie to the dining table and cut her tiny portion of steak into bite-size segments. "Baby Maule!" she sneered. I filled her wine glass and she took a sip: "I hate it! Sharp and sour!" She drained the glass and tried the steak. "Tough!" I glanced at Don. His face registered his misery and on the instant he lost any little appetite he had. Mollie was now so deaf that conversation was impossible. His next letter told me, 'Unfortunately both breathing and eyes so bad I cannot look at anything or write more at the moment. Benny is being of enormous help. Can no longer drive car so he took me to the eye hospital yesterday.'

A handwritten letter told me, 'Thieves have broken into the house. All sound equipment, binoculars, my inscribed 30th wedding anniversary chiming mantel clock etc. Sorry to have to report that both of us are getting feebler and unable to fend for ourselves much longer. Am exhausted after trying to type statement to police and insurance company.' Then came: 'Mollie now almost completely bed-bound and self house-bound. I may be forced in the end to negotiate mortgage on house. Have not yet sold copper, brass, rugs etc, but may be forced to do so finally.'

His anxiety over money had become unreasonable. True, medical attention and chemist's bills were a perpetual on-going drain on income and rates in both Nairobi and Mombasa had been massively hiked at the start of 1981, but Don's income, in the form of dividends, kept pace and I helped out where I could. He was determined to worry himself to death. And then, astonishingly, a well-typed letter dated Boxing Day announced: 'Momentous things have happened! The cook has at last been replaced by a cook/houseman "Joseph" who *seems* a vast improvement. For Christmas lunch yesterday we had sausages, bacon, beans and spinach. Benny and his wife called bringing a new typewriter ribbon — hence ability to type this letter.' He ended with the cheerful 'TTFN (tata for now) as Tommy Handley used to say in ITMA.'

My relief was short-lived. By January gloom had once again settled-in. 'I *hate* all meals. Senility, I suppose also perpetual worry over finance. Benny has been a wonderfully helpful friend. Unfortunately he leaves for Denmark on February 20.'

Benny Wielandt had indeed proved a golden, steadfast friend. He changed library books for the Maules, bringing from the British Council fresh supplies once a week. Arriving at the house he would be met with the repair jobs requiring his attention: leaking taps, blown fuses, clogged shower-heads, the broken lavatory in the guest bathroom — legacy of a short-lived woman housekeeper.

Finally he would settle down to give Don a game of chess. His imminent departure from Kenya was a dreadful blow. He would, however, be able to fulfil one further service for Don.

I was directing *Separate Tables* for the Theatre Group when I received Don's letter in mid-February 1982. He had omitted to date it and this in itself was disquieting. Don always dated his letters. Mollie never dated hers.

He had mislaid an important legal document drawn up by my Nairobi lawyer. Could I forward a copy? 'I am nearing the end of my tether and many Stock Market shares are right down. I have renewed Mollie's Aliens book for two years.'

The Aliens Restriction Act had been operative since 1973. We all had to register and renew our *carnets* every two years. Don himself had no need to do so. Long before this he had become a Kenyan citizen.

'Our voluntary Health Insurance (he meant National Hospital Insurance Fund) has lapsed for want of ready cash or post office out of stamps when attempting to pay. Do you agree to NOT paying insurance on this house?' He added that their telephone had been out of order for days. It was serviceable however two days later when Mollie called me at 7 in the morning.

Don was in a bad way. She feared he was going mad. I made contact with his doctor who promised to keep in touch.

Don was dwelling on his problems, both real and imaginary — the latter taking on alarming proportions. Destitution stared him in the face. Assessments for Income Tax were outstanding; how was he to pay? He could not locate a quantity of Share Certificates. Had they been stolen? Where were they? I applied for Letters of Indemnity on his behalf. He was put on anti-depressants and kept slightly sedated. If fully alert he would seize on a new anxiety. Mollie was unwilling to have him hospitalised. She would be alone in the house. Finally his doctor insisted and Don was admitted to Mombasa Hospital on the evening of February 17 in a very weak condition. I set off in the valiant old VW. Rattling past the dusty dorp that is

Sultan Hamud, my mind flashed back to that first drive to Mombasa. When was it? January 1953 with all of us jammed into the Morris Minor setting off through the night on the first leg of the tour of *Bell, Book and Candle* when Don had said, "This must be Sultan Hamud" and I had savoured the exotic name "Sultan Hamud."

Arriving at the hospital I was shocked at my father's appearance: emaciated and the colour of putty with unseeing eyes. The mane of white hair brushed straight back from his brow, his most distinguishing feature, was now plastered close to his scalp, an uneven parting ploughed to one side. He resembled the man from the gas company, come to read the meter.

The guest room at Bleak House was occupied by a tenant, so I used Don's big study-bedroom. The heat was stifling and mosquitoes whined in the still night air. Traffic rumbled continuously across the new bridge. Sleep was impossible.

Benny came the following day. He was on the point of leaving for Europe. It was Benny who had taken Don to hospital, rendering the final service.

I found my father heavily sedated. He didn't register my presence. He was refusing all food and drink. I worked at his big desk, checking accounts and bringing myself up to date with their affairs. Locating their N.H.I.F. cards, I affixed the stamps I had brought with me from Nairobi. I found the receipt, dated the previous October, for the house insurance. From her bed Mollie gestured vaguely toward the bureau in her bedroom. "There are some papers in there..." I unlocked the fall front to disclose the missing Share Certificates. There had been so much less for Don to worry about but now it was too late.

On the Sunday morning a visitor arrived at the house: the Manager of the Maules' bank. He told me that their joint account showed a credit of over Kenyan £5,500. He suggested that the greater part of this sum should be placed on deposit in Mollie's name. He offered assistance in a variety of ways knowing that Mollie was immobilised in the house. I had to return to Nairobi where work awaited me and the production of *Separate Tables* was handed over to a fresh director but by week's end I was once again rattling past Sultan Hamud, heading for Bleak House. At the hospital I found Don weaker.

The next day, Monday, dawned beautifully as the Indian Ocean lapped at the sandy beach below the house and the birds stirred among the trees and the flowering shrubs in the garden. It was March 1, 1982. I reached the hospital at 8.30. Don recognised me and I suggested bringing Mollie to visit. He seemed indifferent.

Two hours later I wheeled her into his room. He was slumped in a chair at the open door to the veranda. The water of the creek glowed cornflower-blue.

They were knee-to-knee; he in his hospital chair, she in her wheelchair. Both were barefoot.

"Look at me. Look at me properly. Look into my eyes. Can't you see the love for you there? *You* may want to die, but I don't want you to die. For my sake, please stay alive..."

He didn't respond. Had he heard her plea? There was no sign. I felt certain he had heard but was too tired, too weak, too beaten to respond. He was deserting her. The struggle had overwhelmed him.

It felt indecent to be a witness here. I gazed at the water beyond the veranda. The sun glinted on the surface and a lateen sail moved from right to left across my field of vision. I recalled a cry of despair I heard him make the previous year. "Oh God! If I had the courage I'd cut my throat!" Alone in the hospital room with me he had spoken a little. "It's a concentration camp here. They pull me up by my hair." Then, following a long pause, "I can't afford a second opinion. They expect me to eat bacon and eggs with a knife and fork." His glazed eyes turned slowly to the curtains hanging at the window with their bold, 'cheerful' colours. "The mad hatter's tea party!" We were back with Lewis Carroll.

Something caught his eye. "What's that?"

"The shaving cream you wanted."

"They don't let you shave yourself here. It doesn't make any difference. It's too late now..."

It's too late now. He had said this more than once — about nothing in particular. Too late for what? To keep going? To complete something? The Mémoirs, perhaps? Rolled into the typewriter on his desk I found two sheets of foolscap interleaved with carbon paper: the rewrite of Chapter Four. He had been working on the Mémoirs until just recently, trying to get the memories onto paper.

Back in 1979, in April, before the strenuous trip to Nairobi, he had recorded, 'After my second evening whisky I almost always resolve to get down to writing tomorrow. After my third, I am wrapped in a joyful cosy glow of certainty with whole sentences and paragraphs dancing through my mind. My fourth and normally final whisky sends me into a blissful daydream of the magnificent and satisfying work I will do tomorrow. But, alas, when tomorrow comes...' With this last attempt he had reached Chapter Nine but had, as so often in the past, returned to revising and rewriting and stalled at Chapter Four. And now it was too late.

The following day I found him restless and distressed after a bad night, but nevertheless surprisingly lucid and vocal. Later the hospital called. His condition was deteriorating. Could I go?

I found him propped up in bed under an oxygen mask. As I came through the door a flicker of surprised recognition showed in his eyes before they closed again. He made an effort to speak but no sound came. "Daddy." I had not called him Daddy for years. He didn't like me calling him Don, so we had settled, in later years, on Ma and Pa. I took his right wrist, lying on the hospital counterpane and using my thumb, stroked his pulse. "Daddy." Had he heard me or had I too, left it too late?

The breath came painfully, laboriously and the minutes passed. Soon after five o'clock it was all over. His doctor, summoned from his home, told me his heart had given up the struggle, at last.

I collected the few articles: a dressing gown, a sponge bag, his watch strap. Where was the gold Omega watch he had bought in

Lugano in June 1969 on the final overseas leave? He had thrown it away. Told me so himself. Thrown it from his hospital bed. It had skittered across the green polish of the veranda and dropped to the rocky waste ground below. A strange look of cynical humour came into his eyes as he recounted this exploit. "But why?" I asked. The ghost of a shrug twitched his thin shoulders. He didn't answer me. A search was mounted but the watch was never found.

As I returned to Bleak House I was distracted by an amazing sky. Some time later Edward Rodwell's *Coast Causerie* told his readers:

'There was a Turneresque touch to the Island on the day that Donovan Maule passed on; a sunset such as we rarely see at the coast. The western and southern skies were ribboned with golden, red and pearly grey garlandry reaching up into the pale blueness speckled with feathers of cirrus. While driving home that evening a passenger in the car said that Donovan had set his last and best stage backdrop. It was the ebb of the day when windows burn in the reflection of the sun's last rays; when boles of fig and mango, clothed in shadow leave branches and foliage silhouetted against the sky; the hour, as Swahili folk say, is *jua laaga viti:* when the sun says goodnight to the leaves.'

I have never again witnessed such a dramatic sunset.

When I reached home, Mollie in her wheelchair was in the sitting room, facing a wall. As I entered, her face split into an angry grimace. "Why didn't he ask for *me?*"

To assuage the pain I said, "I don't think he asked for anyone."

CHAPTER TWELVE

What of the theatre which still bore the name 'Donovan Maule'? Falkland's first production there opened on August 1 1979 with Alan Ayckbourn's *How The Other Half Loves*. The publicity was deafening, the HOUSE FULL boards were on display at the Gala Charity Première and columns of newsprint trumpeted the success of the 'new' DM. The new régime planned a turn-around of 11 performances per production. Three professionals from UK were flown in by KLM. *The Standard* quoted Falkland: "They simply couldn't have come without KLM." They joined Kenneth Mason and James Ward as members of the permanent company. Local guest artists would complete cast lists where necessary.

Production Number Three would be *Sleuth!* in which Falkland had made his Nairobi début in September 1970.

The greatly hiked annual subscription fee promised members a monthly house magazine compiled by Kenneth. It covered 20 or more pages of art paper including a great many photographs. His column 'Pooter's Nairobi — Day by Day, Night by Night' afforded him wide scope for name-dropping.

Alterations were made to the actual building. Artists' flats became offices housing a General Manager, three accountants and a couple of typists. The entrance from the street was relocated and the box office was moved. Kenneth's glossy magazine proclaimed there were '...constant queues there.'

People who had never previously crossed the threshold of the 'old' DM now had to see and be seen, at the 'new' DM.

Within 10 days the next production was on stage, and then the next; revving up the number of productions revved up costs. Before very long the honeymoon between Falkland and his co-directors, those funding Theatre Arts '80 Limited, was showing signs of strain.

In March 1980 Kenneth's magazine was imploring: 'We need more members — many more.' In August, I met Peri Bhakoo, the company's Chairman, in the theatre's bar during the interval of *Middle Age Spread*. Over a drink he mused, "One year old..."

"Have you enjoyed it?" I asked. He pursed his lips and inclined his head, then sighed, "But financially it doesn't pay."

I allowed a pause then enquired, "What are you going to do? You can't go on pouring money into it — or can you?"

"I think that from the beginning I should have exercised more control." It was said that the company had made an operating loss of K£39,000 to date.

The warning bell sounded and I returned to my seat. By November rumour had it that Falkland had resigned as Managing Director. The theatre was in deep financial crisis and sponsorship from the business world was being sought. A large injection of cash resuscitated the ailing patient and the show went on with Falkland still at the helm, for the time being.

By January 1981 the marriage was over and he was testing the water outside the financially-heated pool provided by Theatre Arts '80.

'PHOENIX PLAYERS LIMITED (IN FORMATION)

'With reference to the non-profit-making theatrical company which you are proposing to form, with the above name... I/We confirm my/our intention of contributing the sum of Kenya Shillings .... to the Company when formed, on the understanding that this does not create any sort of obligation, but is an expression of my/our support for your proposal.

SIGNED ....,'

Completed forms were to be returned to 'Mr. James Falkland, c/o Donovan Maule Theatre.'

In February, 'In response to disquieting rumours about the Donovan Maule Theatre', Nigel Slade called on James Falkland.

'It appears that worries may be groundless. Mr. Falkland announced a programme of shows for the next four months. Asked why the members' magazine had been scrapped he replied that it had proved cumbersome and uneconomical to maintain. More beneficial to the members would be a season ticket scheme ...At the moment they had 1,000 members.'

The Season Ticket scheme, running from March to June, was launched, headlined MORE THEATRE FOR LESS MONEY — but it failed to appeal to theatre-goers.

At the beginning of April the services of the General Manager were terminated. In June Falkland was quoted in *The Nation:* 'The most disturbing thing I find about Nairobi's theatre-going crowd is their lack of commitment.' He was referring to the difficulties in keeping the DM afloat but there may have been a deeper disillusion. What response had he received to his Phoenix Players Company (In Formation) plea? August marked the second anniversary of the 'new' DM, and by October a different approach was being made to the 'theatre-going crowd': Subscription Theatre — 'There will only be Full Members, Temporary Members and Honorary Members. Full Members will pay Sh2,000 for 12 months (Sh1,000 for six months)' A variety of goodies were on offer under this scheme, one of them being a Club Magazine 'to be published quarterly, consisting of about 16 pages.' Furthermore 'Admission to the Club premises will be strictly controlled. Non-members will not be admitted in future.'

At the start, in Kenneth Mason's house magazine dated September 1979, he asked, 'May we request you to bring your membership cards with you on all occasions that you use the theatre either to book seats, attend performances or merely to have a drink and a bite to eat.' This rule had been flouted from the word go. It had long been evident that anyone who cared to saunter in and make use of the bar had done so. Also evident was the lack of control of the bar itself. 'Fiddling' could be observed with the naked eye!

Now, in January 1982, 'Guests will not be allowed to buy drinks at the bar. Only Members may do this.'

Nigel Slade told his *Standard* readers that the new subscription 'entitles a member to two free seats for every show (24 shows are envisaged for 1982), the same for every Sunday cinema show, free programmes... Temporary members will pay Sh120 for a ticket... James Falkland aims to attract 2,400 new members; if the idea fails, that's the end of the DM.' Shortly after Christmas '81 Slade reported: 'About a thousand people had taken out the new subscription.' He ended his piece, 'As the DM will now convey news to members its own way, probably much less will be said about it in future columns here. Certainly, and at the DM's wish, no shows will be reviewed.'

Excluding critics from productions caused a small stir. In January 1982 the second leader in the *Standard* was penned by the Editor-in-Chief, George Githii. 'The oldest theatre in Kenya, the Donovan Maule, has recently closed its doors to the critics ... The new owners of the theatre maintain that their new arrangement has become necessary because of declining audiences. In order to ensure consistent patronage, the reasoning goes, the theatre has had to introduce a scheme which enables patrons to subscribe on a yearly basis; if all seats have been paid for in advance, it seems there are some good reasons to argue that one does not need critics. While it is granted that owners must make money, it is hoped that they will not do anything to alter the character of the theatre by restricting exposure to the audience of informed critics. Critics, like journalists, are an important part of the equation of free society. They should be allowed to exist.'

In March, when I was still in Mombasa following Don's death, a friend in Nairobi wrote: 'The theatre is now in the process of being painted red, obviously proclaiming to the world the state of its finances. More than ever it looks like a strip joint in Soho, very seedy indeed.' In April critics were once again invited to review productions at the theatre. Compiling his 'round-up' of theatrical highs and lows at the end of the year, Slade called the exclusion of critics '...the unwisest move of 1982. It entailed a loss of essential publicity (even bad reviews are useful news) at a time when DM was waiting to attract response to an adventurous new membership scheme.'

So, how did this 'adventurous new scheme' fare? By April, the membership stood at 1,350 — a shortfall from the hoped-for 2,400. Kenneth Mason, writing in his reborn, slimmed-down, non-glossy, quarterly magazine reported: 'Our immediate future is assured, but it is also essential for us to be able to plan well ahead, and this can only be done of we have the comforting assurance of a committed membership... Such long term planning is only possible providing we meet our target of 2,400 members this year.' In July: 'For the assured survival of the Donovan Maule Company, it is essential for the club to have a minimum of 2,200 members by the end of 1982. The present number is 1,350. If we do not reach our target membership figure, the prospect of the DM Theatre Club closure is alarmingly real.'

Annual membership fees, received at the start of the year, were exhausted by the end of June. If the DM was to continue to the end of the year, K£40,000 was needed, right NOW.

How had matters reached this point? Production costs had risen, of course, and the Bar appeared to be one long happy hour where Peri Bhakoo generously stood drinks to every free-loader on the horizon. The ever-cheerful faces of the bar stewards indicated that they too, were on a skilful bonanza of their own. Bar stock-taking (if it was ever attempted) would have defeated any experienced accountant.

The one-time wardrobe department and administrative offices had been gutted to become The Players restaurant; all crimson velvet, mirrors and air conditioning.

A circular bade members attend an important meeting, at the theatre, on Monday, September 20, 1982. Nigel Slade told readers of the *Sunday Standard*: 'A sum of Sh800,000 is needed to prevent immediate closure, which if assured, could result in the DM being, in future, controlled by members, on lease from the owners, Theatre Arts '80. If we bale the DM out, what happens next? We support Phoenix Players, a company in formation and hoping to take over management from Theatre Arts '80 from November 1. Phoenix believes it can take DM through 1983 on a budget of Sh3.6 million. I was told by them two days after the meeting that an agreement "in principle" had been reached with Theatre Arts '80 for the November "take over" to happen.' There followed a news clampdown while "negotiations" between Theatre Arts '80 and Phoenix Players (still in formation!) continued. In October, Phoenix told theatre club members, 'We cannot, at this stage, make a definite statement because negotiations are at an advanced and delicate point. But our hopes are high so please be patient for a little while longer.' Members waited.

On October 23 Theatre Arts '80 reported, 'These negotiations have failed, and Theatre Arts '80 Limited is now considering other methods of ensuring the theatre's future.' On the last day of October Slade's piece in the *Sunday Standard* was headed IT NEEDS MORE THAN CASH TO SAVE THE DM. He went on, 'Recently the owners of the DM Theatre, Theatre Arts '80 Limited, announced that the DM is "not yet" in danger of closing down, as shareholders had injected money into it. The real hope for DM's future is in exact equation with how far Theatre Arts '80 accept Phoenix. It is not too naive to urge that they must — and gladly. There's another question. What of the present manager and "life force" James Falkland? How long will he continue with DM? He is believed to have resigned and then withdrawn his resignation. The situation is not clear and members' confidence will further depend on its being made so.'

On December 19, Phoenix Players — now out of formation and a legal entity — announced that 'in pursuit of its objective which has been to take over the running of the theatre not later than January 1, 1983 on terms acceptable to Theatre Arts and just as important within apparent reach of the members as a whole, it has become apparent that no deal is possible. We understand that Theatre Arts are about to issue a statement about their plans for 1983 and that this will embody an appeal for support at higher subscription rates. Theatre Arts have now told us that they are unwilling to invest any more of their own money and that, in addition to the operating expenses of the theatre (Sh4,200,000 per annum) a minimum of Sh1.2 million per annum must be found to pay interest on accumulated borrowing. For the moment Theatre Arts have chosen to go their own way.'

Theatre Arts '80, in a Circular to Members announced: '...the theatre will remain under our management, and will continue to run as before. Mr James Falkland will continue in his usual capacity as Administrator. We have revised the system of membership for 1983. FULL MEMBERSHIP January 1 1983 to December 1983 Sh2,500 SINGLE MEMBERSHIP Sh1,500...'

Thus ended 1982, a year that saw problems other than those of Donovan Maule Theatre.

Back at the beginning of August that year, on a Sunday morning, I had been startled awake by the telephone shrilling. "Have you heard the news?" The speaker was a friend who lived nearby and who had been with me at supper the previous evening. "There's been a coup. The Army has taken over the country..."

"What do we do?" I asked

"Stay indoors. There's a curfew. The BBC haven't got it yet. Nothing on the 7 o'clock news. Pity. I have very little food in — I intended to go shopping tomorrow!"

I replaced the receiver. A coup? Then I recalled being half-woken during the night by sounds resembling fireworks; little 'pops' of sound. Only they were not fireworks but gunfire. And not too distant. Stay indoors.

I gazed out of the big picture window of my Hill Lane flat. The sun was shining but it was chilly and dew lay heavy on the grass.

News. The radio broadcast news. I tuned to the BBC on one

receiver while VOK, the Voice of Kenya on the other, spewed out reggae. Bob Marley ochestrating a coup? The sound of gunfire, coming in short bursts could be heard. From time to time there was the thump of a heavier explosion.

In the neighbouring compound a chicken grubbed for worms while pigeons, oblivious to gunfire, concentrated single-mindedly on a single issue: SEX. Relentlessly the cocks pursued the females. Tirelessly they forced their attention on the fluttering, evasive hens. A movement in the hedge caught my attention. A thrush was feeding its progeny, of equal or even greater size than itself. The huge open beak urged: Gimme! Gimme!!

Sex and food. Life must be sustained even while others are losing theirs. Abruptly VOK went off the air. At about 10 am jet aircraft shrieked overhead. At 10.30 VOK resumed transmission to proclaim that everything was "under control... forces of law and order had regained the initiative over the rebels. *Not* the Army, but the Kenya Air Force. Citizens should stay in their homes..."

I thought it prudent to conceal the car, my loyal, battered VW Beetle. I locked her away in the garage. For the rest I just hoped that our location at the end of a dirt cul-de-sac would afford us protection. A helicopter whirred overhead. At 2 pm local time the BBC announced, "Kenya radio says that an attempted coup against President Daniel arap Moi has been foiled. Troops loyal to the President fought back. Everything is under control and people should stay calm." At 9.15 Radio Newsreel told me, "The streets in Nairobi are reported calm but with large numbers of troops about. A curfew is imposed. There was fierce fighting at the local radio station. Shops emptied by looters..."

The deep silence, the result of the curfew, from 6pm to 7am, allowed me to sleep undisturbed. The following morning I was up early to cope with whatever had to be coped with. VOK asked people who had abandoned their cars the previous day to please either drive them away or have them towed away. The news bulletin had only just ended when a volley of gunfire sounded nearby.

No sun today. Instead it was chilly, grey and drizzling. I went to my office. It was Monday, the start of a new week and moreover the start of a new month. Company books had to be brought up to date; office routine had to be kept on track. Later I released the car from its hiding place and drove to town, passing several abandoned cars on the way. Some had their bonnets plunged into a ditch, others were on their sides — wheels in the air. Windscreens smashed, trunks yawning open, doors agape. The General Post Office was closed. I intended to clear my post box and mail two letters. No problem parking; there was hardly a soul in sight. The moment I got out of the car there was a sharp crackle of rifle fire. I got my mail and re-entered the VW.

On near-empty Kenyatta Avenue police cars cruised, rifles poking from their windows. On rooftops sharp-shooters could be glimpsed. At the bottom of the avenue the dear old Theatre Royal stood untouched. Right alongside was a shop displaying costly china and glass. A magnificent dining table, set with fine porcelain and crystal for 12 diners remained intact. Just around the corner, outside a flower shop's closed doors, a delivery of fresh flowers stood propped against the shutters.

On Kimathi Street and Moi Avenue the effect of massive looting was plain to see. Heavy metal security grilles had been dragged forcibly from their moorings, smashed glass lay everywhere. Display dummies — pale, nude, dismembered, obscene — lay in the gutters and on the road. Torn plastic bags moved like amoeba, drifting among the débris. Bits of discarded clothing and worn shoes were scattered here and there. At the rear of the National Theatre stood troop-carrying vehicles. Army and GSU personnel were ranged round the neighbouring VOK station. Outside Extelcoms House on Haile Selassie Avenue a body lay sprawled.

It seemed unwise to linger in town — there was always the possibility of receiving a stray bullet in the head. I drove to Hurlingham shopping centre where a few shops operated, restricting entry to five persons at a time. Shoppers were swiftly emptying the shelves of flour, oil, tinned milk and dried milk, tea and coffee, packet soups, sugar. No fresh milk or bread was to be had.

News from the BBC at 2pm reported, "Nairobi is slowly returning to normal." That night I heard the occasional shot in the deep silence of the curfew. Tuesday morning was once again grey and chilly. There were fewer abandoned cars to be seen as I headed once again for the general post office, which remained closed. Suddenly a *Daily Nation* news vendor appeared and was instantly surrounded by a mob of eager would-be readers. To avoid being torn apart he climbed onto the Galton-Fenzi Memorial.

Wananchi pulled at his trouser legs, proffering cash, pleading for four, five, six copies. I managed to obtain one and emerged, dishevelled, from under the rugger scrum.

'The looting was done largely by *wananchi* who raced from their living quarters to "Get rich this day!" Men, women and children rushing by carrying shoes, blankets, *sufurias,* radios, *jembes* and clothing. Shops were strewn over the road as *wananchi* tried to grab loot...'

A *Nation* reporter saw 'several people injured in the city centre, several with gunshot wounds seeking attention from passers-by. But most people were so busy looting that they ignored their pleas for help.'

Long after dark a car drove into the neighbouring E.A. Railways staff quarters. In the silence of the night the noise sounded strange, alien and somehow, shameful.

Wednesday, August 4: BBC news at 7am reported: "Troops still search for rebels. There was a shoot-up in a shantytown area. Nairobi's curfew remains in force and Nairobi remains unnaturally quiet. Despite being urged back to work, people are staying at home." That very evening, following close on the 6pm curfew I heard a sharp volley of gunfire nearby.

On Friday, August 6, the curfew was reduced; it would now last from 9pm to 5am, which allowed a few buses to operate again. The lines of *wananchi* waiting outside the City Mortuary lengthened.

A week later, on Friday August 13, the *Standard* reported the attack on a family in Westlands by a five-man gang. 'The family contacted the police who arrived an hour later and explained that there was nothing much they could do as they were affected by the curfew.'

Firearms abandoned by fleeing rebels posed a further hazard, but there was a 'silver lining' for some: 'Renovators, glassware merchants and security companies have reported an increased demand for their goods and services following the recent disturbances. Stocks of plate glass had built up due to slow demand for new construction in the past few months and glaziers were able to supply the local traders for shop fronts from existing stocks. One shopkeeper commented that the price of shop front glass had almost doubled and the suppliers were insisting on cash payment.'

On August 20, the curfew shrank further — 11pm to 5am. Reporting the events of Sunday, August 1, 1982, an English newspaper spoke of 'the rebels utter ineptitude... The 70 men who seized the Voice of Kenya radio station and where they were due to die under a hail of bullets and grenades a few hours later, were junior airmen who all appeared to be drunk. Nobody was able to find any recordings of martial music so people who switched on their radios that morning heard the military takeover announced to the accompaniment of Western rock and reggae. On the streets airmen were helping civilians loot and vandalise shops. Some shot out locks while others pulled away metal grilles with their Land Rovers.'

On September 3, the curfew was lifted. 'Security' was deemed to be back to normal.

How had Nairobi's theatre and cinemas fared during the month of upheaval? At the DM, *Doctor In Love* would celebrate the third anniversary of Theatre Arts '80. It was scheduled to open at 7.30pm on Wednesday, August 4. They got off the ground the following Saturday and Sunday with special matinées at 2pm. Later, when the curfew was curtailed, performances started at 5pm. Cinemas screened films at 2pm on weekdays and 3pm at weekends. Showing at the 20th Century at the time when the rebels struck was *Those Magnificent Men in Their Flying Machines*.

With day-to-day life declared to be 'normal' once again at the start of September, it was later that month that '...over 400 members of the DM Theatre Club' attended the Important Meeting held in the theatre's auditorium, when '...a Members' Committee was elected and given the mandate to:

'1. Take all steps necessary to prevent the imminent closure of the Theatre and to negotiate with the present owners a lease agreement.

'2. To proceed with the formation of a Company — Phoenix Players Limited — which would take over the management of the Club from the present owners. It is hoped that this will happen not later than November 1, 1982.'

The negotiations were protracted and ended in failure, so 1983 began with the situation at the DM much the same. Theatre Arts '80 remained the owners; James Falkland remained the Administrator and Full Membership would now cost Sh2,500 entitling the Member to seats for every production until the end of the year. In the *Sunday Standard* on January 9, Slade's piece was headlined: DM OWNERS SHOW CONFIDENCE IN FUTURE and he quoted Peri Bhakoo as being 'emphatic that he meant to retain a resident professional company. "We mean to go on offering professional theatre until we are absolutely sure that Nairobi does not want it!" '

Slade was told that 250 memberships had been taken up already. The target was 2,000. Asked what would happen if the support was not forthcoming, Bhakoo replied: "We will have to change the aspect of the entertainment we offer... we would consider turning the theatre over for more use by outside groups and individuals, local and overseas. Mind you, we would offer members a *pro rata* refund first. But let me stress that we don't want to think like that and feel that we won't have to... especially when we were warned by the former owner, Annabel Maule, that a professional theatre was no longer viable." '

Later the same month Margaretta wa Gacheru, writing in the *Nairobi Times,* declared: 'The true meaning of professional theatre is being slightly obscured these days at the Donovan Maule Theatre where a full 50 per cent of the cast of its latest show *The Last Of The Red Hot Lovers* are apparently amateurs.'

At the beginning of May, Slade in the *Standard* noted, '...there are small but unmistakable signs that, for all the assurances given a few months ago, something is amiss. First and most significant, is the departure of three artistes ...they are not being replaced. "There are no plans to bring new artistes," I was categorically told. Secondly, what has happened to the programmes? At present they have degenerated into a single (and untidy) cyclo-styled sheet. Thirdly, I observe that the present production and the following triple-bill are of plays in the "public domain", i.e. plays on which author's royalties are not payable. That may be a coincidence. If it is not, DM has a particularly awkward question to answer. Theatre Arts '80 who have pledged faith more than once, must now make a definite statement.'

In mid-May Margaretta wa Gacheru told her readers, '...radical changes are in the offing for that lovely little theatre on Parliament Road.'

Just two days later a headline in the *Standard* announced: FALKLAND QUITS DM. Slade reported, 'I was given two facts by the chairman of Theatre Arts '80 Limited. One was that he had received the resignation of the Administrator, James Falkland. The other was that no show is planned after the current production ends on Saturday. He undertook to give a full statement in 10 days time.'

On May 24 Slade wrote, 'Yes, the DM, perhaps a tiny but very real light in Nairobi social life, has gone dark after 35 years of significant and in many cases unique existence. Why had this been allowed to happen at all? I promise to relay the answers in the near future, if, that is, there are answers, as there should be.'

Don's Newsletter number Seven, dated December 26 1979, had told his readers, 'Annabel sold the Nairobi theatre. We had been urging her to do this for some time, and were delighted when her letter came telling us that she had done so, and to a true Man of the Theatre who, with a partner, intended to keep the DM running as a place of live entertainment: professional productions, amateur ones, musical concerts. Hootenanny, one-man shows — anything that comes along to keep the theatre going. So far, I am glad to say that it appears to be a financial success, so far as he and his partner are concerned, and I hope it long continues to be so.'

By now Don was no longer alive to know of this outcome and Mollie was too moribund to care.

CHAPTER THIRTEEN

I remained at Bleak House with my mother for the first few weeks of her widowhood. There were days when she seemed to be floating right away from the world. Other days conjured forth vivid memories of touring with *Mrs. Wiggs of The Cabbage Patch* in 1908, recalling actors' names, salaries paid, towns visited.

There was much to do. I located the office of the Registrar of Births, Deaths and Marriages, a dusty office overflowing with even dustier files, up a great many stone steps in an unlovely side street in Mombasa. I joined *wananchi* jostling and pushing, trying to catch the attention of a clerk. For want of an official signature on the Death Certificate I had to return several times.

I arranged for the funeral at nearby Kisauni Cemetery. "It's where we all bury each other," an African told me. It took place on Friday, March 5, as the afternoon sun touched the leaves of the huge mango trees. Mollie didn't attend but she seemed pleased to greet the few friends who came back for tea at Bleak House. I had asked Joseph to prepare egg sandwiches.

Later, after a stiff whisky and soda, she was wheeled back to bed by her *ayah,* Rachel.

Denis and Dorothy Patience, near neighbours on Ras Kisauni Road, remained for a drink. Keen amateur actors in Nairobi prior to their retirement to the coast, they had proved true friends to the Maules since Mollie's fall in October 1978, helping out in a multitude of ways.

Dorothy now sat in one of the two big 'French' armchairs, seen so often onstage at both the little Studio and later at the DM. As I watched, she slowly sank to the ground. A rear leg of the chair had given way. On inspection we found the wood crumbled to dust.

Alarmed, we moved on to other furniture in both the sitting and dining room. Almost every piece was affected. 'Crypto-termites', undisturbed, had been gnawing away for years. A few days later all furniture except beds, was moved out onto the big veranda facing the creek; collected into a mound and enclosed under a big tarpaulin. A 'Pest Control Operator' pumped in some noxious gas.

The burial site was to remain undisturbed for 72 hours. Mollie and I ate our meals on a tiny, white-painted bathroom stool which had escaped the attention of the exterminator.

The denuded rooms in the house revealed the evidence of long neglect: carcasses of geckos and beetles, while gossamer wings and dried leaves floated along the grimy floor tiles. I bought a large tin of floor polish and mobilised the staff. Charles was mutinous. Gone were the happy days when he spent all morning in Mombasa with the *bwana,* extending the shopping as far as he possibly could. This woman, down from Nairobi, expected elbow grease to be applied. Hard work was the order of the day. She even expected him to work as hard as she herself did. This turn of events didn't suit him one little bit.

I switched my attention to Don's desk. I was using his large bedroom study; the guest room was occupied by a tenant. In July the previous year he had written to me: '...I regret to say I just cannot cope any more. Senility has caught up and I can only be dependent on others.' In September came: 'Have had to hand our Income Tax affairs over to local representative of Gill & Johnson. Have not yet had clearance for 1979!'

He had made errors certainly: the mislaid Shares Certificates; the matter of the house insurance... Now I found a note dated November '81 regarding his cheque for the premium, despatched to the brokers. Inadvertently he had filed this elsewhere and then worried that the house was uninsured. But as far as he was able, he was 'coping'. Rolled into his typewriter was the rewrite of Chapter Four of his Mémoirs. At the end of January '82 he told me, 'Joseph, new cook, is still with us. His cooking is considerably better, although I cannot say I 'enjoy' meals — roughly served and, due to essentiality of economy, about equal to prison or workhouse fare. Maybe it's ME — I *hate* all meals. Senility, I suppose; also perpetual worry over finance.' The comparison to 'prison or workhouse fare' was ridiculous. What experience did he have of either? As to his perpetual anxiety over money, in the very same letter he told me he had a credit at the Bank of Sh95,500.

He was determined to worry himself to death. And he had succeeded. I discovered a note: 'All things considered, I hope she will leave the world first, because the one remaining will have the unbearable loneliness; which a selfish man may be able to bear better than an unselfish, adorable woman.' It was dated just six months after Mollie's accident in the supermarket in 1978. Three years later he had abandoned her. I wondered about this. Perhaps the reason was that she was no longer 'adorable' and nor was she any longer 'unselfish' and he could not bring himself to witness her decline.

I expected to bring her up to Nairobi soon and install her at Harrison House, run by the East African Women's League and not far from my flat at Hill Lane. In one of the rooms equipped for geriatrics she would receive round-the-clock attention. Moreover, friends would be able to visit. Her name was on the waiting list.

With this in mind I emptied the bookshelves at Bleak House, cleaning and packing the books into a number of stout cartons and listing the contents of each one. This left the rooms barren and miserable. I worked at Don's desk, with frequent interruptions from my mother. As far as I could, I brought the household 'books' — meticulously maintained by Don — up to date, checking that payments had been made and receipts correctly filed. I knew Pa would have liked it this way. Then there were the letters. Such a quantity of letters. Some arrived in the Nyali post box, others — great bundles of them — forwarded from Nairobi. They all received answers.

At the end of March I returned to Nairobi to catch up on the work awaiting me there.

Mike Elworthy had attended my father's funeral. In the same letter to me typed (and well typed) in January, in which he likened food at Bleak House to that of 'prison or workhouse fare', Don told me, 'the manager of Standard Bank, Treasury Square — M.L.W. Elworthy — called here yesterday, gave me his card and offered to get money to us, also food supplies, just by telephoning him personally! Can't think how he discovered where this house is, but he miraculously found it!'

Mike — I never discovered what the L or the W stood for — came to the house directly after Don's death, to offer condolences and help. Where Benny Wielandt had exited, Mike Elworthy entered and was to prove a marvellous friend over the coming, difficult months. Two weeks after I left Bleak House, the Easter holiday brought visitors to cheer Mollie: Jean Hayes and Elizabeth McConnell, back from her travels. Jean told me, 'Your letter to Mollie reached her a day before we did last Sunday and there she was, sitting on the veranda waiting.

'Tears of joy. I found her looking very much better than I had expected; she has improved daily; in fact, apart from the afternoons in bed, she has been up all the hours we have been. So today we all take off for a picnic in the Shimba Hills; she's taken no persuading. Have just asked Mollie if she wants to add anything; she says how much good our visit has done her. She's a changed person.'

I was delighted. On Easter Monday I telephoned. The joyful picnic trip had not been good for Mollie: diarrhoea on an hourly basis with the doctor being called three times the previous day. I arrived myself two days later. Jean had departed, but Elizabeth was there and able to care for Mollie who was still unwell.

Once more I settled at Pa's desk to bring the accounts up to date. I found an Assessment for Tax for the year 1979 was payable. I also found an ignored dividend cheque lying in a drawer. I searched for receipts required by the Trustee department of the Nairobi bank handling Don's estate. Jean had written, 'Mollie is worrying about money but Elworthy came yesterday and set her mind at rest. I think she has acquired some of the habits of Don in this respect.'

When I had done everything I had to do at the coast I returned to Nairobi. Near Hunter's Lodge, in driving rain, I gave a ride to a woman who had a tiny kitten in a zipped bag, its head poking out at one end to allow it to breathe. Both were soaked. We continued to Nairobi while the windscreen wipers worked at 'hysterical'. I asked where I should drop her. She told me: "The Donovan Maule Theatre."

Early in May Elizabeth sent me a report: 'It is raining non-stop down here which depresses Mollie. Joseph was so drunk that he cooked the evening omelette before 7pm and kept it hot till 8pm. There is quite a roof leak in Mollie's room, between her bed and the window.'

Later that month Elizabeth wrote, at Mollie's dictation, 'Sorry to be so depressing but I miss Don most terribly — although he was not the brightest companion during those last weeks, he was always there and now he's gone forever.'

We were moved up a notch on the waiting list at Harrison House. Jean had told me, 'There is no doubt in my mind that Mollie will be better off in Harrison House; we have discussed it *ad nauseum*. Mollie admits that loneliness is not worth the view.'

At the end of July Elizabeth McConnell moved on. Mollie told me: 'Don't worry about me. I will phone you early in the morning if I need your help urgently.' The following morning, early, the phone rang. I was at the instrument as fast as the favourite out of Trap One at the White City dog-racing stadium.

"Have you heard the news? There's been a coup..."

Knowing that Mombasa remained untouched by the uprising and that Mollie found it near impossible to tune to the BBC on her transistor radio, I didn't fret too much about her. In fact she knew nothing about it until the following Friday.

Later in August she *did* call. A quavering, tearful voice asked, "Can you come down today?"

"Why? What's happened?" She was talking still, she couldn't hear me. With difficulty I got the gist of the matter. She had made an appointment with an eye specialist. How was she to get there? "Ask Mike Elworthy." There was a long pause. I repeated, carefully, clearly "E-L-W-O-R-T-H-Y".

"What?"

"The man at the BANK. Mike *Elworthy;* he will help you." Reluctantly she agreed. "Yes... I suppose... I'm in pain all the time... I get hardly any sleep. I was going to say I'm dreadfully ill, but I'm not. But I'm so weak..."

I stood sweating and trembling. The inability to communicate cast one in the role of a heartless ogre. A housekeeper now occupied Don's room but was in no way a companion, which was what Mollie yearned for. When I calmed down I telephoned Mike. He had it all under control. There was no need to worry.

Within two weeks, though, I was once again by-passing Sultan Hamud, heading for Mombasa in answer to further anguished early morning calls. Mike was away on overseas leave.

What was the problem? Mosquitoes. She had been bitten, then felt 'hot' and taken her temperature. Reading 102 degrees on her thermometer, she telephoned her doctor who was away on leave. His locum came and, using his own thermometer, found her temperature normal. He prescribed Valium. Before setting off for the coast I spoke to him. "She is suffering from 'nerves' ". Hence the Valium. He added, "She needs help to the toilet and the dining table."

Where, I wondered was her *ayah?* Why, I wondered couldn't the resident housekeeper help? I made a series of telephone calls and visits: Harrison House — situation the same, we were on the waiting list. Louise Decker Memorial Home? Inmates had to be mobile and in any case there were no vacancies. Pioneer Ward at Nairobi Hospital? As a last resort, perhaps, but I knew she would hate it.

Before this I had written to her own doctor asking for his professional opinion. On his return from leave he telephoned me: "She is fine. NOT ill... but she is lonely. The Valium seems to have done wonders." I told him I planned to drive down the following day.

At Bleak House I found the *ayah* gone and it was evident to me that the housekeeper would not be staying very much longer.

I tried to shake down Mollie's thermometer but it stuck, stubbornly, at 102 degrees. "Why don't you have a mosquito net?" I asked.

"I hate them! Feel so claustrophobic."

"Well, spray the room."

"I hate the smell."

"At least close the windows. No wonder you're bitten with the windows wide open."

"I'd suffocate".

"Switch on the electric fan."

"I prefer to have the windows open."

As long ago as September 1979 Don, heavy-hearted, noted: 'I am in despair to know what to do.'

In exasperation, I turned to what I knew *I* could do: work at his desk. I found it chaotic. By the simple expedient of getting Joseph to bring the entire drawer to her, where she sat in bed, she had muddled and meddled — it took a long time to sort out. I found another dividend cheque stashed away: unpresented, three months old. I also found she was overdrawn at the bank.

It was a relief to walk back to the nearby Patiences in the evening. Dorothy had offered a bed; there was none available to me at Bleak House.

Don's final letter, written in February 1982: '...I am nearing the end of my tether' came to mind.

The housekeeper resigned. This did not surprise me; it *did* cause me fresh anxiety, though. It left Mollie without help from the start of December. Elizabeth McConnell would be overseas until mid-

January. In any case, we had no lien on her. There were other summonses for her time and sympathy.

Applying her arthritic fingers to a variety of pens, Mollie wrote me letters which were difficult to decipher and invariably distressing to read. 'It becomes increasingly hard for me to write a letter or even write a shopping list [due to] the increasing clumsiness of my fingers. I drop things or knock things over. Twice I upset a freshly poured whisky and soda...' Back in June she had told me, 'My leg is a little better. It remains more or less quiescent until 6 o'clock or so then it begins to feel as though a great number of small mice are running around under the skin pulling wires. A whisky and soda helps to quiet them.' Later the same month: 'I fight an overpowering desire to have a whisky and soda mid-morning to assuage my loneliness and grief at Don's death, but know this won't do. I refuse to become an alcoholic.'

Don's diary of 1979 noted, 'Drugs as well as worry make her a nervous invalid — unable to think clearly.' But memory, clear and lucid, could come flooding back. Early in November 1982 I received a four-page letter. She had come across a book: *Recollections of a Defective Memory* by Fred Kerr.

'Now Fred Kerr was on tour with us, or rather I should say we the three Shiells were on tour with him in Pinero's *Preserving Mr. Panmuir* with Daddy as stage manager (there were no stage directors in those days), Sheila as general understudy and me in a whale of a good part — a horrible prig of a child... We had no idea at the time that Fred Kerr had been a famous star of the Hawtrey type and had been in management with many famous plays of the time. And was on a par with Wyndham and such like famous names.'

Indeed, Fred Kerr was accorded five close-printed columns of credits in *Who's Who in the Theatre*. He had played at just about every theatre in London and not a few in New York. Mollie's letter went on, 'Why he came on tour in Percy Hutchinson's company was a mystery. P.H. was known as the meanest bastard in the business but he always procured the 1st touring rights of the biggest successes in London and made a mint of money and was loathed and envied by everyone.' Right again! *Who's Who in the Theatre* told me, in a mere *two* columns of credits, '...made his first appearance on the stage as a member of his mother's company... subsequently toured with her for many years.' Here lay a similarity with Don's early stage career: touring with Miss Lydia Donovan, his mother.

Hutchinson's credits continued: 'Has toured over 50 West End successes in the provinces.' The fact that he was the nephew of Sir Charles Wyndham may have had something to do with this.

Mollie's letter went on: 'Typical of P.H. had hooked another week on the originally scheduled tour and I was due to rehearse for *The Blue Bird* the first week in December, so Daddy asked for me to be released. P.H. reluctantly agreed so long as we paid for a replacement. Which was fair enough. P.H. told us a few days later that he had found someone to replace me but she wanted £6 a week. Now we, the three Shiells, were getting £6 joint! But we had to pay the wretched girl what she demanded or forego my engagement in *The Blue Bird* which was unthinkable. So we paid and tried to look cheerful...'

This took place in 1912.

Curiously, Hutchinson's entry in *Who's Who* made no mention of a father. '...born Stratford, 1875; son of Emma Hutchinson; nephew of Sir Charles Wyndham.'

Fred Kerr, following an illustrious career on the stage, 'commenced his film career in 1930, aged 72.' This was at just the moment when talkies were taking over from silent movies. Before he died, two years later, he had notched up 14 or more films, the first being *Raffles* starring Ronald Colman.

Mollie's letter explained, 'I'm trying to write this on my knee in bed and the light is making my hand cast its shadow over the paper so I must give up until tomorrow.' I was delighted that she had got thus far and wrote to congratulate her: 'There is certainly nothing defective about YOUR memory.'

Continuing her letter she told me, 'Mike is back. He really is a great joy and comfort so very kind and thoughtful. I'm feeling pretty rotten everything is a great strain.'

Unable to travel to Mombasa — I had the auditors in the office — I arranged for four bottles of whisky to reach her.

'I meant to write you much more about Fred Kerr, but something interrupted me and I left him high and dry on the *Panmuir* tour. He was a sweetie and never attempted to "pull rank". He signed my autograph book (we kids *all* had autograph books and must have pestered everyone's life out) ...I had many famous signatures in that book including Ellen Terry's. Foolishly I lent [it] to the stage manager of some show we were doing. Of course I never saw it again.'

What she did see, though, at the Elworthy home, was the video of the Royal Wedding — between the Prince of Wales and Lady Diana Spencer. 'Had a lovely time yesterday... It's wonderful... I did enjoy it so much.' Earlier she had announced, 'Mike is back which is a great relief and we are arranging for me to see his video of the Royal Wedding in the near future. I was given three times to choose from which would suit me best: either morning ending with lunch, or afternoon with a cuppa, or evening with supper. I was so excited with the idea of being out *after dark!* that I opted for evening. But I soon decided that was crazy. By 7pm it is essential for me to be in bed lying flat for some time, so it's to be the afternoon.'

We agreed that I would not travel to Mombasa for Christmas. 'Of course I don't expect you to come down here, especially as the road is bad.' On Christmas Day, however, she telephoned just as my lunch guest arrived at the flat. "This is the most miserable Christmas of my life!" Four days later a neighbour rang me. Mollie had been "terribly sick" for three days. I managed — when the telephone system co-operated — to make contact with her doctor. "It's malaria, I think; with an upset tummy and diarrhoea.... not eating."

On January 3 the neighbour (the Patiences were out of the country) rang again. Mollie had "had a relapse. The *ayah* couldn't cope". Two days later I set off for Mombasa. Following much heavy rain the road was hazardous but the baobab trees were robed in green.

At Bleak House I found both the refrigerator and the electric kettle out of order — but the evening after my arrival Mollie much enjoyed a whisky and soda and a chicken sandwich. She continued to improve, but would this be maintained following my departure?

I visited Sunset Lodge in Mombasa. I found it austere and unwelcoming and insistent that inmates must be mobile.

I mentioned Nanyuki Cottage Hospital. "I don't want to go to Nanyuki!" I completed a Tax Return for the previous year and took it, with as many vouchers as I could locate, to the accountant in town.

For lunch I cooked fresh prawns which she ate with relish although she told a visitor at tea time that we had had "chicken, tough and horrible!" Joseph returned to duty at 6 o'clock each evening drunk on some local brew and, while remaining friendly, was both erratic and unreliable.

If I cooked, she ate and improved. I got her out of bed and sitting on the veranda, contentedly riffling through a pile of magazines. Prior to returning to Nairobi I altered the staff hours: ensuring that one person was always on hand in the house. Back in my own flat I slept.

She tried to reassure me. In a shaking scrawl I managed to unravel, 'To stop you worrying, I am *all right* eating well without enjoyment but lamentably weak and simply cannot manage a proper letter.'

1982 had ended but her grief over Don's death had in no way diminished. Among despairing letters were those in which she reproached herself: 'I disappoint myself all the time. I thought I had more stamina and self-sufficiency.' Others asked, 'Why can't I be allowed to slip quietly away, and painlessly if possible, in my sleep? I am no use to anyone now only an expense and responsibility...'

In April Mike telephoned me — Mollie should no longer be allowed to handle money; cash was disappearing, unaccounted for.

He proposed allowing her only a little 'pocket money'. He himself would make all other payments. Then, just two weeks later, he reported that my mother was not eating, that her mind was 'wandering', that she was asking for me. Company business: a Directors' Meeting and the AGM retained me for a couple of days. The VW — still valiant but now aged — was put safely into a garage at Hill Lane, surrounded by the ongoing work on the Theatre Archives.

I reached Mombasa late in the afternoon, having travelled by M.P.S. taxi. Outside the Standard Bank in Treasury Square, Mike scooped me up. We reached Bleak House in separate transport. Mollie was surprised, she thought I was due the next day.

I overcame my terror at being behind the wheel of the powerful Range Rover that Mike had left for me and set about the tasks awaiting me.

It rained ceaselessly; washing out the horizon, wiping out the vivid colours of the landscape and seeking out the growing number of weak spots in the roof of Bleak House. On the morning of my departure the rain lifted and the sun shone. Breakfasting on the damp veranda I could see clear down the creek all the way to the Indian Ocean. The old Nyali pontoon bridge had disappeared — all except the piers at either side of the creek. The whole middle section had gone — sold for scrap. Work continued on what remained with match-stick figures from a Lowry industrial landscape busy dismantling steel girders. The incandescent light from their acetylene cutters fizzed and sparked like distant fireworks.

Mollie declared, "I'm spending a ridiculous amount on wages and can't do with less."

We were still waiting for a vacancy at Harrison House. For the moment she was well cared for in her own home. Elizabeth McConnell was back, and occupying the guest-wing was a new tenant, a trained nurse. Before moving in Christine wrote to me: 'I cannot provide the constant companionship that Mollie would like as I have my own life to lead, but would be readily available if she needed me. I'm afraid to put it bluntly, that not many people would be able to stay with Mollie for any duration of time in your room as she is becoming very demanding and difficult and is extremely bad tempered at times. Her memory is failing her now and she is often confused. But despite all this, she has a will of iron and is as tough as old boots and will only do what she wants to do...'

Early in 1980 Don had lamented, 'Mollie has taken almost permanently to her bed, poor darling... Her condition deteriorates alarmingly, both physical and mental.'

The deterioration continued inexorably until this moment, observed so keenly by Christine — all set off by a fall in a supermarket. We brought suit for damages against the shop. The matter dragged on, year after year. The company carried no Public Liability Insurance. We sued the owners who defended the suit. But now, as the case approached a hearing I could not allow my mother to be cross-examined by some smart-ass lawyer who would exploit her mental confusion. At the time of the accident the supermarket management had offered not one jot of assistance, on the contrary, they had locked themselves in their office, immuring themselves from any liability. Only the chance presence of a couple of friends got Mollie off the premises and into hospital: Good Samaritans, neither of whom unfortunately was any longer available in Mombasa to give evidence on her behalf.

Between sojourns in hospital following the fall she had written:

'My dearest dear, This is just to let you know how much I love and appreciate your wonderful, sympathetic understanding and patience with me over this very difficult period in our lives. It will come to an end some time and we will be able to look back on it as an enlightening experience and without bitterness. My everlasting love to you, my very dear and beloved husband.'

Don had struggled on through the 'very difficult period' but it did not come to an end and he could struggle no longer. Now, five years on, she appeared to be dying. She clutched my wrist, "Poor Annabel. She had to come down to watch her father die and now she has had to come down to watch her mother die."

Next day, extraordinarily lucid, she remarked: "I've been trying to think of something witty to say, but all I can think of is, Goodbye." She didn't die. Christine was correct; she was as tough as old boots. This was September and I had to return to Nairobi. At Christmas I was back at Bleak House with some bleak news. Harrison House would not, after all, accept Mollie as a patient. The only reason they gave me was that they had 'changed their policy.' Elizabeth had gone her way once more, after spending two months with Mollie and, worse, Mike Elworthy had left Kenya for good. It was a bleak Christmas.

On the 'festive' day Mollie fretted and fumed because lunch was a little late. She told me she wished to move into "somewhere smaller". I pointed out that with Christine on the premises, able to offer professional services on the spot, it was wiser to remain where she was. Already that year Christine had nursed her through more than one chest infection and a torn ligament in her bad foot. With Mike's departure she had also taken on responsibility for paying staff wages and other accounts. It was better to leave matters as they were. "So," she said, "I have just got to get used to being lonely and miserable all the time?"

Don's room was now rented to a tenant; a very spotty youth who was out a good deal of the time. Mollie had hoped to receive companionship from a 'paying guest' in the adjoining room and I had the unenviable task of explaining that this was unreasonable.

Having had barely any sleep during my short visit, I set off on the return to Nairobi in a newly-acquired Ford Escort. I had sold the VW, sorry to rupture what had been a good relationship. The Ford Escort and I were never on good terms — it gave me near non-stop trouble and expense. This trip to the coast was our first safari together. Soon after leaving Hunter's Lodge and just as I was gaining speed a guinea fowl emerged suddenly from the undergrowth on the left. It hesitated at the edge of the tarmac and I breathed, "Thank God!" but in that instant the bird took wing and smashed directly into the windscreen in front of my face. The glass spread in a cobweb of cracks but remained in place. At reduced speed I drove back to Hill Lane going via the main post office to clear my post box.

My poor mother — what could I do to alleviate her misery? — What she hoped was for me to live permanently with her at Bleak House. I had explored every alternative. Harrison House had seemed the best solution but that door was now closed. "I don't want to go to Nanyuki!" had closed that door, too. My own small flat at Hill Lane could not possibly accommodate her. Forlorn, she had said, "I thought you might think of something..."

The pale parchment of each day stretched ahead of her. Breakfast, on a tray in bed, had come and gone. She had lost interest in reading. She fumbled a cassette into her machine. Distorted sound from the sagging, worn tape split the balmy air. She couldn't hear it. The tape rolled to its finish but kept on rolling, the 'stop' mechanism out of order. No visitors came, or, so she claimed. They came but she had forgotten their presence within minutes of their departure. Don was no longer there... a little nip of whisky might help to dissolve the misery, the boredom, the loneliness. After all, it would soon be lunchtime. And so, at nine o'clock in the morning she would have a small scotch and then, maybe, another.

When I saw the accumulation of miniature white plastic horses, meticulously retained by Joseph in the kitchen, I was dismayed. One day I told her, "You know, you're drinking too much." Her face stretched into a terrible screeching grimace and a harsh sound came from her throat, a sound of outrage: "Me? Drink too much!"

A day or two later, sad and bitter, she said, "What's the use of self discipline at the end of the line?"

1983 ended; already part of history; no longer part of 'now'. In August Humphrey Slade died and became part of history — certainly part of Kenya's history. A keen amateur actor, he played in *The Corn Is Green* — twice. The second occasion was when I directed the play for the Theatre Group in 1980.

1984, the awful Orwellian year, loomed and, from where I was sitting — writing up the 'books' of Annabel Maule Limited while contemplating my mother's plight — filled me with apprehension.

Before January had ended Sir Ernest Vasey became history, dying at the age of 82, the same age at which Don had died. He had appeared in the very first production of The Donovan Maule Players, *The Guinea Pig,* at the Theatre Royal in September 1948. When he became Finance Minister he could no longer spare the time for rehearsals or performances!

Toward the end of the month an old and dear friend arrived from America unexpectedly — letters to announce his arrival had been 'delayed' in the four-day shut-down of postal services while Kenya celebrated 20 years of Independence in December 1983; swiftly followed by further shut-downs over the Christmas and New Year celebrations. Meeting again after 20 years we made sentimental journeys to old haunts, drank wine, laughed, cried and on the last day in January set off for the coast in the Ford Escort — its windscreen restored — and insured against any flak-happy guinea fowl intent on suicide.

On February 1 we found my mother sitting on the patio at Bleak House. We had struck lucky; it was one of her 'good' days. She was delighted to see us. I brought her affairs up to date, delivered a tax return to the accountants, paid her alarmingly high grocer's account (all those little white plastic horses) and filled a bowl with gardenias for her bedroom. A bush at the entrance to the drive was smothered with blooms. She missed having flowers in the house; nobody bothered to pluck so much as a bract of bougainvillaea to bring indoors.

At tea-time Mollie was bright and talkative. "I'm 86 you know!" she told us proudly.

As a molten sun sank behind the coconut palms it was time to leave. She waved at the departing car. I was never to see her again.

By the middle of February the influence of the baleful Orwellian year began to take effect. I had a lesion excised from my leg; nothing dramatic, it was done on the Surgeon's premises under a local anaesthetic and seven stitches closed the wound. On reaching home I found the dressing protecting the wound gone; lost somewhere along the way from mid-town to the parked car. The wound became slightly infected. Antibiotics were prescribed and trustingly I took 'ONE *four* times a day' while coping with problems which followed one upon the other: no water at Hill Lane Flats; finding my post box locked due, so they claimed, to my failure to pay the rent. I did not of course have the receipt available with me to prove them wrong, so further trips back and forth. A few spidery, overlapping lines from Mollie told me she had a kidney infection and, a week later, that she had fallen out of bed 'flat on my back'. By the end of the month I felt ill: throbbing eyes in a throbbing head, leg pains and more. It was no help to be woken at 4 o'clock in the morning on February 28 by the 'understudy' night watchman: the garage at Hill Lane had been broken into. Putting on a ludicrously inadequate 'shift', I went to investigate. The padlocked bolts had been smashed and the doors damaged. Four locked tin trunks had been ransacked, three of them the property of a tenant, currently out of the country. In an unsuccessful attempt to force the lock on the trunk of my car, the bodywork had received punishment. But all was not lost; nearby stood a box with a great many brand-new spare parts for the Escort. A prize for the taking!

At 7.45am the watchman and I reported to Kilimani Police Station. At 10.30, back at Hill Lane, I contacted a carpenter to effect repairs to the garage doors. The Income Tax Department demanded to know why I had not returned a completed Tax Return which they had posted to an incorrect box number.

In the intervals between these alarums and excursions, I sat on the lavatory seat, doubled up with stomach cramps and diarrhoea and still we were without water. I typed a letter to my mother: 'Last week was a real pig!' before hurrying back to the recently vacated lavatory seat. A week later I was admitted to hospital with a nasty dose of enterocolitis — a result of the antibiotic Lincocin. This had been sold to me without any information regarding adverse side effects.

A diary entry for March 15 announced: '1.10pm the drip — in my right hand since last Sunday — was removed. What bliss to be free of that shackle.' 48 hours later I noted: 'Asked to come off the "Light & Gastric" diet. It would fell a buffalo!'

Two days after this I was home again, not restored to health but able to swallow some of the delicacies that Alan Bobbé brought me from his Bistro restaurant and, above all, enjoy the freshly pressed fruit juice that my dehydrated system craved.

But the enterocolitis persisted. I had received treatment in hospital but had not improved and was warned this might be "life threatening". The remedy? Another antibiotic as an antidote to the effects of Lincocin. This was not available in Kenya. It would have to be despatched, URGENTLY, from the UK. The cost, when it arrived, approached Sterling £800. I took dose number one on March 23 at 5pm and set my alarm clock for 11pm when number two was due.

I had just swallowed dose number 15 early on March 27 when Christine telephoned: Mollie had been moribund for the past week. Her doctor thought she was "finished", but she had "rallied".

My temperature yo-yoed down and up: 97.4 degrees — 103 degrees. Attempting to dry-out my soaked bedding I resorted to my hair dryer, succeeding only in burning out the element.

Once again we were without water at Hill Lane. With the arrival of April, I completed the bankrupting regime of Vancocin. I had lost 10 pounds; none, unfortunately, from areas where the loss would have been a blessing. I was as weak as a *small* mouse, but within a few days I could face the idea of food without retching and improved to the level of a medium-sized mouse. There was, though, further trouble ahead. On the last day of April Annabel Maule Limited held its AGM. May 1, was a public holiday so it was not until the following day that I returned to Nairobi Hospital to undergo an operation for a *fissure in ano,* the legacy of the enterocolitis.

On May 3, I was 'prepared'. A young nurse removed the varnish from my toenails. I was dressed in a short hospital gown, pulled on woollen socks and a cap was placed on my head after being asked "Did I wear a wig? Contact lenses? False teeth? Jewellery? Hair pins?"

One evening a large silver dish-cover came through the door of my room, borne by Alan Bobbé. Under it was a delicate crab mayonnaise. Six days later I removed my pain-in-the-arse from the hospital bed to my own at Hill Lane. Weekly visits to the surgeon for checkups kept me in town until I was signed off toward the end of May. The following day I drove to Crescent Island on Lake Naivasha to spend a week convalescing with Jean Hayes.

Now it was June, another public holiday, and the wedding day of two friends, but I was restored to health and could have faced the long haul to Mombasa to comfort Mollie. There had been many requests. One of them stated, 'You live a very short distance away and have a car. It would be easy for you to come and see me.'

She had been unable to grasp the fact that I had been in hospital a second time. When this news eventually sank in she telephoned: "I want to come up and look after you, but I suppose I would only be a liability..."

Christine wrote to tell me Mollie wanted to sell the house and move into a hotel. Mollie wrote, 'I know I'm behaving like an idiot and ought by now to be able to face the future with courage. There are hundreds and thousands of lonely widows who learn to live with it. I must learn to do the same. At the moment I'm full of despair and have no wish to go on living. Don and I were not only a happy man and wife but we were so much more than that. We were partners in everything we did. How are you? I was most distressed that you had' — at this point I could not make out the overlapping lines, until, 'Hope to see something of you... DO write...' I typed a letter the following day and again the following week and the week after that but I had received her final letter.

On Sunday morning, July 1, Christine telephoned. Mollie had died the previous night.

Now — too late — I would *have* to travel to Mombasa. There was much to do. The car needed servicing; company business set up to run in my absence; letters to write. The following day, Monday July 2, was yet another public holiday, Idd-ul-Fitr, when no business could be carried out. A friend came to lunch and later, alone again, as I washed up, tears splashed into the sink.

On the telephone Christine told me that Mollie had died "in her sleep" but after reaching Bleak House I was told that Joseph had found her on her bedroom floor. I knew that she fell often. What had happened? Had she lain there, calling for help, frightened, alone ...and no one came? Above all, I failed to come. I had abandoned her. Convinced as she was that I lived nearby, it was incomprehensible that I didn't come. She had implored me to come.

The previous year, in October, Christine wrote, 'Mollie has been very sick with another chest infection. She has had some rather vivid "dreams" recently and was extremely alarmed — distressed to the point of vomiting all day when she thought you had abandoned her in *Glasgow*... She is definitely getting a little senile at times.'

I could never figure out why it was in Glasgow. There was only one thing that I could be certain about — she had been released from her lonely misery. She had been allowed to die, as she had frequently implored. Whether it had been painless I would never know.

We buried her in Kisauni Cemetery. I had not had the foresight to purchase a plot alongside Don. It distressed me that she was a considerable distance from him. Monkeys in the lofty mango trees peered down at the small gathering below. Rain had threatened all day and the undertaker had a few broken ribbed black umbrellas hooked over his arm, as a precaution.

We returned to Bleak House for tea and egg mayonnaise sandwiches, as we had done following Don's funeral. Joseph possibly considered this food as symbols of *wazungu* funeral rites. His people feasted on meat and traditional beer. The *wazungu* drank tea and ate egg sandwiches. So be it.

That morning I had cleared her post box. In it I found my last letter to her, uncollected, unread.

Once again I settled to work at Don's desk. The waters of the creek at the bottom of the Kisauni property were satin-sheened, battleship-grey in the early morning. Later, with the sun climbing high and the breeze riffling the bougainvillaea, the colours changed: first to aquamarine, then cornflower-blue. Out on the reef white breakers rolled inshore. The coconut palms swayed to the music of the wind... It was perfect weather for the carefree holiday-maker.

Instead I re-visited the familiar offices of the Registrar of Births, Deaths and Marriages; as always dusty, as always crowded.

Mollie's three first names had been wrongly inscribed on the Death Certificate and several visits needed to get this corrected: 'Mrs. Mary Florence Margaret MAULE née SHIELLS — Born November 24, 1897...'

I reflected on this life. Queen Victoria was still on the throne at this time. Just one year earlier in 1896, the Red Flag Act, which demanded that a man walk in front of that dangerous machine, the automobile, waving a red flag to warn of its approach, had been repealed. She had been six years old when Orville Wright made the first flight in an aeroplane. In 1969, when she and Don were in Europe on the final overseas leave, men had walked on the moon.

On Sunday, July 8, I wrote, 'Woke at Kisauni: this day last week darling Mollie was found on the floor in her bedroom dead... Very moving tribute to Mollie written by Nigel Slade.'

Sunday Standard: BEHIND EVERY GREAT MAN WORKS A GREAT WOMAN. 'Mollie died quietly last Sunday. "Don" died in 1982... "He and Mollie"... Don's mémoirs re-echo this over again. So, always did his conversation. "Mollie and I," he would say, as if the "I" were not complete without "Mollie". Nor was it!

'In getting the DM off the ground and keeping it flying higher and higher, Don mainly looked after finances. Mollie did about everything else. Don was concerned with getting their theatre to pay. Mollie was in getting it to work... It was all for Don. They met as children in a railway carriage and disliked each other. Many years later, they met again. Don then pursued her with an ardour that she once whispered to me "wore her out". In Don's diary of the time the fact that he married Mollie on "that" day is underlined in red... Mollie would never have called herself a star. But she was a star in Don's eyes. And being "Mollie", she will always remain a star in mine. She was a truly wonderful lady of the theatre, an exemplary wife and, yes, a really super person.'

I sold Chateau Maule, after a lengthy wait for 'Letters of Administration.' It had become for me the bleakest of houses, full of sorrow. As I made the final departure, the car loaded to the roof with mementos, it came to me that it was just nine symbolic months since Mollie's death. The umbilical cord was severed at last. Now I was free to be myself.

Only now, nobody cared.

Another strange quirk of time and fate: Don's death on March 2, 1982 came just 40 years after that of my brother, Robin, which had occurred on March 2 1942. Robin, their second-born. A lovely blue-eyed boy reflecting Don's looks. Robin, with an early talent destined to take him far in theatre, films and beyond. Robin, with all his life ahead of him but cut short at 17, three years after the outbreak of World War II.

CHAPTER FOURTEEN

With the founders of the Donovan Maule Theatre now dead, what of the theatre they founded? It was near its end too. In November 1982, in a letter to my mother, I wrote, 'God knows what is going on there — money is owed all over town.'

Writs for non-payment of Accounts Rendered came to me, sent by careless lawyers to Annabel Maule Limited. Wearing my office messenger hat I would, personally, return these offending summonses.

In October '82, Theatre Arts '80 issued a statement: 'Negotiations have been going on between Theatre Arts '80 Limited and Phoenix Players about the future of the Theatre. These negotiations have failed, and Theatre Arts '80 Limited is now considering other methods of ensuring the Theatre's future. The Theatre costs about Sh350,000 a month to run. Since December 1981 we have received from Memberships Sh1,876,483 which only covered running expenses up to the end of June. The balance has been put in by shareholders in Theatre Arts '80 Limited, and from a small income which has arisen from the box office. The Players Restaurant has not been financed by the new Membership scheme and not used as much by members as we had hoped.'

'Operating expenses of the theatre Sh4,200,000 per year. In addition, a minimum of Sh1,200,000 per year must be found to pay interest on accumulated borrowing.'

Any shrewd impresario would surely turn his attention to a more viable option. I recalled the occasion in March 1981 when Peri Bhakoo asked me for advice on "...how to run a theatre."

On May 17 1983, the very day when the *Standard* trumpeted FALKLAND QUITS DM, I wrote to Mollie, 'I went to the DM

Theatre last Saturday to see their triple bill: *The Bear; The Proposal* and *A Marriage Has Heen Arranged*. A somewhat sparse evening; the theatre's future seems to be most precariously in the balance and we may soon know the outcome. But when I think of the quantities of cash that have been poured in since I left in 1979 and think of what I might have done with that sort of money, it is all rather saddening. Just where all that money went remains a mystery. And I daresay will remain so!'

Bhakoo told me, somewhat ruefully, that his involvement with the DM had set him back Sh6 million.

MYSTERY AS FALKLAND BOWS OUT headed Nigel Slade's piece on Sunday, May 29. 'The latest and sole item of news to emerge from the mist of mystery that surrounds the DM Theatre has come from the administrator, James Falkland. His resignation was made public 10 days ago but the actual date of his departure was not announced. Now it appears that he will leave sooner than might have been expected...'

Falkland spoke of "A considerable divergence of opinion in matters of policy between the directors of Theatre Arts '80 Limited (DM's owners) and himself.. He feels ...he should be replaced in his position as administrator as soon as possible." A statement, promised by Theatre Arts '80's Chairman, Mr. P.K. Bhakoo, has not at time of writing materialised... No news of any show opening at the DM (inactive all last week) has yet reached me. Let us hope that this uncertainty can be resolved soon. Members' subscriptions (paid for the whole year) are affected.'

The Chairman of Theatre Arts '80 chose to make his statement to another newspaper, *The Sunday Times*. On the same date, May 29, 1983, Margaretta wa Gacheru told her readers: 'Contrary to the view that the Donovan Maule Theatre has "died" with the formal resignation of James Falkland, the Donovan Maule will continue to run, irrespective of Falkland's departure on May 31. What will be "no more", according to Peri Bhakoo, the Theatre Chairman and controlling shareholder, is an in-house English

Repertory company at the DM. (The name of the place may very well change in the future as well). The Directors of the DM will take on a whole new attitude and approach to theatre presentation and live entertainment in general. In fact they have already begun to open their doors up wide to any and all performing artistes who might like to present high quality productions at their venue... be they Kenyan Africans, Asians and European... or they may be from abroad... as long as they sustain the high standards so strongly associated with the DM. As Bhakoo sees it, re-establishing the DM as a versatile venue for theatre groups and other performing artistes will only work if he sustains a style of professionalism that will keep up its international reputation. That is why he intends to get hold of "the best" and most broadminded theatre manager as soon as possible to co-ordinate the theatre's show calendar. Bhakoo already has several names in mind; it is to that person that he will hand over the responsibility of seeing that the DM continues to run as one — if not the very best theatre on the entire continent.'

Splendid and laudable sentiments... Margaretta's article went on, 'It is a radical step that Bhakoo is about to take allowing his professional repertory company to die a quiet death. But it is something that his closest family and friends advised him to do as far back as 1981 when James Falkland first voiced his desire to retire from the DM as Managing Director. Back then Mr. Falkland was virtually running his own "one-man-show", in charge of not only the Theatre itself: but the bar, the catering unit and even the DM flats — and being given a veritable blank cheque by Bhakoo to do so. That was the way the two men's relationship had begun back in 1979, when they bought the DM from Annabel Maule, one of the first people to say that English repertory theatre had no future in Kenya. Bhakoo was the "businessman" and financial backer behind the scenes who had virtually no say in the daily management of the organisation while Falkland took charge of everything from the hiring and firing of both the professional and the technical staff. It was for Falkland, for instance, to decide if amateur groups like the Nairobi City Players or Bhakoo's own brother Kul's group, NATAK, could or could not put on a production at the DM. Invariably the answer was "no", for reasons best known to Mr. Falkland. But it was that kind of absolute power that Bhakoo had allowed Falkland to use in the past — despite his having hold of the financial strings of the whole operation. Bhakoo did observe that there might have been a conflict of interest which began once an organisation was formulated by the name of Phoenix Players Limited, a concern whose ambition it was to initially lease and later to buy the Donovan Maule Theatre.'

On June 12 Margaretta told her readers, 'Good news is being brewed up for the Donovan Maule Theatre membership as well as for all those concerned with progressive developments in local theatre generally. The latest word on one of the best theatre venues in the whole of Africa is that the DM's owner-chairman Peri Bhakoo, has just issued a statement especially directed to the club membership to the effect that the theatre is about to go back into operation in the near future. Bhakoo wants the public to know that the DM is not dead and that the members' interests are being looked after. Currently he is working out both short and long term arrangements for the Theatre. In the short run, he is planning to have a special "Jubilee" production on June 17, to mark the 25th anniversary of the opening of the Donovan Maule Theatre. What is more, he is making sure that however long or short it takes to reorganise the Theatre's administration that same amount of time will be added on to their membership in 1984.'

The "Jubilee" production, a slender two-character adaptation of an English classic novel, played for only four performances. I was invited to attend the Gala evening on Friday June 17. Bhakoo's hospitality was generous — hot and cold canapés came round during the interval and there was dinner later in the Players Restaurant. I noted that Theatre Arts '80 Limited now listed three directors, all named Bhakoo.

The following week Phoenix Players presented their first

production in the basement of The Professional Centre; while Eva Ndavu, writing in the *Daily Nation,* reported, 'The Donovan Maule Theatre... seems in near collapse these days as the Theatre Arts '80 group struggles for survival.'

The theatre's death throes were protracted and painful to witness. In July *Makabeti,* a modern English adaptation of Shakespeare's *Macbeth* opened, the brainchild of Luka Wasambo Were. The initial idea was a good one: 'Shakespeare is alive for our times and not restricted to his own age.' The execution of the show was something else. The costumes ranged from contemporary battle fatigues to Victorian Colonial Governor's dress uniform and further... A London 'Bobby' wore the familiar blue uniform lavishly embellished with quantities of bobbled lampshade trim. I was startled out of my torpor when a little lady playing 'Mrs. Madafu' (Lady Macduff) came on wearing the elaborate velvet and brocade evening dress made for me as Queen Mary in *Crown Matrimonial,* set in 1936.

Slade, on July 30, wrote *'Makabeti* is interesting... in terms of overall presentation it is a mess; it was a pity to see a good idea all but disappear under what seemed to be a disorganised ransacking of the DM's wardrobe and a hotch-potch of a set.' A week later he told his readers, 'Mr. P.K. Bhakoo, Chairman of DM's owners, Theatre Arts '80 Limited, frankly admitted that he had not formulated any long-term plans as yet. However, he did stress his undertaking that staged entertainment would continue. As to the form of this entertainment, Mr. Bhakoo was reticent. He understandably did not wish to declare himself until his aims were fully finalised. He did, however, refute a recent report that DM would by policy become an "open house" to any group. "The reporter took what were merely considered possibilities as solid facts". Asked if he would refund any subscriptions *pro rata,* he replied: "Not yet. If we do re-introduce professional theatre, members will receive a *pro rata* extension of membership. However, if I decide against this, then certainly we'll refund on "requests". Meanwhile, he says, research is going on into what sort of entertainment Nairobi really wants. "Once we know that, we'll supply it."'

Whether the show on offer in August was the result of such 'research' cannot be known. Three short plays sandwiched two very long intervals. The plays were of the 'existentialist' genre. As I returned to my seat following the second lengthy interval, the lady sitting next to me, a Club member, declared loudly, "This is NOT what I paid for!"

Any possibility of "professional" theatre being revived at the DM — if such a possibility was being considered — would have been quashed by British Actors' Equity Association's latest demand: a "minimum" weekly wage of £100 and an instruction to its members to 'sign no contracts beyond September 5, 1983.'

In October, Slade wrote, 'Many theatre-goers are waiting for the DM to "re-open", i.e. Be what it was. That hope, I think, can be kissed goodbye with conviction proportionate to duration of "darkness" there and the silence of its owners.'

In December the British Council brought to Nairobi two professional productions: *Educating Rita* and *Duet For One*. Two characters only and each in a single setting. Eminently suited to the DM Theatre, they were instead staged in the barren expanse of the National Theatre. A spokesman at the Council told Slade: "We wanted to present a show, which we're importing, at DM. Yet telephone calls toward fixing this were ignored and we've had to look elsewhere." 'This,' Slade told his readers, 'does not seemingly square with the recently declared policy of "open doors for all" and further justifies the refunds demands.'

At the end of the year a 'Letter to the Editor' of the *Sunday Standard* was headed WHAT IS GOING ON AT THE DM? 'A founder member of the DM, I started seeing their plays when originally staged in a room over a grocery store in what was then Government Road. I have since (with delight) enjoyed the amenities of a "proper" theatre. But now everything is altered and nothing seems to happen at the DM. I am still a member of the DM under a scheme which was proposed by the new owners (Theatre Arts '80

Limited) and which has not yet expired, but no entertainment has been offered for more than two months... The DM Theatre is not being used for the purpose for which it was built. I have always been proud to take overseas visitors to the Donovan Maule — there is no doubt that it added another dimension to Nairobi's reputation as a first class tourist centre, and one which many other independent African States cannot offer. What can be done — what is being done, to restore the DM (which also has a historical value) to its proper place?'

As we embarked on the baleful Orwellian year 1984, Slade took A LOOK AT THE OLD YEAR declaring, 'The most "dramatic" thing about it was the darkening of the Donovan Maule Theatre, after more than 35 years of existence... Answers to questions as to why DM "stopped" are still as much awaited as appeals for them seem to be ignored.'

At the start of February I was at the Coast and saw my mother. In March I was in Nairobi Hospital. On the evening of March 19, home again but 'not restored to health', Peri Bhakoo telephoned. "Can we talk? Can we meet? I must tell you that there is not one word of truth in the piece that Nigel Slade wrote in yesterday's *Standard*..." Slade's headline read DM COSTUMES UP FOR SALE and continued, 'A friend of mine has been to the DM godown and tells me that it is now possible to select what one wants and arrange to negotiate their purchase with the Chairman of Theatre Arts '80 Limited, Mr. P.K. Bhakoo... What does this infer? ...And how does one feel? Subscriptions were not refunded when the shows stopped... Not only has no announcement been made for the last six months but requests for it have been ignored, as have those for refunds. Now equipment essential to any theatre is to leave this particular theatre. How does one feel, I ask? What a shabby ending to such a lovely place, and, yes, such an important place...'

I lay in bed listening to Bhakoo "...not a costume or light is for sale... It is true the building is for sale... Can we talk?" I could feel sweat running off my back onto the already damp bedding. I told him I was too ill at this moment and would have to end the conversation. I took my temperature; it was sky-high. I tried to sleep... the DM's costumes were up for sale... There was no truth in the announcement that the DM's costumes or lights were up for sale... The building was up for sale... he had asked me to direct a play... when was that? Earlier... last year perhaps? Questions... denials... plays... theatre... theatre...

My real concern, the one right at the forefront, the one I had to resolve, was my mother's situation. This was solved for me when she died three months later. The theatre took longer to die.

As the year drew to a close the comatose body that had been a vibrant playhouse gave a twitch. Theatre correspondents in the national press closely monitored the patient's progress: ACTION RETURNS TO THE DM THEATRE - THE DM COMES TO LIFE - DM ALL SET FOR A COMEBACK '...even if immediately it does not seek to be what it was. What will please and impress many is the offer to all those who were members in 1983 — you can be a member for the whole of 1985 free of charge... There is also the mention of employing an eminent, intelligent and experienced Director. This is with the hope of eventually setting up a cadre for professional theatre.'

More laudable sentiments. More promises.

In mid-January 1985 came a *production!* Well, hardly a production. A 'cabaret' was presented, not on stage, but in the restaurant, now named The William Shakespeare. Two of Nairobi's leading critics walked out.

In March, Slade wrote, 'As to that hoary old question "What's happening at The Donovan Maule Theatre, I'm afraid I cannot tell you. I cannot say for sure that the DM will be a theatre much longer — not even an empty one!' July '85: 'The Donovan Maule Theatre has been a closed and empty building for some time now. Rumour has it that it will be sold to become a supermarket or discotheque. That will be a sad day indeed for theatre-lovers in Nairobi! At the start of 1985 the Donovan Maule Theatre blew a proud trumpet, promised a programme and announced membership rates. After that — phut!'

The body had stopped twitching. The scavengers moved in. On a morning of bright sunshine early in 1986 I saw that the theatre's exit door, the one that gave onto St. John's Gate, was open. I entered the familiar building and knew myself to be quite alone. The place had been abandoned. Stepping over builder's rubble and rubbish, I made my way to dressing room number 5 — "Our dressing room, Mollie's and mine. Direct access to the stage, you see and it'll double as an office, so I can do the Royalty Returns during my stage waits..."

The wash-basin was gone, wrenched from the wall. The twin mirrors had left their silhouette against a now empty wall. Gaping holes with wire-ends hanging showed where lights had been. Shelves and wardrobe doors had gone. The floor was a mass of smashed masonry and torn paper. "Now through here... that's the proscenium arch opening. You're standing about centre stage!"

I was startled to find it bathed in sunshine: the roof overhead was gone. Builder's rubbish was piled against the cyclorama and the charred embers of a dead fire blackened the floorboards.

I stood quite still surveying this: the setting for a production of *Mother Courage...* I felt tears, hot, angry tears splashing on my cheeks. Turning away I picked my way over heaps of broken cement and splintered wood, heading for the club lounge and bar. It was the same here.

Everything removable had been removed leaving only dirt, dust, débris. As I turned my gaze to the curved wall flanking the entrance to the auditorium, I found myself staring at Mollie and Don. The portraits, presented by the company on the occasion of their 30th wedding anniversary in July 1950, the portraits of no value to anyone, remained hanging there, dusty and crooked, presiding over the ruin of their theatre.

I reached to unhook them, one after the other, releasing a shower of grit with every movement. Carefully I carried them out to my car. Nobody challenged me because nobody noticed.

In the months that followed, further looting and destruction occurred. Anyone could now enter the shell of the Donovan Maule Theatre. But what remained?

Not until 1988 was the empty husk of this playhouse laid to rest. In April a team of wreckers — "Apollo Eleven" — came with the tools of their trade. Sweating in the heat, they swung picks and pressed down on juddering pneumatic drills, filling the air with dust and noise. It was a long, slow job; that theatre had been built to last and would not easily succumb.

Following their departure, heaps of masonry and rubble remained to litter the area: 'Site between Jackson & Connaught Roads. 2 front corner plots nearest to Legco. 1/6th acre, 75 ft. x 120 ft. deep.'

It wasn't long before Africa reclaimed her own. Green shoots pushed their way through the mounds of smashed concrete. Saplings reached for the blue Kenyan sky, nourished perhaps by the pesky underground river which had so frequently given us grief.

APPENDIX

Productions by the Donovan Maule Players

Number

1948

1	The Guinea Pig	Warren Chetham-Strode	September 13
2	Robert's Wife	St. John Ervine	November 15

1949

3	The Chiltern Hundreds	William Douglas Home	January 3
4	Saloon Bar	Frank Harvey	April 4
5	This Happy Breed	Noel Coward	June 6

Presented at the Theatre Royal, Delamere Avenue

6	Outward Bound	Sutton Vane	November 23

1950

7	Jeannie	Aimee Stuart	February 4
8	The First Mrs. Fraser	St. John Ervine	February 25
9	Pink String & Sealing Wax	Roland Pertwee	April 17
10	George & Margaret	Gerald Savory	May 15
11	Miss Mabel	R.C. Sheriff	June 17
12	The Lady's Not For Burning	Christopher Fry	July 26
13	Blithe Spirit	Noel Coward	August 28
14	Pygmalion	G.B. Shaw	October 2
15	Traveller's Joy	Arthur McCrae	November 8
16	This Was A Woman	Joan Morgan	December 26

1951

17	The Man With A Load of Mischief	Ashley Dukes	January 24
18	Tomorrow's Child	John Coates	February 28
19	Pick-Up Girl	Elsa Shelley	April 4
20	Present Laughter	Noel Coward	May 9

21	Tobias And The Angel	James Barrie	June 25
22	Goodness, How Sad!	Robert Morley	August 6
23	The Importance Of Being Earnest	Oscar Wilde	September 12
24	His Excellency	Dorothy & Campbell Christie	October 17
25	The Holly And The Ivy	Wynyard Browne	November 21

1952

26	The White Sheep Of The Family	L. du Garde Peach & Ian Hay	January 9
27	Gaslight	Patrick Hamilton	February 27
28	Castle In The Air	Alan Melville	April 2
29	Captain Carvallo	Denis Cannan	May 14
30	Time And The Conways	J.B. Priestley	June 27
31	Born Yesterday	Garson Kanin	July 29
32	Young Wives' Tale	Ronald Jeans	September 16
33	The Hollow	Agatha Christie	October 21
34	Bell, Book & Candle	John van Druten	November 25

1953

35	The Little Hut	Andre Roussin, adapted by Nancy Mitford	January 6
36	Dial "M" For Murder	Frederick Knott	February 17
37	Who Goes There?	John Dighton	March 31
38	The Young Elizabeth	Jeannette Dowling & Francis Letton	April 24

Presented at the National Theatre

39	A Horse! A Horse!	L. du Garde Peach	June 2
40	A Phoenix Too Frequent & Hands Across The Sea	Christopher Fry Noel Coward	July 21 July 21
41	Claudia	Rose Franken	August 25
42	The Day's Mischief	Lesley Storm	September 22
43	Private Lives	Noel Coward	October 20
44	Mate In Three	L. du Garde Peach	November 17
45	Charley's Aunt	Brandon Thomas	December 15

1954

46	The Deep Blue Sea	Terence Rattigan	January 26
47	Relative Values	Noel Coward	February 23
48	Gigi	Colette, dramatised by Anita Loos	March 23
49	The River Line	Charles Morgan	April 27
50	To Dorothy, A Son	Roger MacDougall	June 1
51	The Sacred Flame	Somerset Maugham	July 6
52	I Am A Camera	Christopher Isherwood, dramatised by Jon van Druten	August 3
53	Affairs Of State	Louis Verneuil	September 7
54	The Heiress	Henry James, dramatised by Ruth and Augustus Goetz	October 12
55	Both Ends Meet	Arthur McCrae	November 16
56	The Happiest Days Of Your Life	John Dighton	December 21

1955

57	Anastasia	Marcelle Maurette, adapted by Guy Bolton	January 25
58	Dangerous Corner	J.B. Priestley	March 1
59	The Mousetrap	Agatha Christie	April 5
60	A Question Of Fact	Wynyard Browne	May 10
61	The Seven Year Itch	George Axelrod	June 14
62	Waiting For Gillian	Ronald Millar	July 19
63	Simon And Laura	Alan Melville	August 23
64	Murder Mistaken	Janet Green	September 27
65	You Never Can Tell	G.B. Shaw	November 1
66	Two Dozen Red Roses	Aldo de Benedetti, adapted by Kenneth Horne	December 6

1956

67	Escapade	Roger MacDougall	January 10
68	Someone Waiting	Emlyn Williams	February 14
69	The Reluctant Debutante	William Douglas Home	March 20
70	Misery Me!	Denis Cannan	May 1
71	The Donovan Maule Theatre Scandal	Howard Bromley-Chapman, adapted by Malcolm Farquhar	June 12
72	The Burning Glass	Charles Morgan	July 24
73	Sabrina Fair	Samuel Taylor	August 28

74	The Scandalous Affair Of Mr. Kettle And Mrs. Moon	J.B. Priestley	October 9
75	South Sea Bubble	Noel Coward	November 20

1957

76	Spring Meeting	M.J. Farrell & John Perry	January 8
77	The Spider's Web	Agatha Christie	February 19
78	The Waltz Of The Toreadors	Jean Anouilh	April 9
79	Plaintiff In A Pretty Hat	Hugh & Margaret Williams	May 14
80	Eden End	J.B. Priestley	June 25
81	We Must Kill Tony	Ian Stuart Black	July 30
82	The Little Hut	Andre Roussin, adapted by Nancy Mitford	September 3
83	The Touch Of Fear	Dorothy & Campbell Christie	October 8
84	Dear Delinquent	Jack Popplewell	November 12
85	Doctor In The House	Richard Gordon, dramatised by Ted Willis	December 17

1958

86	The Queen And The Rebels	Ugo Betti, translated by Henry Reed	January 28
87	Come Live With Me	Dorothy & Campbell Christie	March 18
88	Hedda Gabler	Henrik Ibsen, adapted by Max Faber	April 28

Final production at the Studio Theatre, Government Road
Opening of The Donovan Maule Theatre, Connaught Road

89	Separate Tables	Terence Rattigan	June 17
90	Look Back In Anger	John Osborne	July 15
91	Nude With Violin	Noel Coward	August 12
92	The Chalk Garden	Enid Bagnold	September 9
93	Roar Like A Dove	Lesley Storm	October 14
94	The Doctor's Dilemma	G.B. Shaw	November 11
95	Odd Man In	Claude Magnier, adapted by Robin Maugham	December 9

1959

	Wolfit/Iden Season	Scenes from Shakespeare	January 6
96	Venus Observed	Christopher Fry	January 27
97	Not In The Book	Arthur Watkyn	February 24
98	Present Laughter	Noel Coward	March 24
99	Subway In The Sky	Ian Main	April 21
100	Rebecca	Daphne du Maurier	May 19
101	Breath Of Spring	Peter Coke	June 16
102	The Whole Truth	Philip Mackie	July 14
103	Who Is Sylvia?	Terence Rattigan	August 11
104	The Grass Is Greener	Hugh & Margaret Williams	September 8
105	A Dead Secret	Rodney Ackland	October 13
106	Down Came A Blackbird	Peter Blackmore	November 10
107	Murder On Arrival	George Batson	December 8

1960

108	Lock Up Your Daughters	Adapted by Bernard Miles from Fielding's Rape Upon Rape	January 6
109	The Pleasure Of His Company	Samuel Taylor & Cornelia Otis Skinner	February 6
110	The Summer Of The Seventeenth Doll	Ray Lawler	March 15
111	When We Are Married	J.B. Priestley	April 12
112	The Ring Of Truth	Wynyard Browne	May 10
113	The Amorous Prawn	Anthony Kimmins	June 7
114	Five Finger Exercise	Peter Shaffer	July 12
115	Candida	G.B. Shaw	August 9
116	The Sound Of Murder	William Fairchild	September 6
117	Dry Rot	John Chapman	October 4
118	Random Harvest	James Hilton	November 8
119	The More The Merrier	Ronald Millar	December 6

1961

120	A Lady Mislaid	Kenneth Horne	January 3
121	The Rape Of The Belt	Benn W. Levy	February 1

122	Rookery Nook	Ben Travers	March 1
123	The Rainmaker	N. Richard Nash	March 29
124	She Stoops To Conquer	Oliver Goldsmith	May 3
125	The Aspern Papers	Henry James, adapted by Michael Redgrave	May 31
126	Simple Spymen	John Chapman	June 28
127	The Caretaker	Harold Pinter	August 2
128	The Miracle Worker	William Gibson	August 30
129	Arsenic And Old Lace	Joseph Kesselring	September 27
130	Doctor In The House	Richard Gordon, dramatised by Ted Willis	October 25
131	Go Back For Murder	Agatha Christie	November 22
132	Oliver!	Lionel Bart	December 21

1962

133	The Marriage-Go-Round	Leslie Stevens	February 14
134	Bus Stop	William Inge	March 14
135	Laura	Vera Caspary & George Sklar	April 11
136	Champagne Complex	Leslie Stevens	May 9
137	The Irregular Verb To Love	Hugh & Margaret Williams	June 6
138	The Deep Blue Sea	Terence Rattigan	July 11
139	Boeing-Boeing	Marc Camoletti	August 8
140	The Gazebo	Alec Coppel	September 6
141	The School For Scandal	Richard Brinsley Sheridan	October 16
142	Signpost To Murder	Monte Doyle	November 7
143	Beyond The Fringe	Alan Bennett, Peter Cook, Jonathan Miller, Dudley Moore	December 5

1963

144	The Complaisant Lover	Graham Greene	January 9
145	The Hostage	Brendan Behan	February 6

146	Kill Two Birds	Philip Levene	March 6
147	Don't Tell Father	Harold Brooke & Kay Bannerman	April 3
148	Wake Up, Darling	Alex Gottlieb	May 1
149	Billy Liar	Keith Waterhouse & Willis Hall	May 29
150	My Three Angels	Sam & Bella Spewack	June 26
151	Woman In A Dressing Gown	Ted Willis	July 24
152	The Mousetrap	Agatha Christie	August 21
153	Hobson's Choice	Harold Brighouse	September 18
154	Doctor At Sea	Richard Gordon, dramatised by Ted Willis	October 16
155	Dial "M" For Murder	Frederick Knott	November 13
156	Look After Lulu!	Georges Feydeau, adapted by Noel Coward	December 13

1964

157	The Private Ear The Public Eye	Peter Shaffer	January 7
158	Private Lives	Noel Coward	January 28
159	Come Blow Your Horn	Neil Simon	February 18
160	Arms And The Man	G.B. Shaw	March 10
161	Something To Hide	Leslie Sands	March 31
162	The Merchant Of Venice	Shakespeare	April 28
163	Don't Listen, Ladies!	Sacha Guitry, adapted by Stephen Powys & Guy Bolton	May 27
164	Mary, Mary	Jean Kerr	June 24
165	Trap For A Lonely Man	Robert Thomas	July 22
166	Blithe Spirit	Noel Coward	August 19
167	The Winslow Boy	Terence Rattigan	September 16
168	The Reluctant Peer	William Douglas Home	October 14
169	Night Must Fall	Emlyn Williams	November 11
170	Goodnight, Mrs. Puffin	Arthur Lovegrove	December 9

1965

171	Meet Me By Moonlight	Anthony Lesser	January 6
172	The Big Killing	Philip Mackie	February 3

173	A Man For All Seasons	Robert Bolt	March 3
174	Sailor, Beware!	Philip King & Falkland Cary	April 7
175	Silver Wedding	Michael Clayton Hutton	May 5
176	Waters Of The Moon	N.C. Hunter	June 2
177	Ten Little Redskins	Agatha Christie	June 30
178	The Heiress	Henry James, dramatised by Ruth & Augustus Goetz	August 3
179	Diplomatic Baggage	John Chapman	September 1
180	The Importance Of Being Earnest	Oscar Wilde	October 6
181	The Hot Tiara	Janet Allen	November 3
182	Hay Fever	Noel Coward	December 1

1966

183	Dirty Work At The Crossroads	Bill Johnson	January 6
184	Witness For The Prosecution	Agatha Christie	February 9
185	Saint Joan	G.B. Shaw	March 9
186	The Amorous Prawn	Anthony Kimmins	April 13
187	A Clean Kill	Michael Gilbert	May 11
188	The Cherry Orchard	Anton Chekhov	June 8
189	Don't Utter A Note	Anton Delmar	July 6
190	Ring Round The Moon	Jean Anouilh, adapted by Christopher Fry	July 27
191	The Hollow	Agatha Christie	August 31
192	Barefoot In The Park	Neil Simon	September 28
193	An Inspector Calls	J.B. Priestley	October 26
194	How's The World Treating You?	Roger Milner	November 23
195	A Christmas Carol	Charles Dickens, adapted by Trevor Smith & Mollie Donovan Maule	December 24

1967

196	Wait Until Dark	Frederick Knott	February 1
197	Say Who You Are	Keith Waterhouse & Willis Hall	March 1
198	Uncle Harry	Thomas Job	March 29
199	White Lies And Black Comedy	Peter Shaffer	April 26

200	The Unexpected Guest	Agatha Christie	May 26
201	The Rivals	Richard Brinsley Sheridan	June 21
202	There's A Girl In My Soup	Terence Frisby	July 19
203	Thunder Rock	Robert Ardrey	August 16
204	On Approval	Frederick Londsdale	September 13
205	Who's Afraid Of Virginia Woolf?	Edward Albee	September 15
206	Horizontal Hold	Stanley Price	October 18
207	Rattle Of A Simple Man	Charles Dyer	November 15
208	One For The Pot	Ray Cooney & Tony Hilton	December 13

1968

209	Heartbreak House	G.B. Shaw	January 17
210	A Severed Head	Iris Murdoch & J.B. Priestley	February 14
211	The Promise	Aleksei Arbuzov	March 20
212	The Killing Of Sister George	Frank Marcus	March 22
213	Boeing-Boeing	Marc Camoletti	May 1
214	Relatively Speaking	Alan Ayckbourn	May 22
215	Twelfth Night	Shakespeare	June 19
216	Spring And Port Wine	Bill Naughton	July 24
217	The Flip Side	Hugh & Margaret Williams	August 21
218	Gaslight	Patrick Hamilton	August 28
219	Dear Liar	Jerome Kilty	October 2
220	Dear Brutus	James Barrie	October 3
221	The Creeper	Pauline Macaulay	November 13
222	The Boy Friend	Sandy Wilson	December 19

1969

223	Not Now, Darling	Ray Cooney & John Chapman	January 22
224	The Secretary Bird	William Douglas Home	February 26
225	The Man Of Destiny & The Master Of Two Servants	G.B. Shaw George Mully	March 26
226	Pink String And Sealing Wax	Roland Pertwee	April 23

227	Bell, Book & Candle	John van Druten	May 21
228	Busybody	Jack Popplewell	June 18
229	Little Boxes	John Bowen	July 16
230	Halfway Up The Tree	Peter Ustinov	August 13
231	The Italian Girl	Iris Murdoch & James Saunders	September 10
232	Uncle Vanya	Anton Chekhov	October 7
233	On The Spot	Edgar Wallace	November 5
234	Loot	Joe Orton	December 3
235	Anne Of Green Gables	Maud Montgomery, adapted for the stage by Donald Harron	December 31

1970

236	His, Hers & Theirs	Hugh & Margaret Williams	January 28
237	Present Laughter	Noel Coward	February 25
238	According To The Evidence	Felicity Douglas & Hugh Cecil	March 25
239	The Man Most Likely To...	Joyce Rayburn	April 22
240	Who Killed Santa Claus?	Terence Feely	May 20
241	Oh Men! Oh Women!	Edward Chodorov	June 24
242	Duet For Two Hands	Mary Hayley Bell	July 22
243	She's Done It Again!	Michael Pertwee	August 19
244	Sleuth!	Anthony Shaffer	September 16
245	The Lady's Not For Burning	Christopher Fry	October 21
246	How The Other Half Loves	Alan Ayckbourn	November 18
247	East Lynne	Mrs. Henry Wood	December 23

1971

248	The Jockey Club Stakes	William Douglas Home	January 20
249	The Duchess Of Malfi	John Webster	February 23
250	A Song At Twilight	Noel Coward	March 24
251	Dead On Nine	Jack Popplewell	April 21

252	The Taming Of The Shrew	Shakespeare	May 26
253	All For Mary	Harold Brooke & Kay Bannerman	June 23
254	A Boston Story	Henry James, dramatised by Ronald Gow	July 21
255	Move Over, Mrs. Markham	Ray Cooney & John Chapman	August 18
256	Born Yesterday	Garson Kanin	September 29
257	The Winslow Boy	Terence Rattigan	October 27
258	Breakfast With Julia	Burton Graham	November 24
259	Canterbury Tales	Chaucer, adapted by Nevill Coghill & Martin Starkie	December 22

1972

260	Suddenly, At Home	Francis Durbridge	February 2
261	Getting On	Alan Bennett	March 8
262	No Sex, Please - We're British	Anthony Mariott & Alistair Foot	April 5
263	Forget-Me-Not-Lane	Peter Nichols	May 17
264	The Imaginary Invalid	Moliere	June 14
265	There's A Girl In My Soup	Terence Frisby	July 12
266	The Philanthropist	Christopher Hampton	August 16
267	They Don't Grow On Trees	Ronald Millar	September 13
268	Johnny Belinda	Elmer Harris, adapted by Sorrel Carson & John Hanau	October 18
269	The Noble Spaniard	Somerset Maugham	November 15
270	Virtue In Danger	Paul Dehn, from Vanbrugh's "The Relapse"	December 20

1973

271	On Monday Next	Philip King	January 24
272	Night Must Fall	Emlyn Williams	February 21
273	Dead Easy	Jack Popplewell	March 29
274	And The Bride Makes Three	Frank Barbara	April 25
275	The Government Inspector	Nikolai Gogol	May 23
276	Ladies In Retirement	Edward Percy & Reginald Denham	June 20

No.	Title	Author	Date
277	It's In The Bag	Claude Magnier, adapted by Robin Maugham	July 18
278	Don't Start Without Me	Joyce Rayburn	August 15
279	A Short History Of The English People	Frank Harvey	September 12
280	Foursome Reel	Peter Whitbread	October 17
281	My Fat Friend	Charles Laurence	November 14
282	Hay Fever	Noel Coward	December 19

1974

No.	Title	Author	Date
283	Murder Mistaken	Janet Green	January 16
284	Sailor, Beware!	Philip King & Falkland Cary	February 13
285	Lloyd George Knew My Father	William Douglas Home	March 13
286	The Late Christopher Bean	Emlyn Williams	April 17
287	Two And Two Make Sex	Richard Harris & Leslie Darbon	May 15
288	Party To Murder	Olive Chase & Stewart Burke	June 19
289	Roar Like A Dove	Lesley Storm	July 17
290	In Praise Of Love	Terence Rattigan	August 14
291	Why Not Stay For Breakfast?	Gene Stone & Ray Cooney	September 11
292	Who Saw Him Die?	Tudor Gates	October 16
293	Mary, Mary	Jean Kerr	November 13
294	Doctor In The House	Richard Gordon, dramatized by Ted Willis	December 18

1975

No.	Title	Author	Date
295	The Circle	Somerset Maugham	January 22
296	Habeas Corpus	Alan Bennett	February 19
297	The Gentle Hook	Francis Durbridge	March 19
298	Time And Time Again	Alan Ayckbourn	April 16
299	My Three Angels	Sam & Bella Spewack	May 14
300	Crown Matrimonial	Royce Ryton	June 11

301	Rope	Patrick Hamilton	July 16
302	The Pay-Off	William Fairchild	August 13
303	A Touch Of Spring	Samuel Taylor	September 10
304	Mrs. Gibbon's Boys	Will Glickman & Joseph Stein	October 15
305	Boeing-Boeing	Marc Camoletti	November 12
306	Tons Of Money	Will Evans & Valentine	December 17

1976

307	The Importance Of Being Earnest	Oscar Wilde	January 14
308	Darling, I'm Home	Jack Popplewell	February 18
309	The Day After The Fair	Thomas Hardy, dramatized by Frank Harvey	March 17
310	Move Over, Mrs. Markham	Ray Cooney & John Chapman	April 14
311	The Daffodil Man	Martin Worth	May 19
312	I'll Sleep In The Spare Room	David Lawton	June 16
313	Rosencrantz And Guildenstern Are Dead	Tom Stoppard	July 14
314	A Bit Between The Teeth	Michael Pertwee	August 11
315	The Dame Of Sark	William Douglas Home	September 8
316	Murder Most Logical	Peter O'Donnell	October 13
317	An Englishman's Home	Stephen Mallatratt	November 10
318	The Murder Of Maria Marten or The Red Barn	Brian J. Burton	December 8

1977

319	The Bed Before Yesterday	Ben Travers	January 5
320	The Platinum Cat	Roger Longrigg	February 2
321	Table Manners	THE NORMAN CONQUESTS Alan Ayckbourn	March 2
322	Living Together		March 22
323	Round And Round The Garden		April 13

324	Night Watch	Lucille Fletcher		May 25
325	French Without Tears	Terence Rattigan		June 22
326	The Mating Game	Robin Hawdon		July 21
327	The Queen's Highland Servant	William Douglas Home		August 17
328	Rat Trap	Bob Baker & Dave Martin		September 14
329	Away Match	Martin Worth & Peter Yeldman		October 12
330	They Walk Alone	Max Catto		November 9
331	See How They Run	Philip King		December 7

1978

332	The Sunshine Boys	Neil Simon	January 11
333	Scarlet Ribbon	Rae Shirley	February 8
334	Confusions	Alan Ayckbourn	March 8
335	Pygmalion	G.B. Shaw	April 5
336	Hands Across The Sea and The Browning Version	Noel Coward Terence Rattigan	May 3
337	The Hot Tiara	Janet Allen	May 31
338	Sleeping It Off	Georges Feydeau, adapted by Guy Slater	June 28
339	Hindle Wakes	Stanley Houghton	July 26
340	Equus	Peter Shaffer	September 1
341	The Lion In Winter	James Goldman	September 20
342	The Murder Game	Constance Cox	October 25
343	The Glass Menagerie	Tennessee Williams	November 22
344	Plunder	Ben Travers	December 20

1979

345	Bedroom Farce	Alan Ayckbourn	January 17
346	Gigi	Colette, dramatised by Anita Loos	February 14
347	Rattle Of A Simple Man	Charles Dyer	March 14
348	Clouds	Michael Frayn	April 18
349	The Killing Of Sister George	Frank Marcus	May 16
350	Why Not Stay For Breakfast?	Gene Stone & Ray Cooney	June 13

INDEX

Adagala, Seth 167,168
Alban, Gwen 3,8,16,199 (See also Barret, Mrs. Edward)
Albee, Edward 119
Albery, Donald 96
All For Mary 137,285
Amorous Prawn, The 93,95,279,282
Anouilh, Jean 75,278,282
Ardrey, Robert 119,283
Arms And The Man 5,25,184,281
Arusha 34,36,41
Ascanius, SS 1,2
Aspern Papers, The 94,95,280
Ayckbourn, Alan 175,229,287,288

Baggage 115,142,151,157,181,188, 190,193,218
Banbury, Frith 185,186
Barret, Mrs. Edward 3 (See also Alban, Gwen)
Barry's Hotel 43,44,45
Baynton, Henry 89
Bed Before Yesterday, The 174,175,287
Bedroom Farce 197,198,288
Bell, Book & Candle 24,25,28,33,34, 57,62,65,74,209,276,284
Best, Geoffrey 20,23,28
Bhakoo, Kul 267,268
Peri 230,233,240,265,266, 268,271
Billy Liar 101,281
Block Tubby 6
Bobbé, Alan 260,261
Boeing-Boeing 99,280,283,287
Bolt, Robert 106,282,
Born Yesterday 68,276,285
Boston Story, A 137,139,144,285
Boy Friend, The 88,124,283
Breath Of Spring 88,279
Browning Version, The 183,288
Burkitt, Doctor 4
Burning Glass, The 73,277
Burrell, George 3,6,7,8,9

Busia 54
Byrne, Lady Joseph 219
Sir Joseph 219

Cable & Wireless Broadcasting Station 3,4,7
Cameo Cinema 8
Candida 92,184,279
Canonero, Milena 220
Canterbury Tales 143,199,285
Capitol Theatre 2,6,7
Caretaker, The 95,280
Charter Flights 113
Chetham-Strode Warren 7,275
Chiltern Hundreds, The 9, 275
Christie, Agatha 28,75,112,118,276,277 278,280,281,282,283
Christine 254,255,256,260-262
Christmas Carol, A 114,115,282
Circle, The 199,286
City Square 71
Clandestine Marriage, The 88
Claudia 68,276
Coke, Peter 88,279
Come Live With Me 79,278
Compact 98
Confusions 183,288
Connaught Road 23,70,85,91,102,274
Conservatoire of Music 4
Corn Is Green, The 257
Council, British 182,223,270
Council of Repertory Theatres 99,109
Counsell, John 92, 143
County Lane 152
Coward, Noel 9, 21,74,156,275-279 281,282,284,286,288
Crown Matrimonial 165,177,210,269,286

Dahms, Gary 149,150
Daily Nation 90,92,94,97,98,155,160, 175,186,189,231,238,269
Dame Of Sark, The 173,287
Day's Mischief, The 68,276

Dead Easy 199,285
Dear Departed,The 6
Deep Blue Sea, The 68,99,277,280
Delamere Avenue 2
Delhaye, Jacqueline 164
Dempster, Jeremy 31,33,35,37,40,42,
  43,44,49,52
Dexion Special 36,37,38,39,43,44,46,
  49,53,61,63,64
Dial "M" For Murder 24,276,281
Dickens, Charles 96,135
Diplomatic Baggage 109,282
Doctor In The House 77,161,162,163,278,
  286
Donovan, Lydia 2,77,78,89,206,251
Donovan Maule Players 5,9,55,62,64,67,
  68,70,87,154,170
Donovan Maule Theatre 8,72,73,76,79,
  84,86-88,98,105,108,123,
  130,131,136,137,140,143,
  154,158,163,171,172,196,
  198,207-210,216,217,221
  230,235,241,247,265,266,
  268,269-273
Don't Tell Father 101,281
Douglas, Home William 9,177,275,277,
  281
Dresdel, Sonia 78,79,85
Dry Rot 93,209,279
Duke Street 70
Durban 101,106,117,191

East African Standard 3,6,9,17,54,71,77,
  79,90,92,93,95,100,107,109,
  146,158,160,174,183,189,
  194,202,210,229,232,239,
  241,265,271
East Lynne 2,78,132,206,284
Eastleigh Airport 27
Eaton Terrace 4,9,11
Egypt 1,9,13,75
Eldoret 60,61,63,64
Elworthy, Mike 246-248,252,256
Empire Cinema 3
England 4,73,99
Entebbe 55,57,58
Equator 27,43

Equity Actors' British Association
  122,147,154,180,195,196,
  197,201,202,270
Equus 185,186,187,288

Falkland, James 131,135-138,172,202,
  207,208,210,229,230,232,
  234,235,240,241,265-268
Feydeau, Georges 102,281,288
Fischer, Oswald 81
Francis, R.D. (Kay) 160
Fry, Christopher18,21,275,276,279,
  282,284

Gacheru, Margaretta wa 241,266-268
Garland, Ambren Mrs. 67
  Christopher 165,166
Gathwe,Tirus 167
Gazebo, The 99,280
Gibbs, Dorothy (Dee) 156,198-200
Gichure, Joseph107,133,143,160
Gigi 107,198,199,200,277,288
Girl And The Drug, The 147
Githii, George 232
Githua, James 137
Glass Menagerie, The 194,196
Government Inspector, The 152,285
Government Road 7,11,14,15,17,76,155
  270,278
Gregory, Doctor J.R. 4,6,8
Guinea Pig, The 7,82,188,217,258,275

Hands Across The Sea 183,288
Hanwell, Nadine 148
Happiest Days Of Your Life, The 107,209
Harvey, Frank 9,154,155,275,286,287
Havoc 90
Hay fever 156,282,286
Hayes, Charles 68
  Jean (née Parnell) 13,23,68,
    117,120,121,190,246,261
Hedda Gabler 79,80,82,209
Heiress,The 69,277,282
Hellenic Glory 175,178
High Commission, British 159
Hill Lane Flats 129,133,134,259
Hindle Wakes 183,185,288

His Excellency 18,20,23,84,166,276
His, Hers & Theirs 130,284
Hollow, The 28,276,282
Hostage,The 100,107,280
Hot Tiara, The 183,282,288
Houghton, Stanley 7,183,288
How The Other Half Loves 284
Hughes, Mrs. E.D. 5,25
Hurle-Hobbs, Basil 13,14,16,22,33-37,
    39,41,43,47- 49,52,58,61,63
    64,68
Hutton, Fred 188

I Am A Camera 69,277
Imbuga, Francis 167
Immigration Act 121
Importance of Being Earnest,The 8,199
In Praise Of Love 158,160,161,286
Independence 67,95,195,103,258
Indian Ocean 34,131,179,226,254
Irregular Verb To Love, The 99,286
Italian Girl, The 129,284

Jackson Road 23,70,85,274
Jeannie 16,18,275
Jinja 58-60,63
Jockey Club Stakes, The 133,284
Johannesburg 3,9,80,100
Johnny Belinda 148,149,285
Juba 27

Kabete 4
KADU 92
Kakamega 51,53
Kampala 54,55,56,57,58,59,98
KANU 92,93
Karanja, Mugambi 186
Karmali, John 83
Keen, Angela 164
Kenny, Desmond 96,97
Kenworthy, Eva 3,4,17,18,77
    George 3,4
Kenya 1-6,9-10,19,23,31,34,38-41,43,
    44,56,60,65,68-70,72,85,88
    89-93,95,97,98,100,102-103,
    105-106,110,112,119,121,
    126,127,133,136,138,147-
    149,159,161,163,172,176,
    182,184,
Kenya Cultural Centre 100,172
Kenya Society for Deaf Children 148
Kenya Weekly News, The 9,40,41,119,160
Kenya,Writers Association of 172
Kenyatta, Jomo 23,29,91,92,95,102,186
    189
Khartoum 13,14,27
Kiboro, Donald 106,107
Kill Two Birds 100,281
Killing Of Sister George,The 202,207,217,
    288
Kimmins, Anthony 95,282
Kinangop 34,143,200
Kisauni Cemetery 243,262
Kisumu 14,51,52,53,54
Kitale 47,50,60

Lady's Not For Burning, The 18,209,275,
    284
Lake Naivasha 20,121,130,200,261
    Victoria 53
Lawler, Ray 91,279
Legion, British 9
Lion In Winter, The 185,187,288
Lion, Leon M. 94
Little Boxes 129,284
Little Hut, The 24, 276, 278
Lloyd George Knew My Father 158,160,286
Lock Up Your Daughters 90,97
London 1,2,4,7,10,18-22,24,27,33,67-
    69,72-73,77-79,86,88-92,94-
    96,98,100,106,111,117,121,
    124,125,130,133,138,143,
    155,161,162,166,174,177,
    183,185,190,195,212,250,
    269
London Evening Standard 18,20
Look After Lulu 102,281
Look Back In Anger 86,278
Lufthansa Airlines 122,152

Macmillan, Harold 91,93
Makerere College 54,56,57
Malaga 108
Malta 13,27

Man For All Seasons, A 106,282
Markham, Sir Charles 11,18,84,115,130,
    191
Mason, Kenneth 69,82,91,97-99,109,
    123,143,208,229,231,233
Master, James 67
Mau Mau 19,29,34,42,47,69
Maule, Annabel 8,24,40,115,117,126,
    127,130,132,133,135,
    136,151,158,163,174
    191,209,210,215-217
    241,258,260,265,267
    Chateau 137,139,141,142,
        146,151,156,169,
        175,178,179,180,190-
        194,205,207,264
    Robin 264
Mboya, Tom 126
McCabe, Mike 95,101
McConnell, Elizabeth 218,246,247,249,
    254
McCrae, Arthur 9,19,275,277
Medicks, Theatre Royal owner 2
Merchant Of Venice, The 105,209
Military Hospital 2
Miracle Worker, The 107,280
Moi, Daniel arap 134,236
Molo 42,45,46,47,48,50,51
Mombasa 1,2,9,23,29,31,33-36,69,73,
    80,85,101,111,115,
    117,129,131,133,
    135-137,139,142,
    143,145,146,154,
    156,157,169,173,
    175,178-180,182
    184,194,208,224
    Club 136
    Hospital 85,111,205,224
Mombasa Times, The 33
Moshi 34
Mount Kenya 38,40,41,43
Mount Kilimanjaro 34,36
Move Over, Mrs. Markham 138,139,154,
    285,287
Mua Park Road 3,19
Murder Mistaken 158,277,286
Muthaiga 3,27,74,100

Mutisya, Simon Wambua 160
Mwenda, Kyale 119
Mwenesi, Steve 167
My Fat Friend 156,157,286

N.A.A.F.I. 2,7
Nairobi 1-3,7,11,14-15,18,20,27,36,37,
    39,50,53,54,60,63,
    67,69,70-73,75-77,
    79,81,84,86-92,
    94-95,99-101,105,
    107-109,111-113,
    115-119,121-124,
    132-133,135-136,
    143,144,147,149,
    151-152,156,161-
    163,165,202,208-
    209,270-272
    City Players 77,202,268
    Club 115,208,209
    Hospital 117,135,156,163,
        248,260,271
    Provision Store 7,14
Nairobi Times 241
Nakuru 19,24,45,46,62
Nanyuki 36,37,38,39,40,43,68,119,253
    257
Nash, Richard N. 93,280
National Theatre 4,5,10,25,27,67,76,77
    88,98,100,138,167,172,173,
    237,270,276
New Stanley Hotel 8,90
New York Times 89
New Theatres Limited 3,9,14
New Venture Theatre 11
New York 2,24,25,68,79,89,90,99,250
NEWSLETTER 131,141,142,
    151,213,214,222,242
Ndavu, Eva 3
Ngala, Ronald 70,92
Ngui, Tim 199
No Sex, Please We're British 164, 285
Norfolk Hotel 5
Norman Conquests, The 175
Nyali pontoon bridge 131,145,178,
    179,212,219,254
Nyeri 19,23,40,68,69

Okumu, John Sibi 167
Oliver! 95,96,97,98,99,114,280
Omee's Supermarket 192,219
Omollo, George 135
On Stage Magazine Programme 82,99, 123,143,155,185,187, 188,189,192,207,215
Onzere, Barnaba 23
Osborne, John 86,278
Otiende, J.D. 105
Out Of Africa 219
Outward Bound 15,16,17,83,275

Paris 2,68,102,198,220
Parliament Road 102
Parnell, Jean 13,23,68
Patience, Denis 243,249,252
    Dorothy 243,249,252
Phoenix Players Limited 230,231,234, 240,265,268
Pickles, Vivian 19
Piggott, Bill 79,94,95,97
Pink String And Sealing Wax 124,283
Pinter, Harold 95,280
Playhouse 2
Port Said 11,72
Present Laughter 21,275,279,284
Private Lives 68,276,281
Punch 96
Pyewacket 25,28,31,34,37,40,42,43,44, 45,46,52,53,56,60,61,64,65
Pygmalion 19,183,184,275,288

Queen And The Rebels, The 78,79,278
Queen's Highland Servant, The 177,288
Queen's Hotel 3

Railway Players 16,67
Rainmaker, The 93,94,167,280
Ras Kisauni 144,178,179,243
Rat Trap 178,288
Rattigan, Terence 79,160,277,278,279, 280,281,285,286,288
Rattle Of A Simple Man 199,288
Reporter 94,105,107,120
Richardson, Sir Ralph 27

Right To Strike, The 18
Ring Round The Moon 112,282
Ripon Falls Hotel 58,61
Rivals, The 118,283
Riverside Drive 75,82,108,117,127,132
Robert's Wife 8,9,275
Rodwell, Edward 146,228
Rookery Nook 93,280
Rosencrantz And Guildenstern Are Dead 172, 287
Royalty Theatre 94,133
Ryan, Molly 45,47,48
Ryton, Royce 165,286

Saint Joan 209,282
Saloon Bar 9,154,275
Scarlet Ribbon 183,288
School For Scandal, The 99,209,280
School of Dramatic Art 6,7,8,14,15,70 217
Separate Tables 79,82,85,86,224,226,278
Shaffer, Anthony 131,284
    Peter 185,279,281,282,288
Shakespeare, William 20,26,87,88,105, 106,123,134,269,272,281, 283
Shaw, George Bernard 5,19,25,92,184, 275,278,279,281,288
She Stoops To Conquer 94, 280
She's Done It Again 131,135,284
Shields, G.B. 135,136,144,152,153,154
Shiells, Sheila 19,70,88,250,251
Short History Of The English People, A 154, 286
Signpost To Murder 100,280
Simon, Neil 281,282,288
Simple Spymen 95,280
Slade Humphrey 109,257
    Laurie 109,118,124,178
    Nigel 109,135,160,183,189, 194,202,208,230, 232,233,234,241, 263,266,269-272
Sleeping It Off 183,288
Sleuth! 131,229,284
Smith, Trevor 114,282
Soldiers Of The Queen, The 89

South Africa 87,95,160,190,191
South Sea Bubble 74,278
Spider's Web 75,278
St John's Gate 152,165,273
Stage, The 26,80,111,158,201,202
Stag's Head Hotel 45
Starehe Boys Centre 134
State of Emergency 27,29,34,91
Stoppard, Tom 172,173,287,
Studio,Theatre The 13-18, 20,21,22,24,
    25,63,69,74,77,78-80,155,
    278
Suez 1,75,175
Sultan Hamud 32,225,226,248
Summer, Of The Seventeenth Doll, The 91
Sunday Nation 70,97,98,130,131,149,
    158,163,167,184,197,198
Sunday Post,The 4,5,6,68,71,80,90,97,129
    131,132
Sunday Standard 233,234,240,263,270
Sunday Times,The 126,266
Sunshine Boys, The 183,288

Tamburlaine The Great 87
Taming Of The Shrew, The 134,136,210
Tanganyika 24,33,34,87
Taru Desert 32
Taylor, Samuel 167,277,279,287
The Love of Four Colonels 77
Theatre Arts 68
Theatre Arts '80 Limited 68,214,230,
    234,235,239,240,241,265,
    266,268,269-271
Theatre Royal 2,5,7,8,9,11,83,92,123,
    143,154,217,237,258,275
This Happy Breed 9,275
Thomson's Falls (now Nyahururu) 43,45
Thorndike, Dame Sybil 73
Thunder Rock 119,283
Tom Mboya Street 69
Tomorrow's Child 21,275
Torr's Hotel 2,8
Touch Of Spring,A 167, 287
Traveller's Joy 19,275
Travers, Ben 174,280,287,288
Travis, Alderman Harold 84
Turi 24,46

Twelfth Night 123,210,283
Two And Two Make Sex 160,286
Uganda 24,33,54,55,56,57,61, 98,133
Uganda Herald 54,57
Uncle Vanya 129,284
Under the Sun 4
Unexpected Guest,The 118,283

Vasey, Sir Ernest 188,258
Victoria Street 7,14,69,76
Virture in Danger 149,151,285
Voi 34

Waibu, Njoroge 153
Waltz Of The Toreadors, The 75
Ward, James 118,131,143,148,149,155,
    158,167,174,185,198,199,
    207,229
Wasambo, Luka Were 269
Watene, Kenneth 167
Waters Of The Moon 108,282
Watson, Michael 33
While Parents Sleep 95
White Rhino Hotel 19
Whitehouse Road 91
Whittle, Donald 31,35,37,43,45,49,52
Who Goes There? 68,276
Who's Afraid Of Virginia Woolf? 119,283
Why Not Stay For Breakfast? 207,288
Wielandt, Benny 182,223,225,246
Wigmore, Oliver 96
Wilde, Oscar 170,276,282,287
Wilkinson, Frederick 72,75,80,83,130
Williams, Hugh & Margaret 130, 279
    Tennessee 194
Wilson Airport 10
Windsor,Theatre Royal 92,143,166,177
Wolfit, Sir Donald 87,88,279
Woodley, Sir Richard 100
Women's Royal Naval Service 166

Young Elizabeth, The 67,69

£ 4. 0. 0

Wednesday Sept 22, 1824

Sir,

The proposal I have to submit to your consideration, is this — To have the services of myself, Mrs Willmott and her two Daughters, the eldest fifteen Years of Age, to fill the situation of Chorus Singer &c — The Youngest Ten Years of Age as Actress & Dancer — all four for the comparatively small Sum of Five pounds P Week —

As you wish to retrench your expences, here is an excellent opportunity of so doing and at the same time of obliging one of your Faithful and devoted Servants —

The Sum at the first view, may appear great — but consider, Sir — four persons and one of them holding no less a situation than that of Prompter To the Theatre Royal Drury Lane

I remain
Sir,
Your Obt humble St
John Willmott

To
R. W. Elliston Esqr.

A tough business: theatre.

This letter, dated 1824, offers the services of four hopefuls for the all-in price of £5 per week.

See the end of this book for an easier-to-read transcription.

It appears (see overleaf) that John Willmott's offer was accepted, but only £4 per week would be paid.

Transcription

Wednesday September 22 1824

D/Sir

The proposal I have to submit
To your consideration, is this - to have the services
of myself, Mrs Willmott and her two Daughters,
the eldest fifteen years of Age to fill the situation
of chorus Singer and - the Youngest Ten Years of Age
as Actress and Dancer - <u>all four</u> for the comparatively
small sum of five pounds per week -

As you wish to retrench your expenses,
here is an excellent opportunity of so doing, and
at the same time of obliging one of your <u>faithful</u>
and <u>devoted</u> servants.

The sum at the first view may appear great -
but consider, Sir - <u>four persons</u> - and one of them
holding no less a situation than that of
<u>prompter</u> to the <u>Theatre Royal Drury Lane.</u>

      I remain
      D/sir
      Your Obt humble St.

      John Willmott